IMAGES
of America

RED OAK

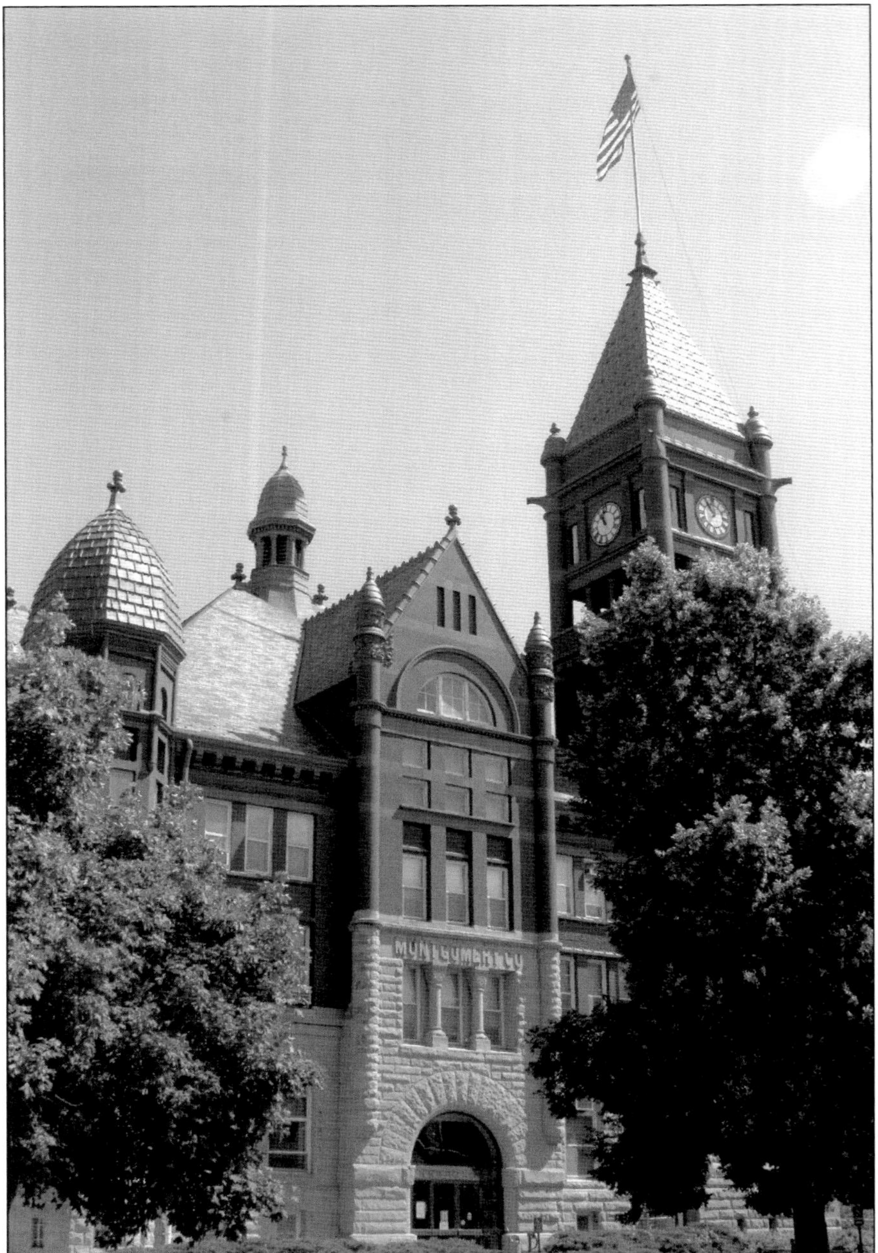

Montgomery County Courthouse, built in 1890, has long been a symbol of Red Oak. It was built of Missouri limestone, red pressed brick, and terra-cotta with a slate roof. The framework and supporting beams are of steel. The courthouse has long been an anchor of stability and endurance, spirit and pride. (Courtesy of the B. Senden photographic collection.)

On the cover: Please see page 30. (Courtesy of the Montgomery County Historical Society photographic collection.)

IMAGES
of America

RED OAK

S. M. Senden

ARCADIA
PUBLISHING

ISBN 978-0-7385-6131-8

Published by Arcadia Publishing
Charleston SC, Chicago IL, Portsmouth NH, San Francisco CA

Printed in the United States of America

Library of Congress Catalog Card Number: 2008931966

For all general information contact Arcadia Publishing at:
Telephone 843-853-2070
Fax 843-853-0044
E-mail sales@arcadiapublishing.com
For customer service and orders:
Toll-Free 1-888-313-2665

Visit us on the Internet at www.arcadiapublishing.com

This book is dedicated to all those who have been fortunate enough to call Red Oak their home; past, present, and future. And to people like Betty McKenzie, who had a dream and had the courage of her convictions to make her dream become a reality. The Montgomery County Historical Society Museum was her dream, now it is a reality.

Contents

Acknowledgments

The statements contained herein are based on facts gathered through memoirs, newspaper articles, and records of the period, often there was more than one date or story about some point in history and they did not always agree. There was such a wealth of history and events down through the years that it was not easy to fit everything in. Forgive me if I have omitted your favorite story, person, place, or memory. I would like to express my appreciation to all those who helped make this book possible: the Montgomery County Historical Society, all photographers, and storytellers. I would like to name a few of those people, forgive me for omitting someone: W. W. Merritt, Oliver Perry Worsely, Minnie Ashby, Henry Binns, Florence Binns, H. H. West, Ralph Spencer, Betty McKenzie, Elaine Artlip, Roy Marshall, Chris Pelley, Charlie and Cheri Notz, Roger Harnack, Charles and Norma Wilson, Helen Murphy and Nancy Murphy, Amy Krasne, Bettie Larson, Carroll Petersen, Maggie Dawson, John Palmquist, Paul McCoy, and James Hoskinson. Special thanks are given to Ted Gerstle, who made that phone call, to John Pearson for excellent technical support, to Darwin Williams for his laughter and his patience, and to Brad for his love and support.

INTRODUCTION

Iowa was a part of the Louisiana Purchase in 1803 but the area was closed to white settlers until the end of the Black Hawk Wars in 1832. In 1836, the government relocated the Iowa Nation, who had lived on the land for generations, to a reservation so that the eastern part of the territory might be settled. It was from these people that the name of the territory was given.

In 1837, the United States moved the Pottawattamie, Chippewa, and Ottawa Nations to southwest Iowa. The Pottawattamie, led peacefully by Billy Caldwell, left the village of Chicago, resettling into five villages in the Council Bluffs area traveling through what was to become Montgomery County. Eastern Iowans considered western Iowa to be a vast, mysterious wilderness, peopled thickly with vague and dreadful phantoms of imaginary uninhabitableness, and that the area would never be worth anything.

Before the 1830s, few whites had traveled across the vast prairie of tall grasses, meandering rivers, thick groves of oaks, black walnuts, and cottonwood trees that grew in the deep, fertile soil. Gentle rolling hills with stunningly beautiful vistas stretched out between the Mississippi and Missouri Rivers, wild game was plentiful, and the Omaha and Otoe people camped on the Missouri River hunted in this land, but there is no evidence of permanent settlement inland.

In 1846, the Pottawattamie sold their land and moved across the Missouri River into Nebraska. On Monday, December 28, 1846, Iowa became the 29th state admitted into the Union. Montgomery County was surveyed in 1851 and officially became a county in 1853.

The identity of the first white people to cross the prairie was not recorded, but they came, they liked what they found, and some began to settle in the new state of Iowa. Elk, deer, wild turkeys, and other game were plentiful on the prairie and the soil was rich, thick, and black. In 1851, W. C. Matthews was among a hunting party that came to the area where the Red Oak Creek, named for the thick groves of oaks that blazed a fiery red in the fall, emptied into the meandering Nishnabotna River, a Native American name that means "crossed in a canoe." On this hunting trip, he recalled that they found the carcasses of two huge elk with magnificent racks intertwined. They would be an easy marker to find when he returned to settle in what was to become Red Oak Township.

Pleasant Jones squatted on some land in 1852. On March 11, 1854, James Shank filed the first recorded claim in the area. Jones did not formally file a claim until 1855 and in 1857 sold his land to Daniel Remick, who purchased it from him hoping that the rumors he heard were true about the advent of the railroad.

Frankfort had been chosen as the location for the Montgomery County seat, a courthouse had been erected, and a city was beginning to grow up around it with great hopes for the future.

However, late in 1853, everything changed. Col. Alfred Hebard was commissioned to do a topographical survey for an east–west route for the railroad from Burlington, on the Mississippi River, to where the Missouri and Platt Rivers merged, placing stakes every 500 feet. Frankfort, beautifully situated on a rise, was passed by. The railroad's path went three miles to the south on a more level grade, and the area around the junction of the Red Oak Creek and the Nishnabotna River was seen as an ideal location for the railroad to travel. It was already on the only east–west stage route that passed through the area. Remick is said to have heard Hebard remark about a site in Red Oak, "Here will be the depot."

In 1855, a post office was established at Oro, a few miles north of Red Oak, and Joseph Zuber was the postmaster. His wife, Mary Jane Wiley Zuber, is credited with having named the area for the abundance of beautiful Red Oaks growing along the creek. In 1857, the roller mills were built along the Nishnabotna.

In 1857, Remick pledged 40 acres for a town site. Within six days, the Shanks, whose land was parallel to his, did the same with another 40 acres, thus was the settlement of Red Oak Junction first established. In that same year, Joseph Zuber built the first house, it served as a hotel called Red Oak House. In 1858, Charles H. Lane opened the first store for business to serve the four houses of Red Oak Junction. They built the town on the hopes and dreams of the future where the rivers met, and soon roads and rail lines would meet as well. The dream of the railroad was put on hold as the Civil War spanned five Aprils in time.

For years there had been a great rivalry between Red Oak Junction and Frankfort. Red Oak had hopes to become the county seat, especially with the promise of the railroad that would come through Red Oak and bypass Frankfort. The railroad meant a town would either grow or perish. With that in mind, there was a movement to have the county seat removed from Frankfort to Red Oak Junction. When it was put to a vote and after the ballots were counted Frankfort emerged as the winner. But H. Campbell pressed for a recount that included all the ballots. There were many cast aside, considered to be incomplete and therefore invalid; the ballots had only the name Red Oak on them, not the full and official name of Red Oak Junction. After a recount of all ballots with both Red Oak and Red Oak Junction were counted. Red Oak emerged as the winner, and it was ordered that the county seat be removed to Red Oak Junction. The records were to be moved by June 1865 and the courthouse by January 1866. Frankfort was not pleased and dragged their feet about the transfer and the removal of the courthouse to Red Oak Junction.

A group of Red Oak men, their patience worn thin, decided that they would go to Frankfort and remove the courthouse themselves. They loaded it upon skids, and began the trek back to Red Oak. A blizzard hampered their progress. They were forced to abandon the building to the blowing snow, letting it slip down a hillside in the whiteout, as they sought shelter. When they returned to look for the building, it was gone. No one could find it. It was a month before the courthouse was finally located buried deep in drifted snow. At last they brought it to Red Oak and installed it on the square.

On March 21, 1869, Webster Eaton put out the first copy of the *Montgomery County Express* from the offices of the Adams County Gazette. He purchased a used Foster Hand Press and type, carted it overland in a wagon from Centerville, and set up shop in Red Oak in April 1869. Within a year, the name was changed from *Montgomery County Express* to the *Red Oak Express*. He wrote, "Red Oak Junction can hardly fail to become an important point, especially if she is so fortunate to get a Rail Road, of which there is a strong possibility."

One

The Pioneer Days

Minnie Ashby was born in Illinois in 1859 and came with her parents to Red Oak in the early 1860s. Her father was marshal for a year while they were building the railroad. In 1927, she recorded her childhood memories of growing up in Red Oak. What follows is an excerpt from those reflections.

Come with me for a ride in a prairie schooner across the hills and valleys of the prairie to the little town on the banks of the Nishnabotna River and a creek called Red Oak with only a wagon track to follow and no bridges to cross the *Tarky* and smaller streams, no houses along the way.

My parents pitched camp under a dome of large cottonwood trees. There was no lumber so they drove to Council Bluffs and built a small house on the corner of Corning and First Streets where we lived for one year then moved because there was so much water surrounding the house and mud! There were no sidewalks anywhere. For those were pioneer days.

A little brick one room schoolhouse was north of town. The Methodist church was way up on the side hill and was the only church in town. The parsonage was on the corner of Sixth and Reed Streets.

Uncle Laz Harding had a hotel where the Griffith Inn is. At Washington and Seventh stood the Exchange Hotel. The barn where the stage coaches stopped was at the corner of Washington and Eighth Streets. The Post Office was at the southeast corner of the square where Ivan Ellwood's store and the building was called the Blue Front, then The Central House and Shanks Drug Store. On the west side stood Lane's General Merchandise store and Roberts Dry Goods Store. On the North side was the Court House and Kerrihard's Dry Goods Store, on the east a Drug and Book Store with several other small buildings.

I won't try and tell you where the saloons were but there were more than plenty. Especially the year the rail road was built. The *Paddies*, as they were called, came to town Saturday nights for a grand spree. The way they raced their horses and yelled and whooped frightened the children. My father, Joshua Ashby was Marshall. Those wild men seemed to think him all right, would listen to him and go home when he told them to. Those were wild and wooly times.

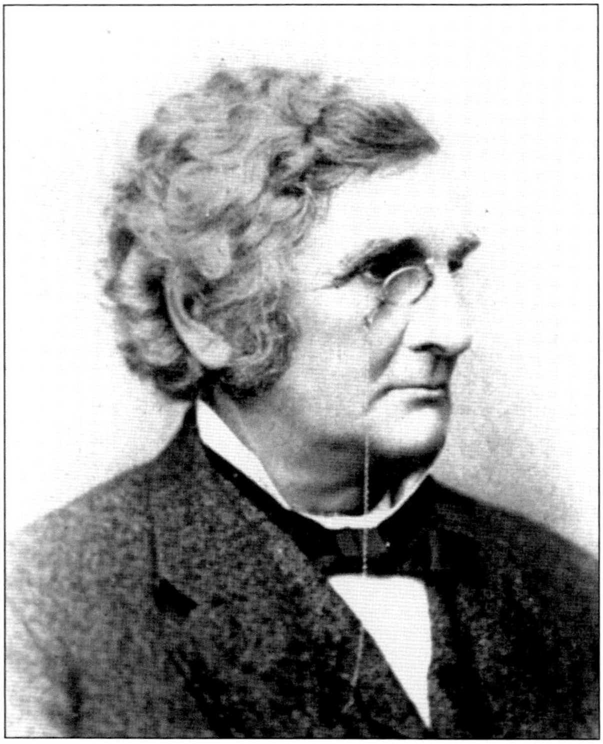

Col. Alfred Hebard is considered to be the father of Red Oak. In 1853, he did a topographical survey for the railroad mapping out a proposed path for the tracks to follow from Burlington west to the junction of the Platt and Missouri Rivers. When they finally built the railroad after the War between the States, his survey route was followed with very little deviation from his original path. He returned to live in Red Oak Junction and built an exquisite mansion at 700 Eighth Street, on the hill overlooking the town. The house is still standing today.

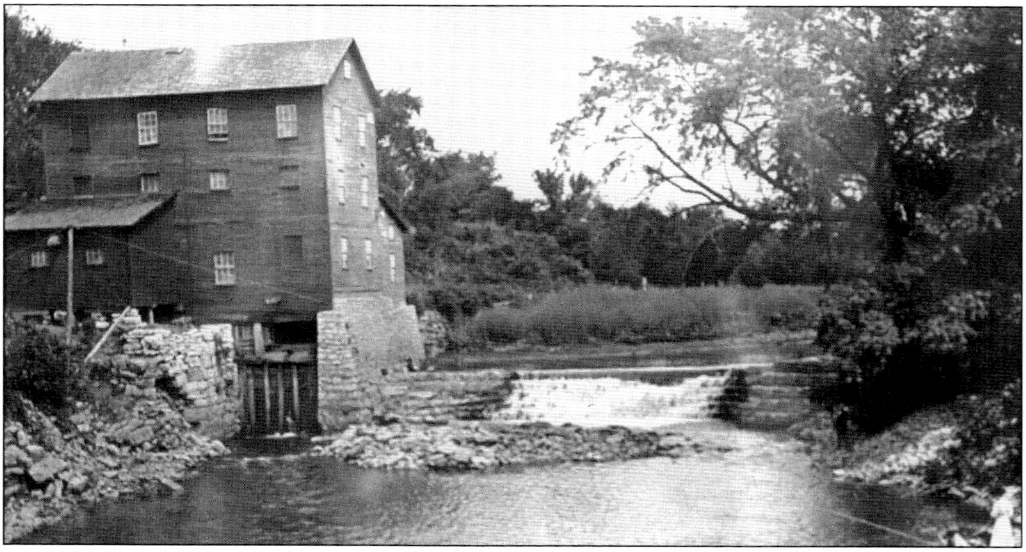

In 1855, David Silket built a sawmill on the Nishnabotna River, north of where Red Oak would be. The same year, the post office was established with Joseph Zuber as postmaster. W. H. Kerrihard built a sawmill in 1856. In July 1857, a ferry business began by the sawmill. Silket built the first gristmill to meet the demands of settlers. The mill changed hands many times, burned to the ground, was rebuilt again, and after another fire, the Tenney brothers created an amusement area called Riverside Park. The ledge below the mill, by the dam across the river, was always a good place to catch plenty of fish.

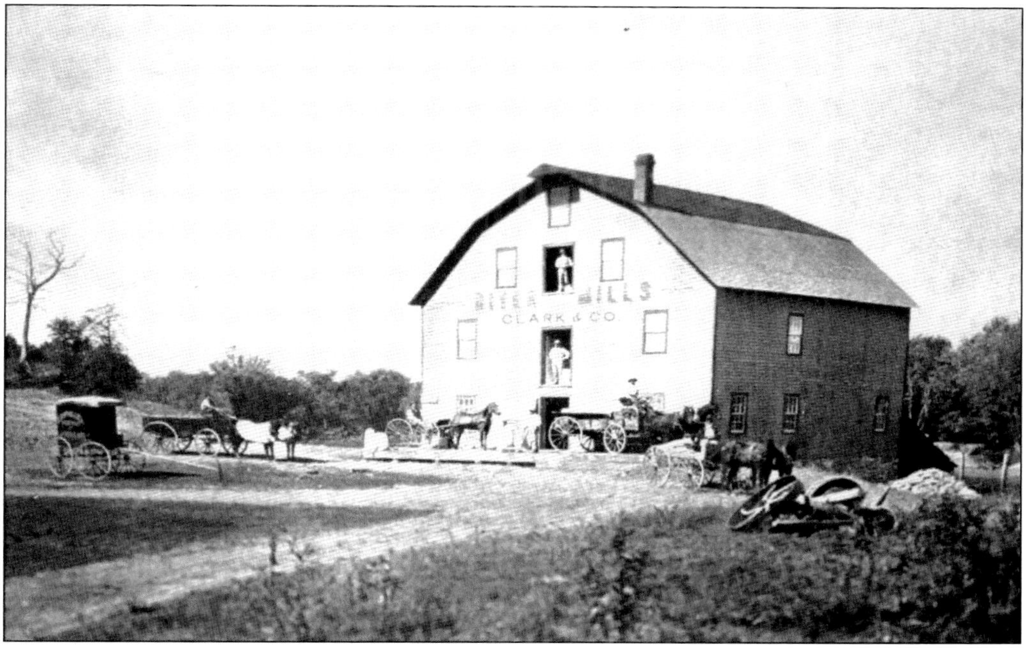

An article written in 1894 named the River Roller Mills, owned by Clark and Company (which purchased it from a Mr. Manker), as the oldest milling plant in the county with a capacity of 80 barrels a day. These early mills used waterpower to grind the grain. About 1870, the roller process was brought in from Hungary. Steel rollers with grooved surfaces would turn against one another squeezing the hard wheat berries. The flour produced was known as patent flour.

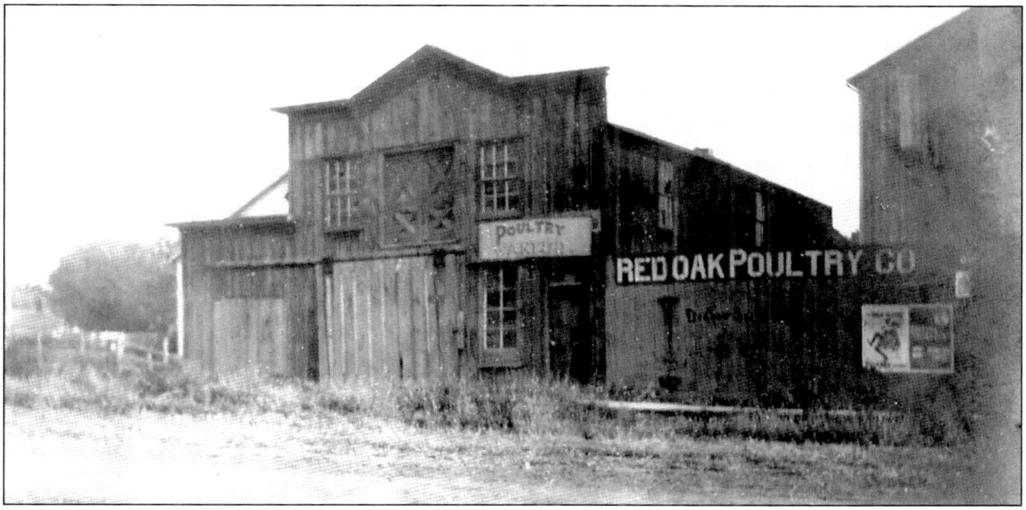

Henry C. Shank was 21 when he came to Red Oak with his parents on June 15, 1854, to farm. He owned a planing mill located around Eighth Street and the Red Oak Creek. It was equipped with a planer or sticker, turning lathe, rip- and jigsaws, a grinding stone, and a mortising machine. Shank lived in the first house ever built in the vicinity of Red Oak. From 1857 to 1865, he was engaged in the sawmill business. He built the first two bridges ever built across the Nishnabotna River. In 1865, Shank opened a drugstore. By 1946, the mill had become Gray's Paint and Auto Body Shop.

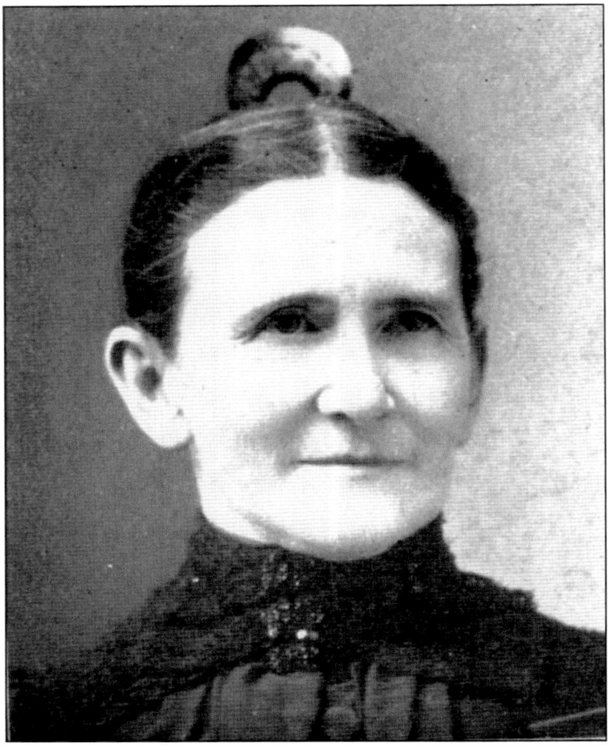

Sophronia W. Dean had come with her parents to Pottawattamie County after finishing high school. She had a gift for teaching and became the first schoolteacher in Montgomery County in the summer of 1856 for 35 scholars. When she married Henry C. Shank on April 15, 1858, she retired from teaching. In 1859, her husband began to saw lumber at his mill, most of it was native walnut, and in 1860, he built her the first frame house in Red Oak, located at 702 Grimes Street.

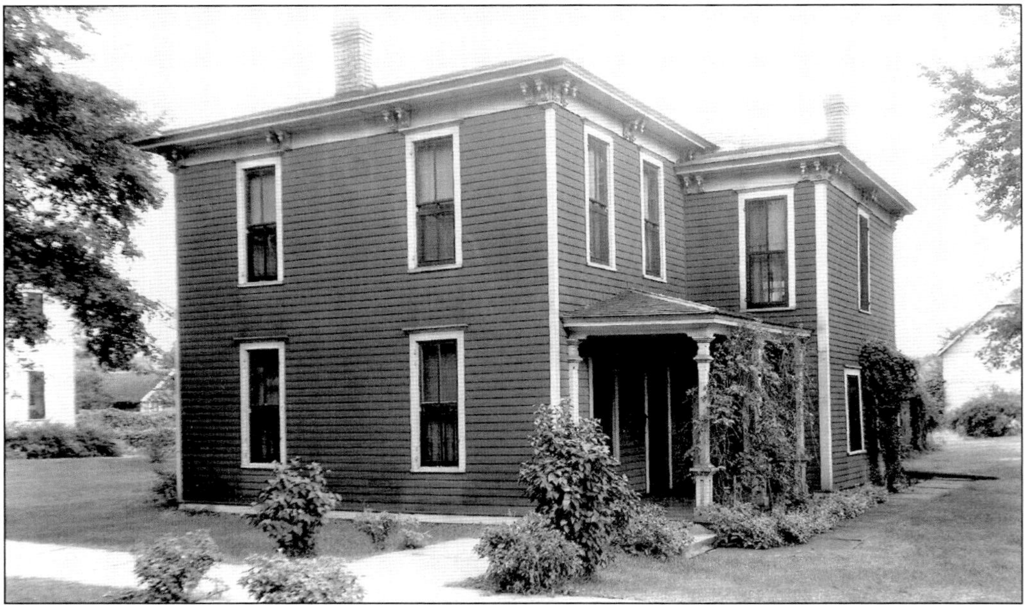

For many years, the Shanks' home was the oldest house in Red Oak. The original house was simple and small, but as their family grew, Henry C. Shank made many alterations to the house over the years. They raised nine children in this home. Shank was a careful craftsman; he did not use nails, but pegged together the entire building. He used mostly native walnut to construct their home. Sadly this house is no longer standing.

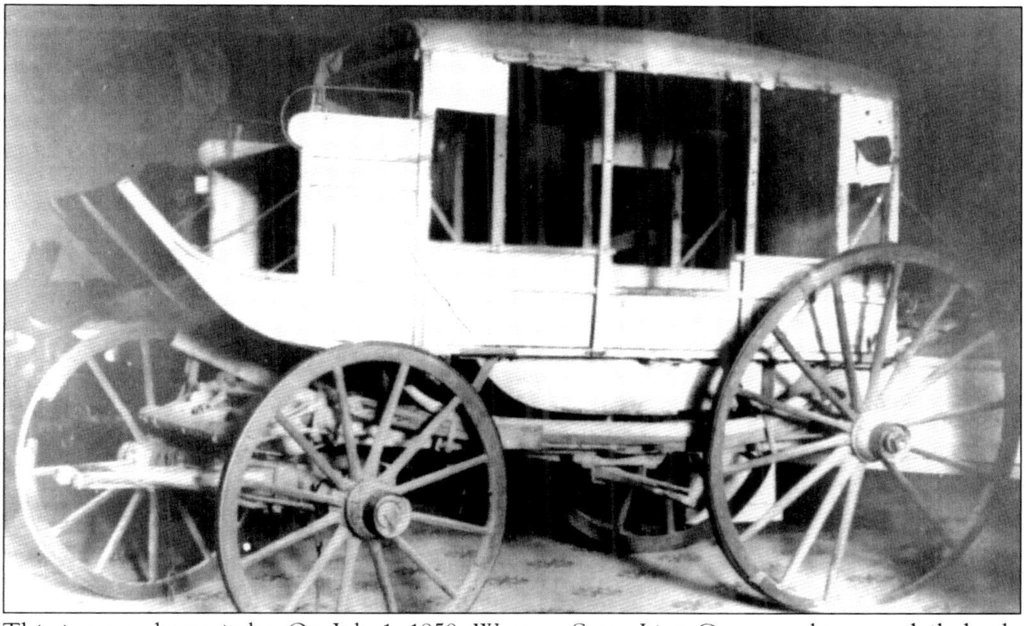

This is a two-horse jerky. On July 1, 1858, Western Stage Line Company began a daily hack, establishing a stagecoach station in 1860 on the northeast corner of Fourth Street and Washington Avenue. The stagecoach man was called "Buckskin Tracy" because of his buckskin suit. Most drivers were said to have a wife in every town. Old rumors tell that as a result of his adventures in Red Oak, a boy was born and named Buck. The first train from the Chicago, Burlington and Quincy Railroad (CB&Q) came to town on November 4, 1869, and the stagecoach closed. Buckskin Tracy stored some coaches and gave others away, many had bullet holes from the Younger gang, the Jesse James gang, or Native American attacks.

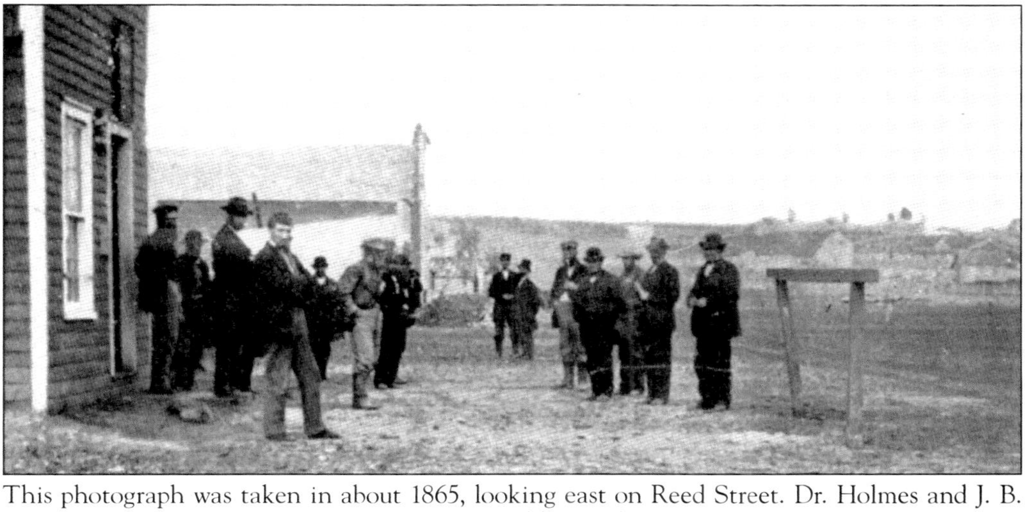

This photograph was taken in about 1865, looking east on Reed Street. Dr. Holmes and J. B. Packard's houses are in the distance. Minnie Ashby recalls, "The old paint mill that stood on the northwest corner of Washington Avenue and Sixth Street where a red paint was ground from the red clay and was called Packard's paint from the man Packard who expected to make a fortune from selling it. Strangers used to think that because so many houses were painted with that red paint was why the town was called Red Oak."

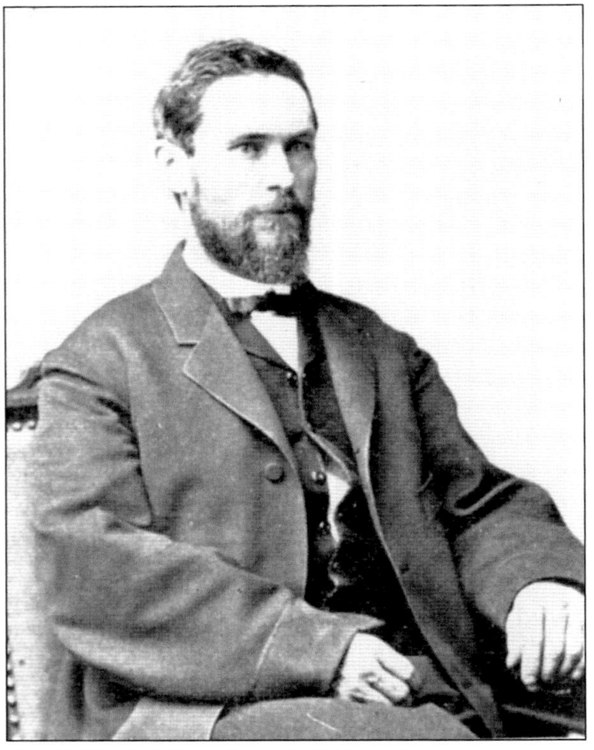

In 1856, Charles H. Lane, an enterprising young man, came to Red Oak Junction and established his mercantile business to serve the four houses that made up this new town in its infancy. Samuel Riggs was the mail contractor who rode on horseback once a week to deliver the mail. In 1858, the post office was moved from Oro and the Red Oak Junction Post Office was christened. Joseph Zuber continued as postmaster.

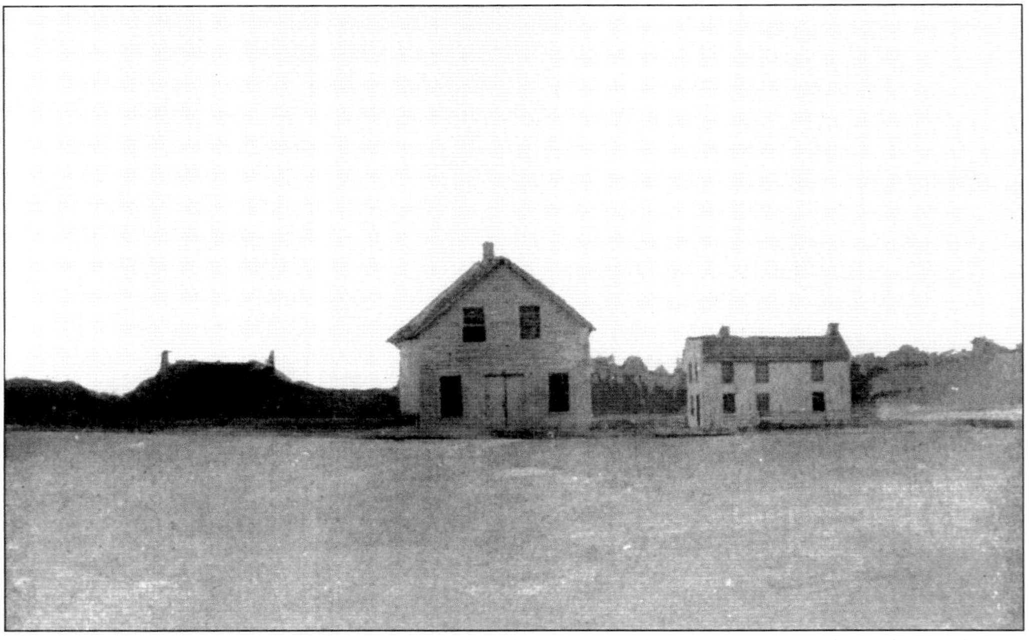

Lane's building was the first business in Red Oak Junction. He ran a mercantile and was also an implement dealer. His little store stood on the west side of the square. A Mr. Holt joined him in business a few years later. By 1868, a man stood on the east hill and counted 51 houses in town. There were also seven saloons by then.

John W. Patterson came to Red Oak in 1853 and was the first grand worthy master of the Masonic lodge from 1861 to 1867. The first Masonic lodge, the Blue Lodge of Red Oak, Lodge No. 162 Ancient Free and Accepted Masons, was organized on November 16, 1861. The charter was granted on June 5, 1862. The 10 charter members included: W. W. Merritt, John Patterson, G. A. Gordon, J. M. Hewett, William Dunn, Charles Bolt, John Ivens, William Focht, Isaac Dans, and R. M. G. Patterson. The first officers were John Patterson, grand worshipful master; G. A. Gordon, senior warden; J. M. Hewitt, junior warden; William Dunn, treasurer; and W. W. Merritt, secretary.

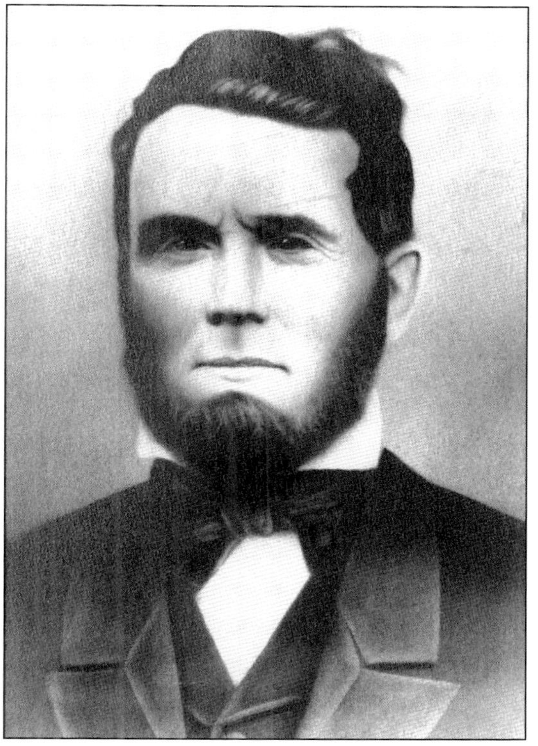

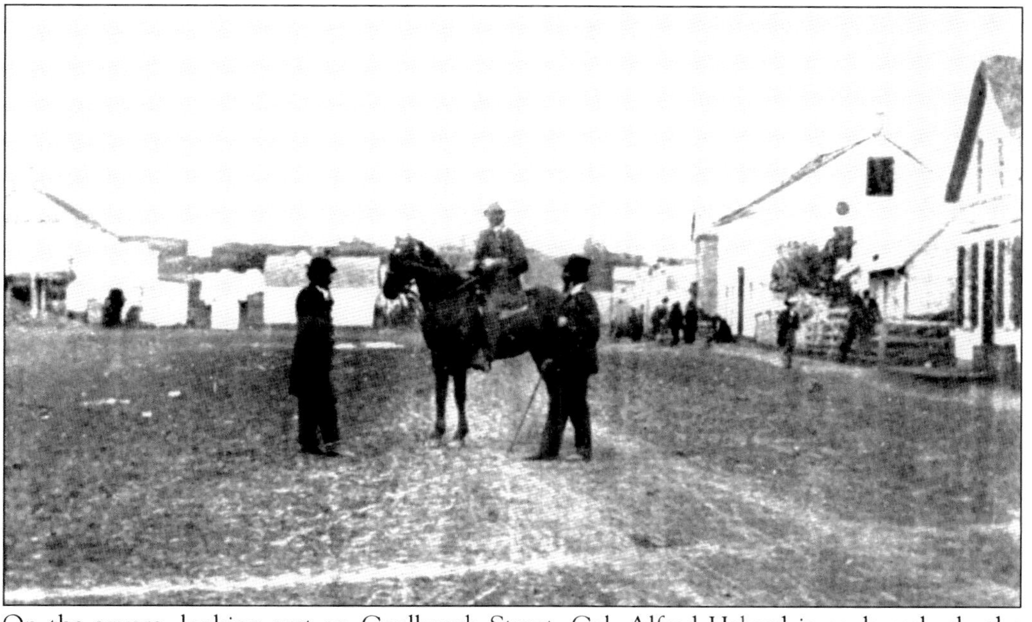

On the square, looking east on Coolbaugh Street, Col. Alfred Hebard is on horseback, the Harding Hotel is in the center, and the Masonic hall is to the left. Ralph Spencer's memoirs relate the story of how Coolbaugh Street was named. A Mr. Coolbaugh was a chief engineer for the CB&Q and, supposedly, if he saw to it that the railroad came through Red Oak Junction, they would be sure to name a major street in his honor.

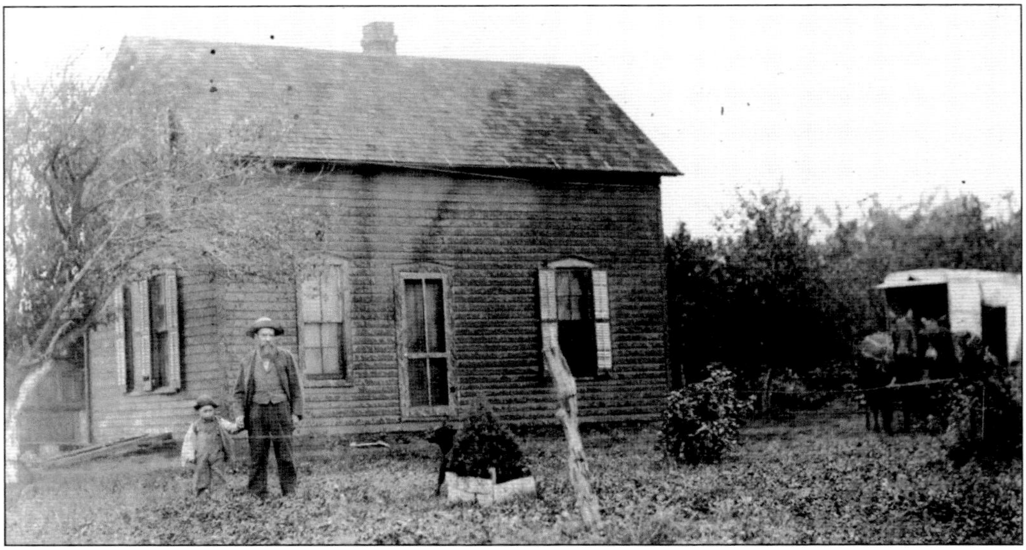

This early frame house in the Red Oak area is much like so many early homes roughly made of timbers cut at the local sawmill. Minnie Ashby recalls, "Then those early days, year after year, we had terrific hail storms that beat the gardens and the crops into the ground and spilt the young apple and cherry trees so they had to be replaced, and broke all the window lights on the north side of buildings."

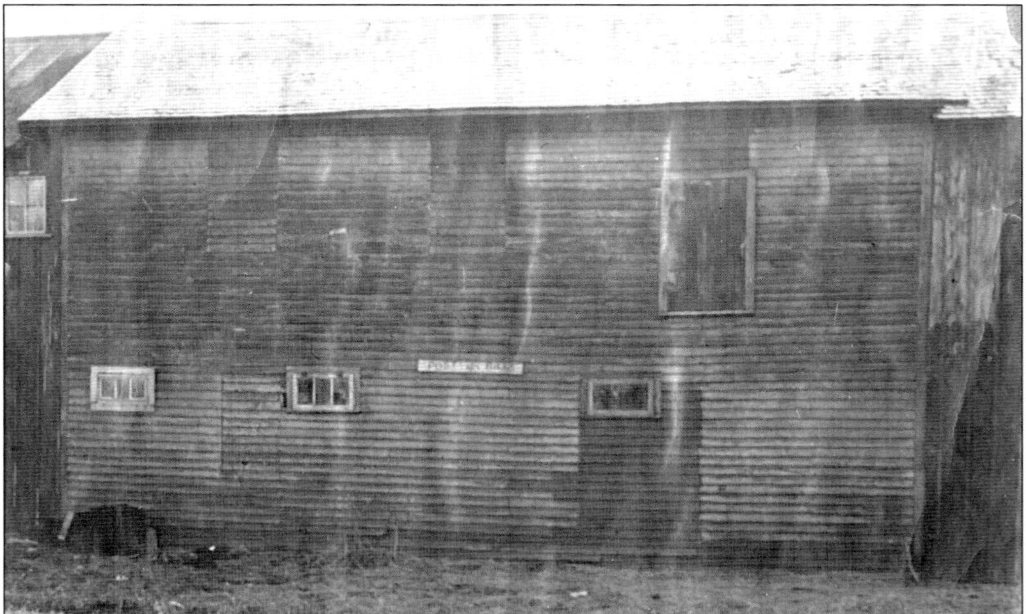

The first official courthouse for Montgomery County was built in Frankfort in the summer of 1856 by Henry C. Shank. It was sold to the county in 1857 for $1,500. When Red Oak became the county seat in 1866, Frankfort did not want to part with the courthouse. So a group of Red Oak men stole it, placing it on skids hitched to 30 yoke of oxen. A blizzard came up, and they abandoned their endeavors. They returned to finish their task, however, the courthouse was lost. It took a month to locate it buried in snow drifts. They placed it on the square in Red Oak.

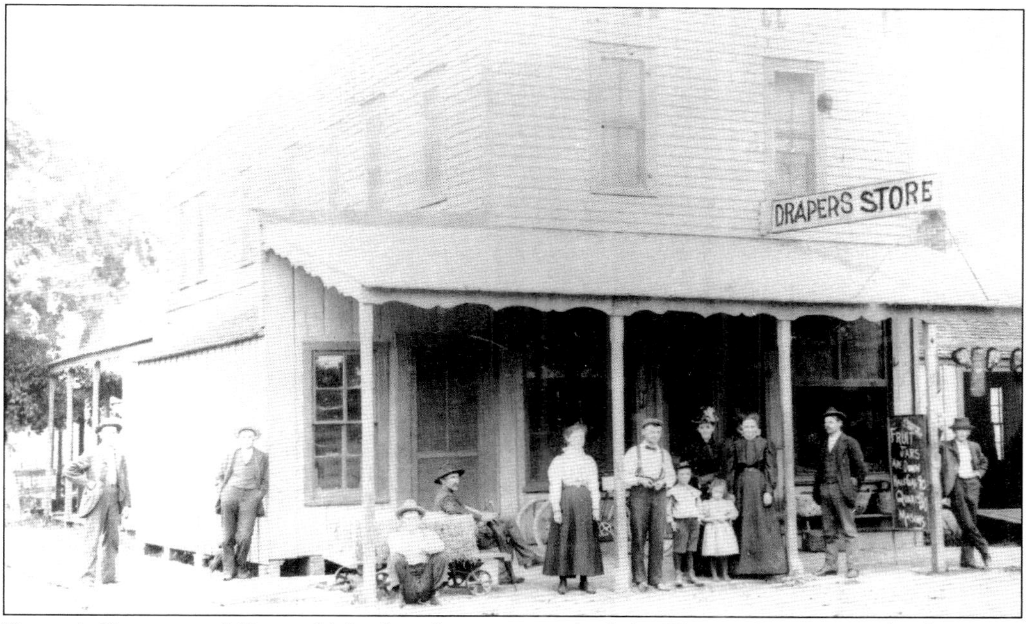

Draper's Grocery and General Merchandise store was built by Thomas B. Draper, who first came to Red Oak with the Burlington Missouri Railroad as a bridge foreman. He liked the town so much, he returned with his wife and family in 1869 and built the store with quarters for his family upstairs. It was located at 101 West First Street, which was later renamed Broadway. It is one of the oldest buildings in town still in use.

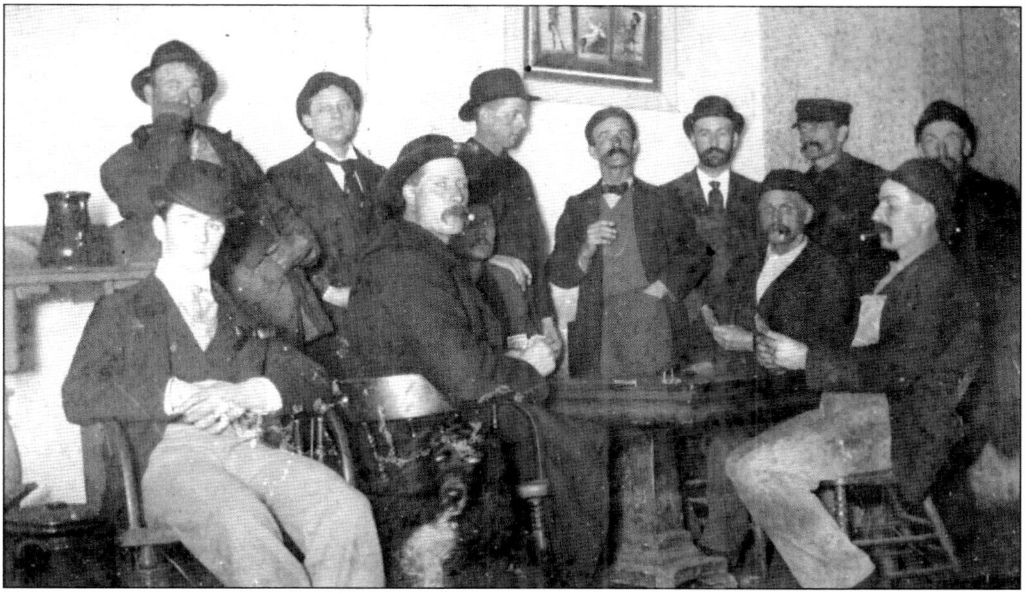

In the 1860s there were seven saloons in Red Oak Junction and business was brisk. Red Oak Junction's unsavory reputation was second only to Deadwood. Oliver P. Worsley recalled, "Whenever a rainy day came and the men could not work they would come to Red Oak Junction and most of them get drunk. Fighting would start among them and I would venture to say that I have seen as many as fifty fights in one day here."

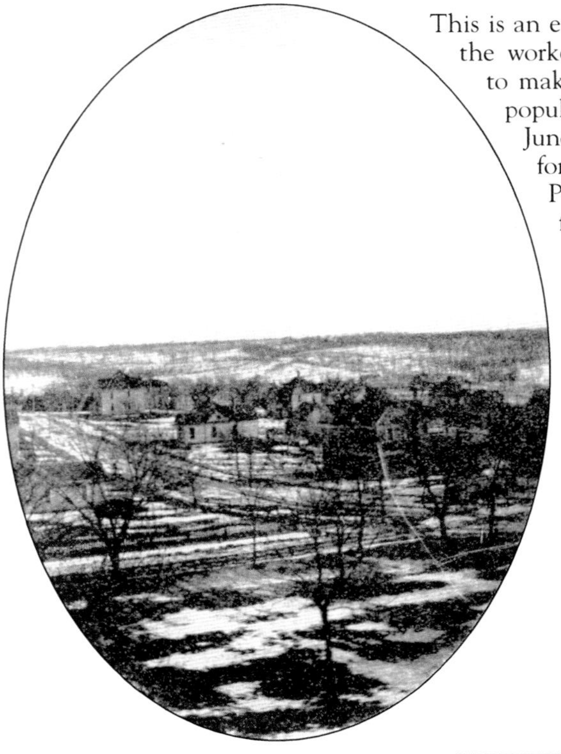

This is an early view of East Joy Street. In contrast to the workers tearing up the town, churches began to make a claim on the hearts and souls of the population. Sheldon Jackson came to Red Oak Junction by covered wagon from Pennsylvania for health reasons. He established the Presbyterian church on June 15, 1869. The first Presbyterian worship services were held at Third and Joy Streets. The first pastor was Dr. Samuel McAfee with a salary of $1,000 a year. Their first building was built at Fourth Street and Hammond in 1870.

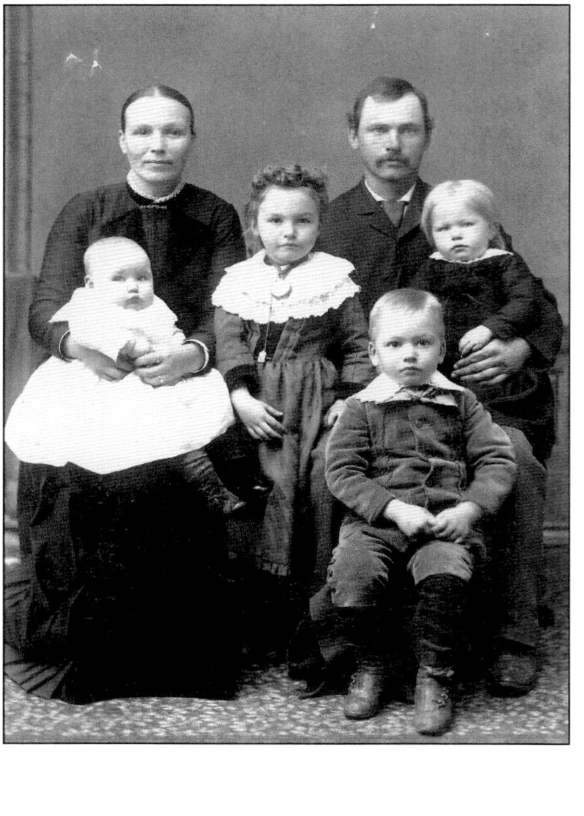

Pioneer families began to come to the growing settlement of Red Oak Junction. They came with dreams for a better life for themselves and for their children. They built homes, schools, churches, businesses, and farms. They are the bedrock upon which the young town built itself into a thriving city.

Two

RED OAK JUNCTION

Once the railroad was completed in 1869, the workers moved on to build another segment of the rail lines that were crossing the nation. Red Oak Junction outgrew its reputation as a wild western town and began to attract people who came seeking their fortune in the world, with dreams in their hearts. Some would meet with great successes and a few would experience failure, but they would change Red Oak forever, usually that change was for the better, and some would even bring Red Oak into national prominence.

Established as the county seat on March 20, 1866, Red Oak Junction had grown sufficiently to earn the designation of a city. Col. Alfred Hebard, who first saw the area when he surveyed for the railroad, returned and built an elegant brick home on the hill overlooking the growing city below. George West, one of many architects and builders who came, built Hebard's home, and over the years, West also built many other elegant mansions and many commercial buildings in town. These buildings reflected the prosperity that Red Oak was experiencing.

New businesses were established, future landmarks, such as Hotel Johnson, were constructed, and old businesses were sold, some closed while others expanded. Two young men, Thomas Murphy and Edmond Osborne, came to Red Oak to purchase one of the three newspapers in Red Oak and, from a desire to stretch an investment in an expensive woodcut of the new courthouse, revolutionized an industry and became one of the largest and longest term employers in Red Oak.

But there were hard times too. Minnie Ashby recalls that "the grasshoppers came between us and the sun so that it seemed twilight at noon. They ate up everything green. Once I saw them stop a freight train in the railroad cut this side of Hawthorne. Now you think they piled up so high that the engine couldn't get through. Not so, the wheels of the engine cars crushed the hoppers and greased the rails so that the wheels couldn't move along any more that your car wheels can in sand or mud."

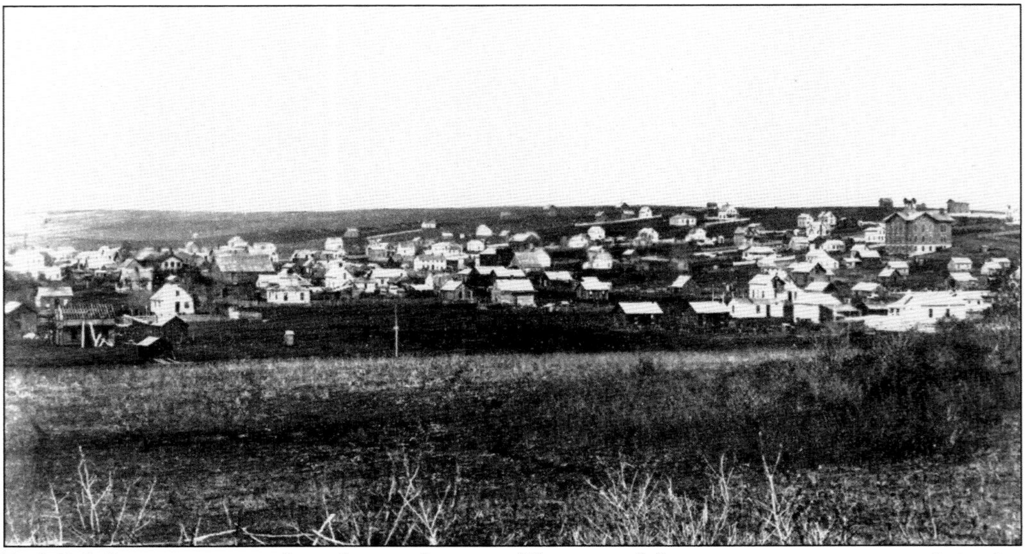

Red Oak Junction is seen here from a distance. The town did not amount to very much in the 1860s, when Oliver Perry Worsley arrived. He wrote, "I crawled out of a stage coach in front of the station on the south side of the square and found myself in Red Oak . . . I went to the old Red Oak House, which was the next-door to the station and applied for a room. Having been shown to a large garret, which contained about twenty beds, I went to sleep in the one assigned to me and left no call for the morning. When I awoke next morning, late, I was the only occupant of the room."

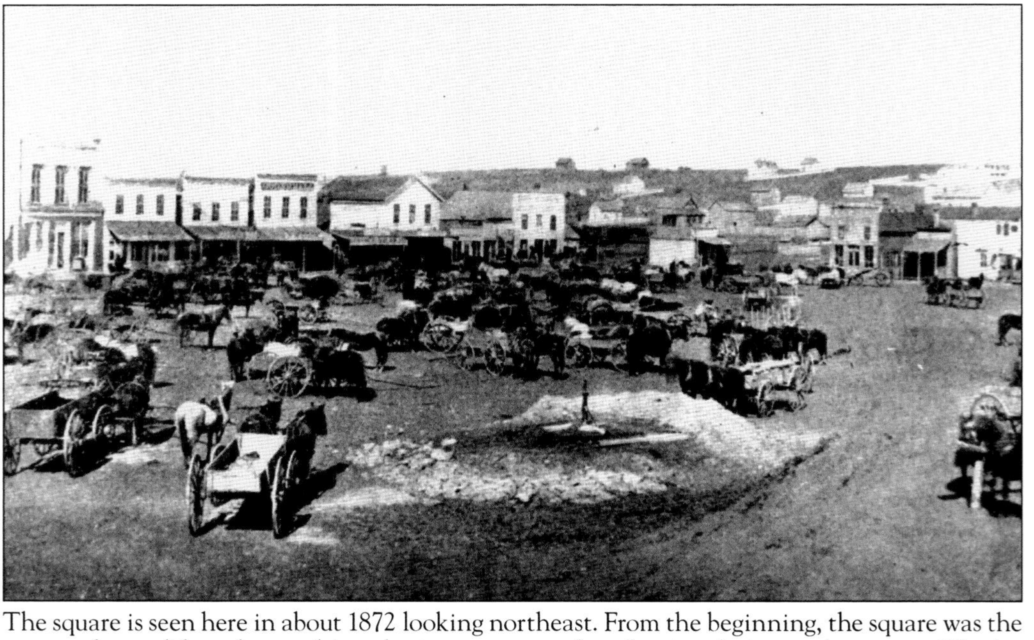

The square is seen here in about 1872 looking northeast. From the beginning, the square was the center of town life and everything else in town was referred to in relation to the square. Worsley recalls that "the north side of the square was vacant until you come to where Sanford's store is located and there Good & Richards had their law office in a frame building. The old court house that was brought down from Frankfort stood next."

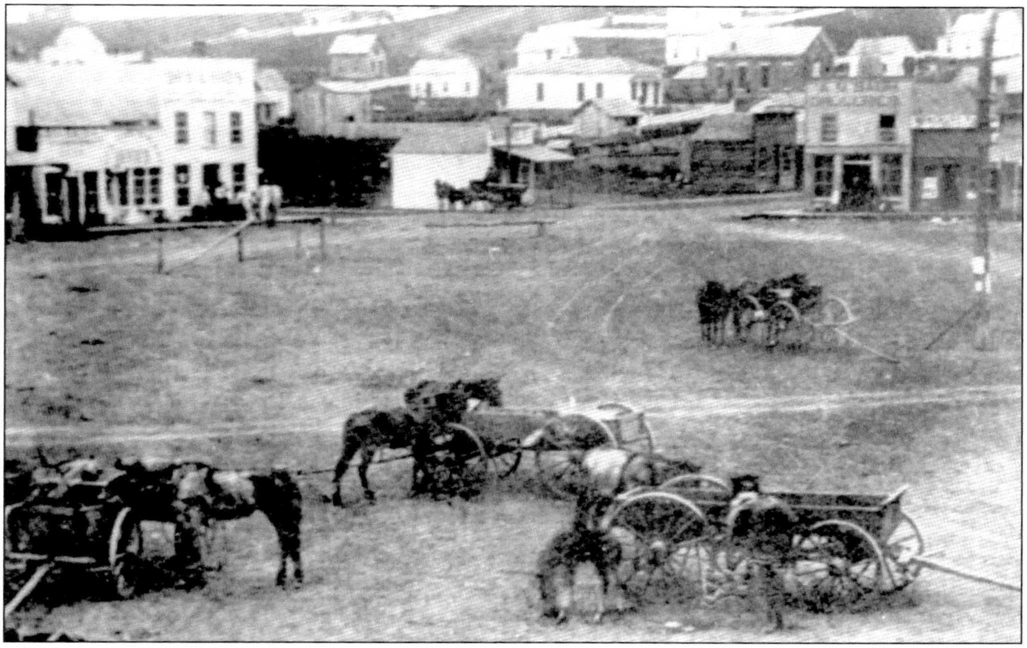

The south side of the square was the least developed; there was a brick building where D. W. Montgomery conducted a general store. Then west of that was the Red Oak House, built in 1857 by Joseph Zuber with the big garret room and the 20 beds, with the stage station and office, then Henry Shank's drugstore, and that was all there was on the south side.

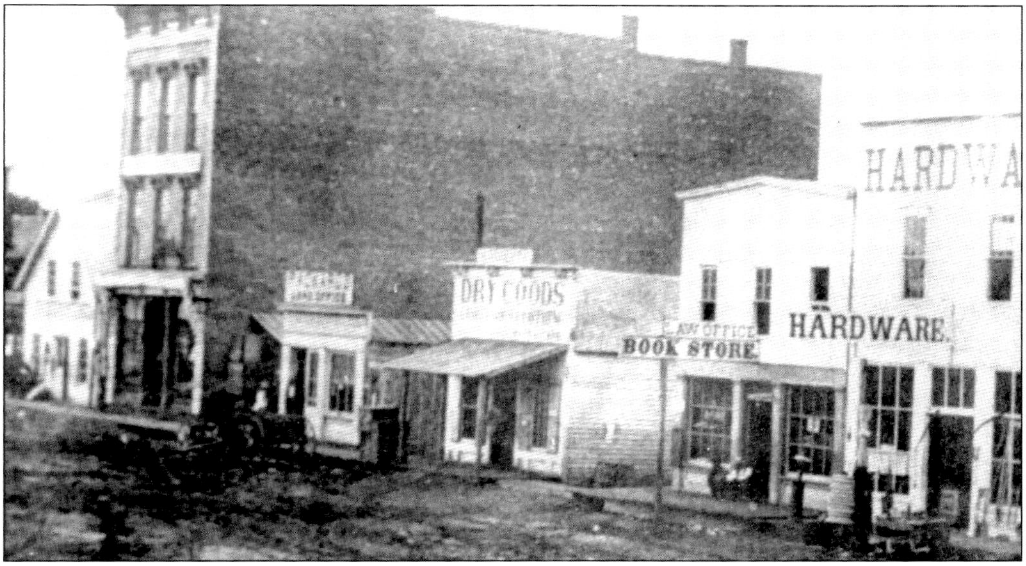

Worsley wrote, "The East side of the square boasted the best buildings in town. It was all vacant north of the alley, but about where Myer's furniture store is located was a two-story building, the first floor being occupied by an Ottumwa store company, while the Masonic lodge used the second floor. This was the best building in the town. On the corner, Cooley & Wiley had a store and east from there, was a drug store owned by Geo. Holmes. Where the Griffith Inn now stands was a hotel, conducted by Las N. Harding."

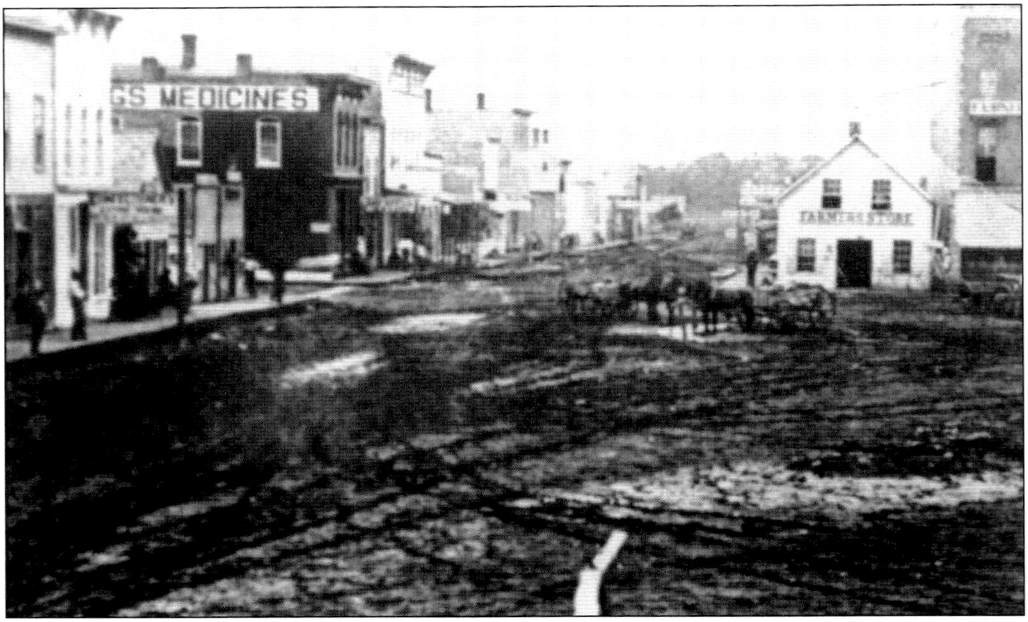

This is Oliver Perry Worsley's summary of how things were about 1870: "On the West side of the square, where Robinson's store is, was where C. H. Lane had his general store and the post office was also located there. Then it was vacant until you come to the Rogers building next to the alley, where H. Roberts & Son had a general store. Then, where the Farmer's Mercantile Co. store is, Web Eaton was putting up a building to house his newspaper office."

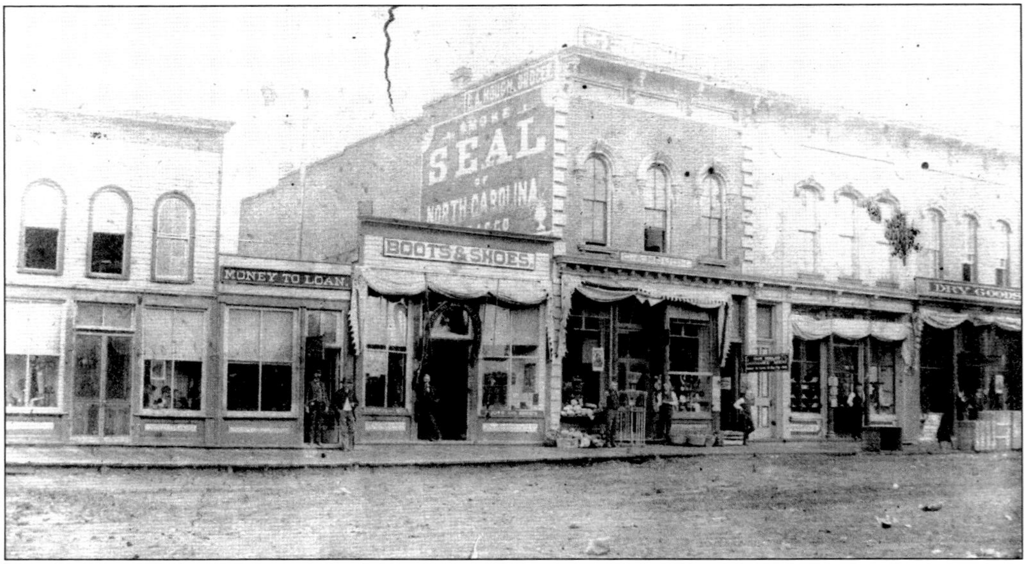

This is an early 1870s view of some shops on the square. They are one of the two millinery shops in town, the Farmer's Mercantile offering farm loans, the sign in the window advertises "Money to loan"; next to that is the only shop for boots and shoes, one entered under an oversized horseshoe that reads "Bring luck to all who enter here"; next door is C. A. Hough Grocer; an insurance agent with offices upstairs; the IOOF building; and Roberts and Sons dry goods concern, which was one of five general mercantile shops in town, was on the alley.

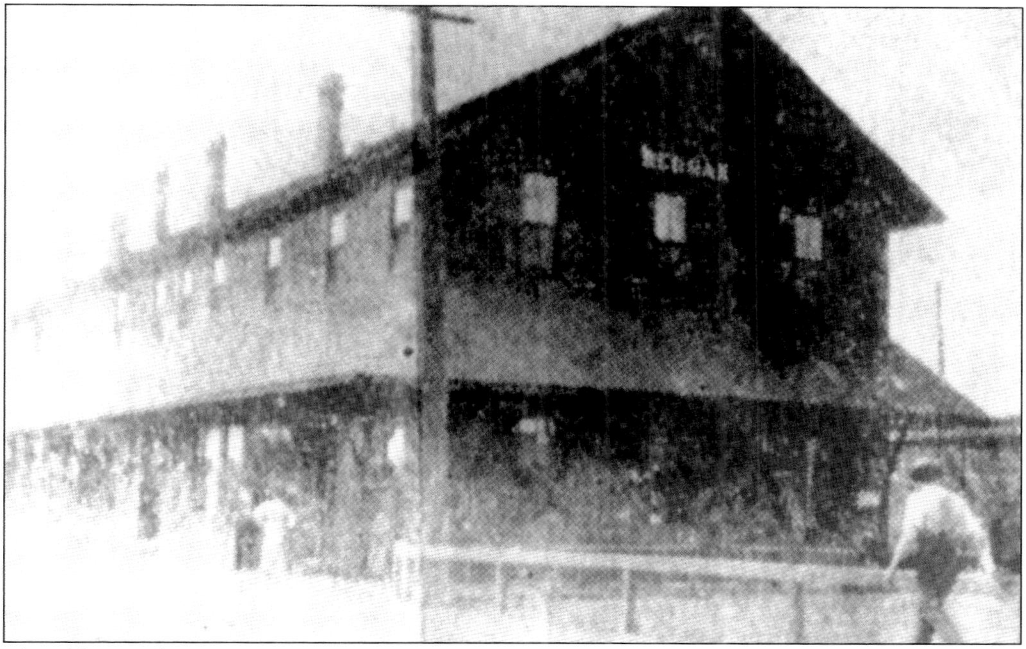

The old train depot is pictured here. In May 1856, Congress created a grant to aid in building the railroads across the nation. About 1852 or 1853 the Burlington Missouri Railroad organized with the hope of obtaining some of that grant money to build a rail line from Burlington to where the Missouri and Platt Rivers converge. The Michigan Central Railroad and the CB&Q were already in joint interest. Under the auspice of these three companies, Col. Alfred Hebard went out in the fall of 1853 to survey a route. In 1868, Hans Thielson, chief engineer, made the final survey, varying little from Hebard's original plan.

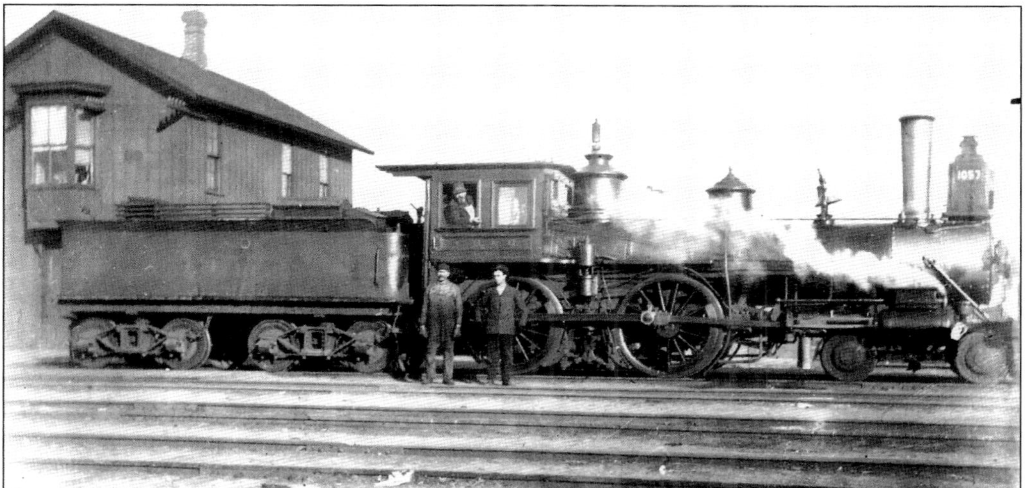

The first train came through Red Oak on November 4, 1869, with a load of lumber for Justice Clark and passengers S. A. Henry and his wife, and Mrs. George Logan. The line was up and fully running by December 25, 1869. The railroad meant the difference between life and death for the struggling settlements on the prairie. Frankfort would soon become nothing but a memory and Red Oak would grow and prosper.

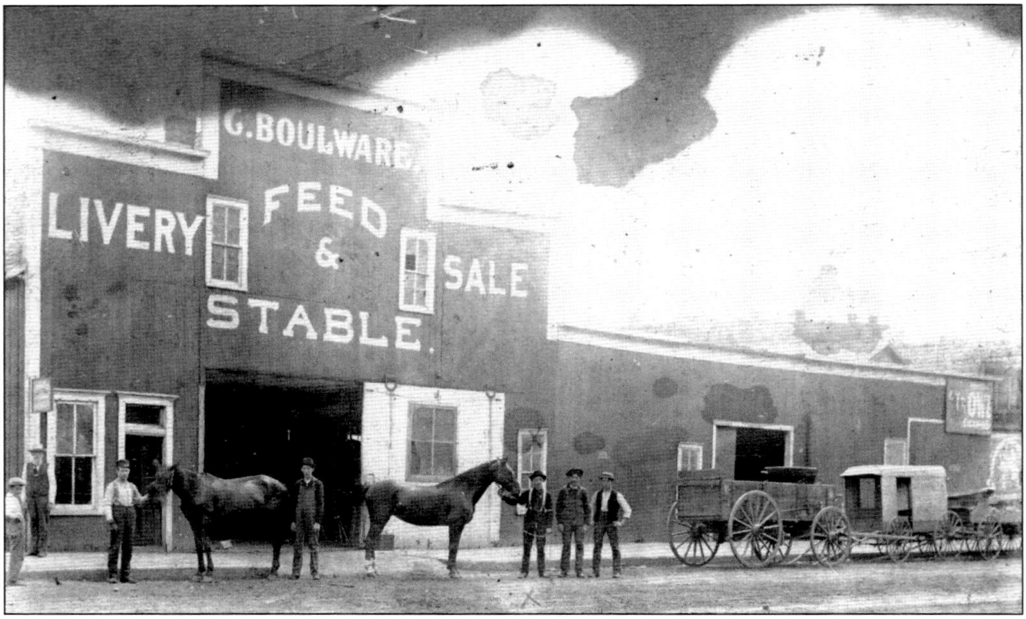

The G. Boulware Livery Barn was at Fifth and Reed Streets. J. K. Mallory was the proprietor. On the back in pencil, as best can be made out, are the names as follows: Old Man Holt, Emery Millpollen, Dr. Joe Ingsmond, John Eiler, Morgan Frank and Emmast horse to the right—A. C. Hinchman. Hinchman was a druggist in town, and the story often told was that one could go into his store, place $2 on the counter, and get a bottle of whiskey. Iowa was a dry state at the time, and it is said that he made enough money bootlegging to build an elegant mansion on Eighth Street.

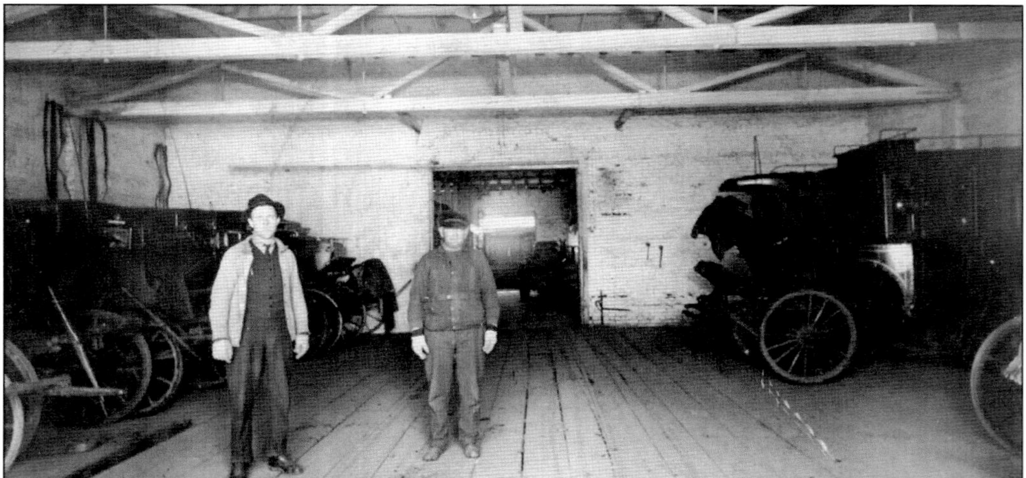

William Thomas came to the area in 1875 and became a leading merchant in town. Hawkins and Thomas sold men's furnishings. In 1890, he established the Thomas Transfer Company at 100 West Coolbaugh Street with more than 40 horses. He was one of the organizers of the Red Oak National Bank, served on the board of supervisors, was on the city council for six years, and served as mayor from 1911 to 1915. His administration was noted for practical reforms and improvements.

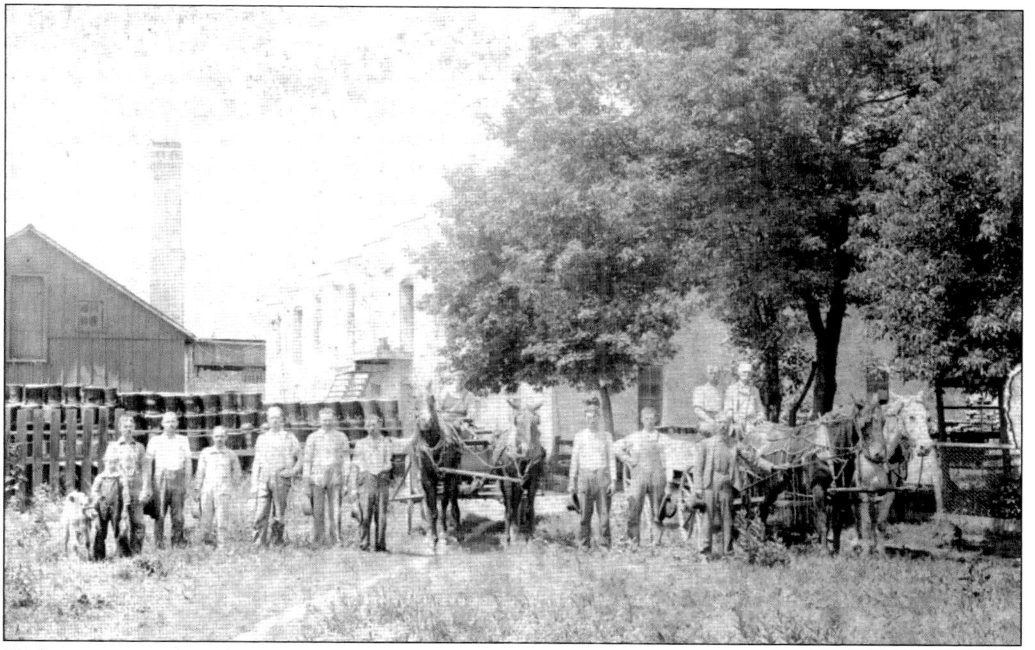

Webster Eaton, founder of the *Red Oak Express* newspaper, and his brother established one of the first industrial concerns in Red Oak between 1868 and 1871. In 1874, they established the Red Oak Pottery Works on West Coolbaugh Street and the Red Oak Creek and leased it to W. H. Close until his death in 1896. Close was succeeded by J. C. Curtis, who managed the business and added brick and tile manufacturing. R. E. Cook and F. A. Weatherhead also had brickworks in the southeast part of town.

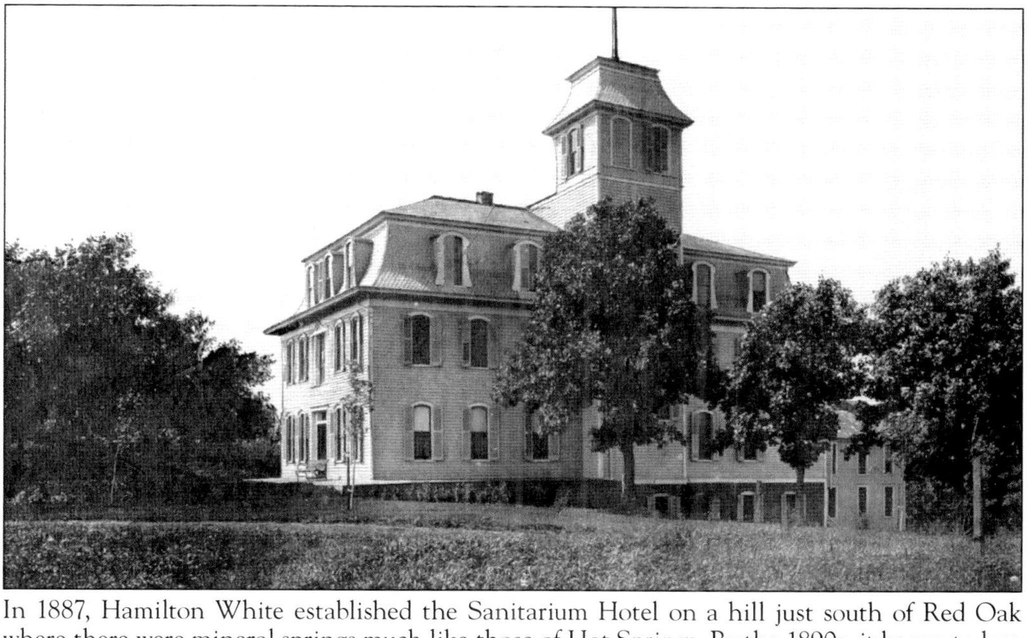

In 1887, Hamilton White established the Sanitarium Hotel on a hill just south of Red Oak where there were mineral springs much like those of Hot Springs. By the 1890s, it began to lose popularity and his venture finally failed around 1900.

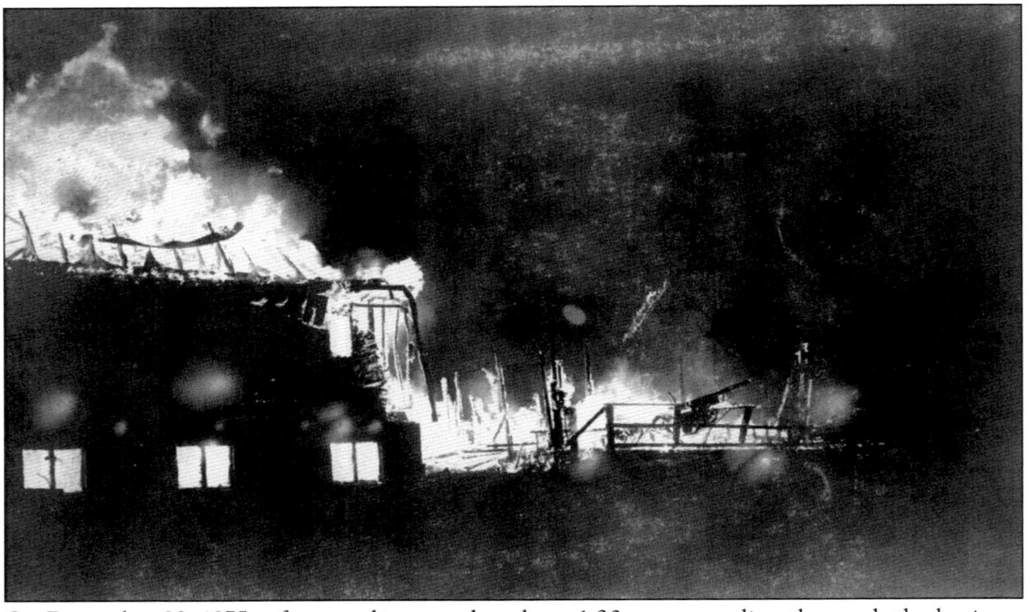

On December 23, 1875, a fire was discovered at about 1:30 a.m. spreading thorough the business section of town. The fire destroyed the east side of the square save for Dr. Wheelcock's drugstore, which survived by pulling down the nearby building. By January 7, 1876, the fire department was organized. It had one truck, which was equipped with 200 feet of hose, an 80-gallon chemical tank, and four ladders, and a three-wheeled truck, which was equipped with a 100-gallon tank, 150 feet of hose, 24 rubber buckets, two hand hooks, and four portable extinguishers. Water was pumped by hand from cisterns or wells.

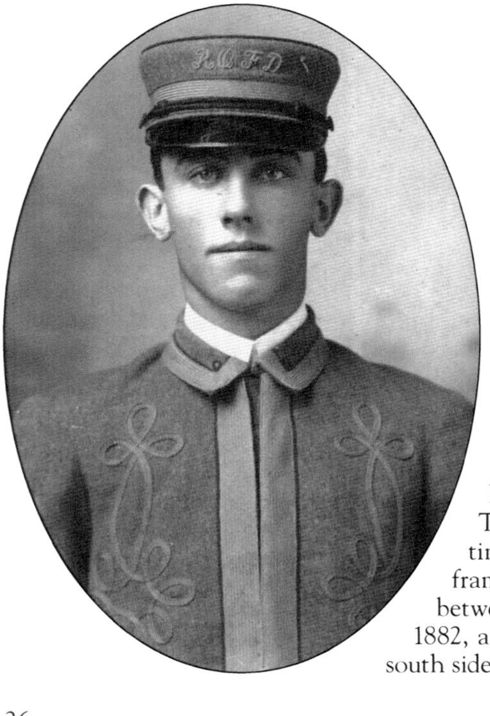

When the fire department was first organized it had two drivers and 67 members, but by 1903, it had grown to 84 members with three divisions. The city was to have two men at the station at all times. On September 18, 1876, another fire destroyed frame buildings on both sides of Coolbaugh Street between Second and Third Streets. In September of 1882, another fire raged through Red Oak. In 1902, the south side of the square burned to the ground.

Until a firehouse could be built at Washington Avenue and Fourth Street, the equipment was stored in a small shed on the Webster School grounds. The horses and equipment were on the first floor, and stairs led up to the fireman's quarters. Necessity being the mother of invention, the idea of the fireman's pole was invented in Chicago by a black man in a small firehouse in the mid-1800s.

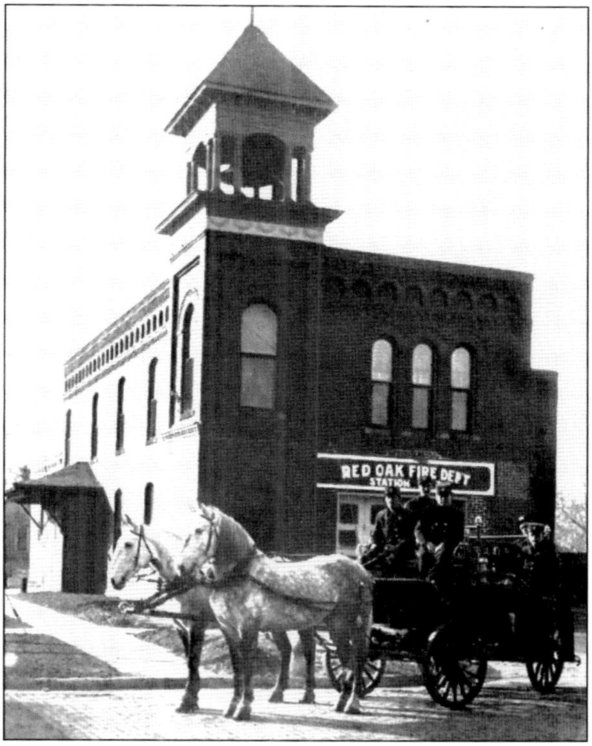

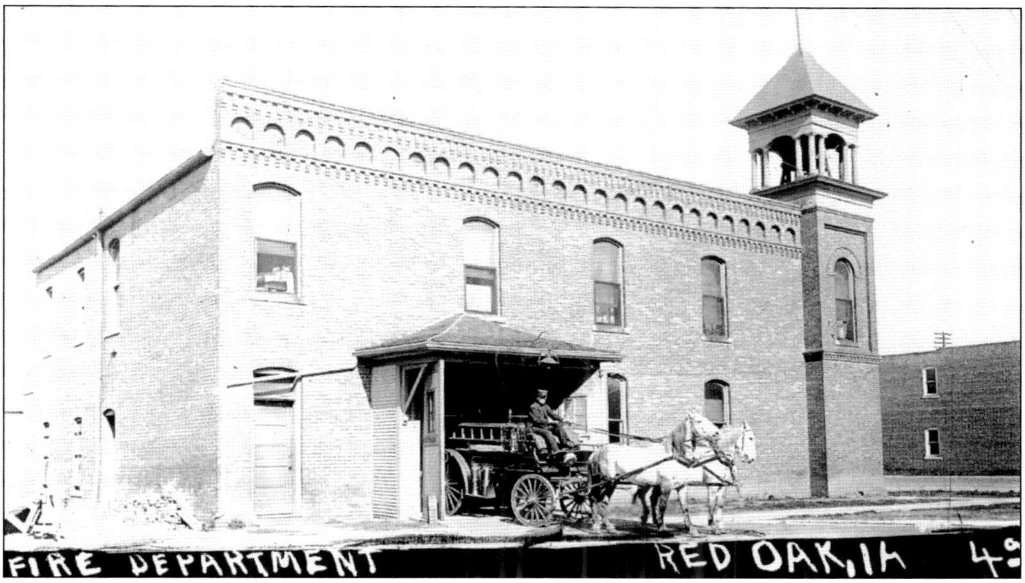

Harry Winn poses for the camera with Dude and Dandy at the state-of-the-art firehouse. Dude and Dandy served the firehouse from 1912 to 1918. At first drays were used, and then horses that were specially trained to jump into their harness without coaxing, hook up to the wagon, and run out the door. After 1879, when there was a fire, the pumping engineer at the steam-driven waterworks gave a succession of short blasts on the steamboat whistle at the pumping plant and opened the pumps to full capacity.

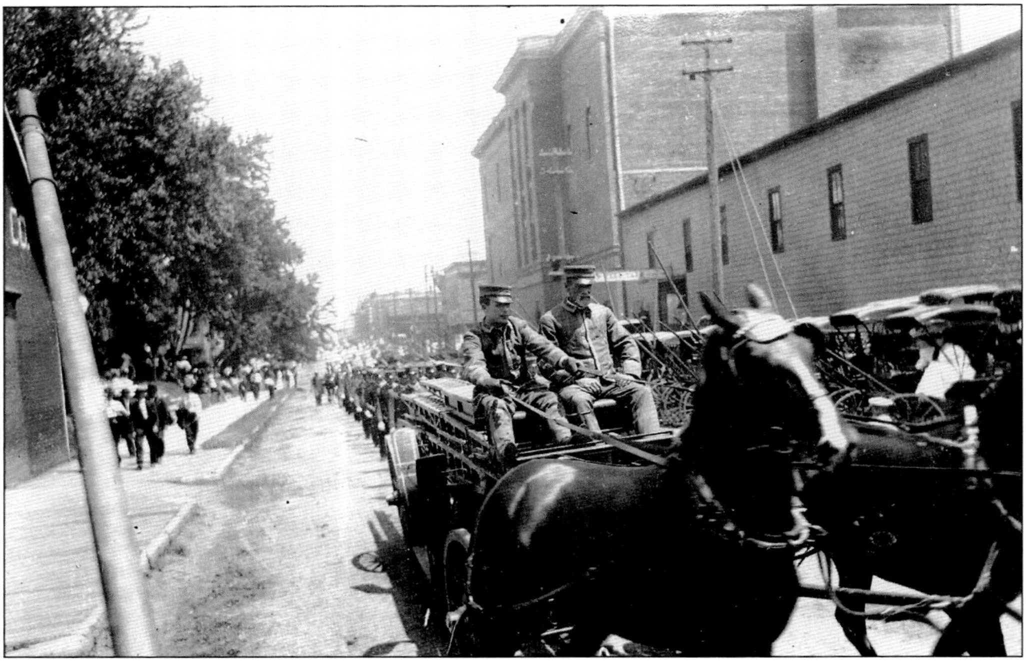

Pac and Pac pull a fire engine through town. They served until 1912, when they were sold and other horses, Dude and Dandy, were used until 1918, when all equipment was motorized.

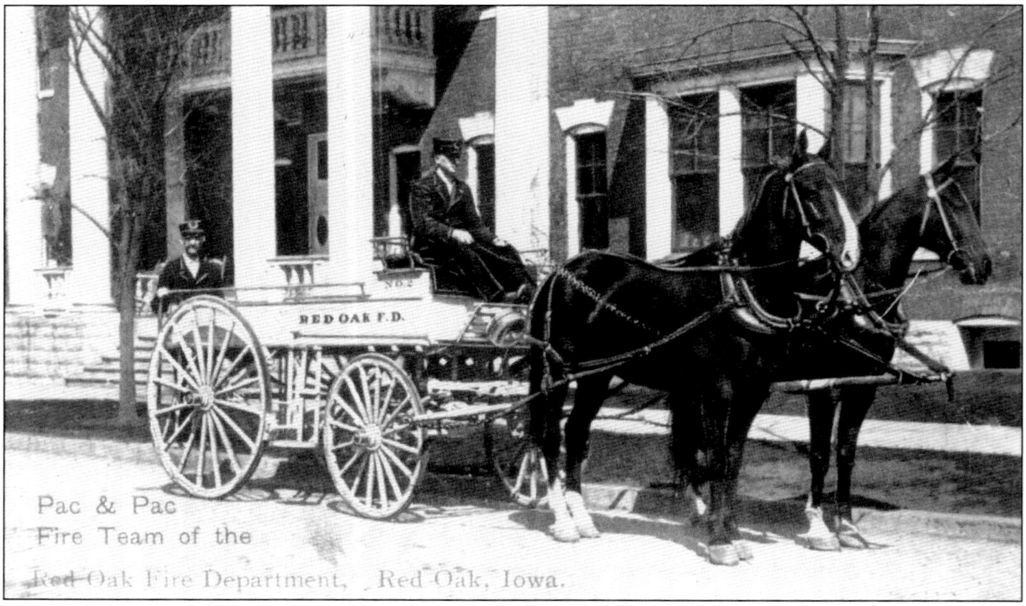

Pac and Pac were the pair of well trained horses that served the fire department for many years. They were purchased from John Blue on the recommendation of E. E. Powell. Pac and Pac were often taken to races and always won first place at any of the southwest Iowa tournaments in which they entered. Pac and Pac pose with a fire wagon in front of the Colonial Hotel with George Millhollin the driver and Mark Adams in the rear.

B. F. Everhart had a barbershop at Third and Reed Streets in the 1890s. Iowa had been an important part of the Underground Railroad and the people of Red Oak and Montgomery County helped many a slave seeking freedom as the bushwhackers pursued them from Missouri. Because the Underground Railroad relied upon secrecy, unfortunately little is recorded about the brave efforts made by those who were involved.

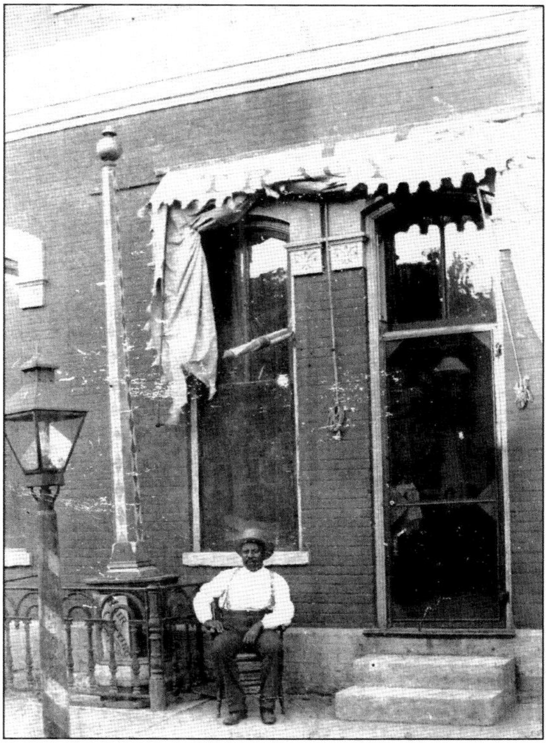

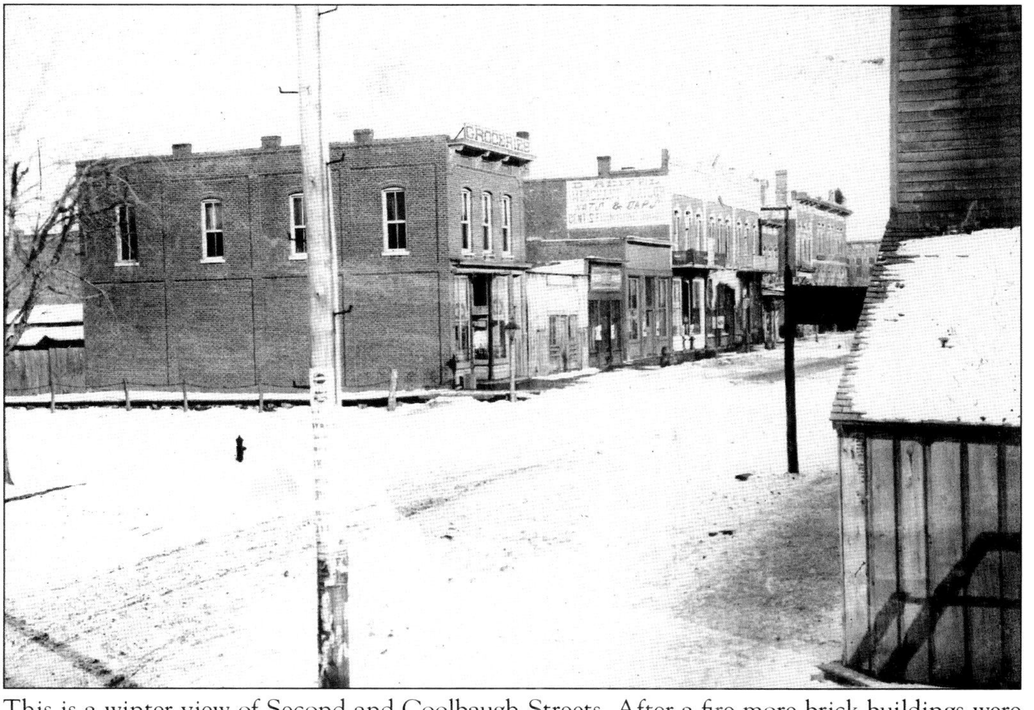

This is a winter view of Second and Coolbaugh Streets. After a fire more brick buildings were erected. Pictured is a grocer and D. Reifel's Clothing Shop and tailor's shop.

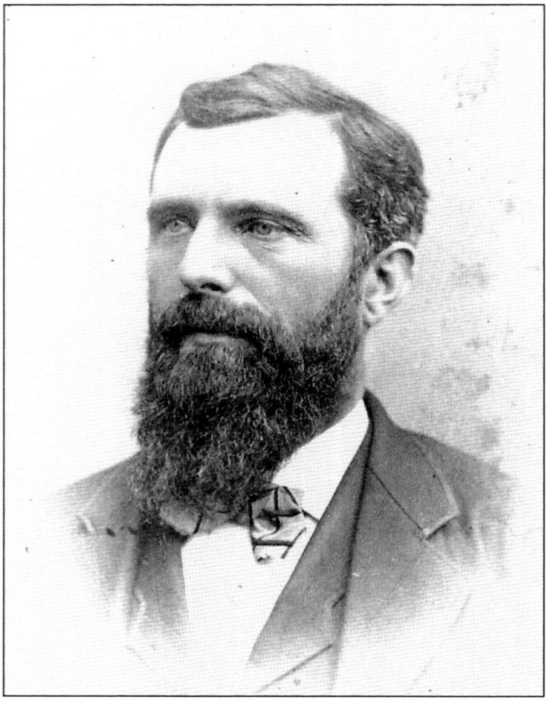

Thomas Griffith was a driving force in Red Oak. Born in Wales in 1840, he immigrated in 1866 and came to Red Oak in 1869. He was involved in farming, real estate, banking, and loans. Through good management and wise investment, he became a wealthy man. In 1880, he married Mary Negus of Fairfield. She was the daughter of Judge Charles Negus, a prominent Democrat of his day. As mayor, public health and cleanliness were important, and road grading, drainage, better sidewalks, and paved streets around the square were a few of Griffith's improvements.

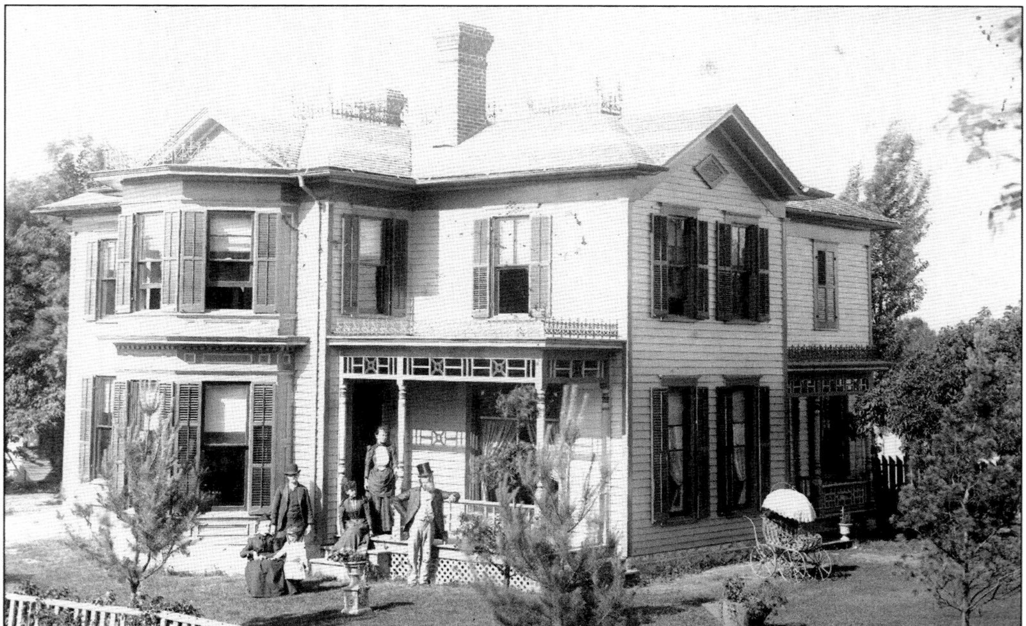

Thomas Griffith's home at 510 Coolbaugh Street is seen about 1888. From left to right are Marion Eleanor Negus, Blanche Martha Griffith, Lyman Smith Nagus, Susan Ella Nagus, Mary Cary Griffith, and Thomas Griffith. This house is no longer standing. Thomas swapped this house for another one at 602 Eight Street, which is still much as it was when he lived there.

Judge Smith McPherson was born in 1848, graduated from Iowa State University in 1870, and began clerking in his uncle M. L. McPherson's law offices in Council Bluffs. He settled in Red Oak and practiced law with W. T. Carlton. He was appointed district attorney from 1874 to 1878 and was elected Iowa attorney general in 1880. In March 1910, John Mabray stood before him in a federal courtroom in Council Bluffs. Mabray was the head of a confidence ring. Mabray operated out of his Big Store, headquartered in the Merriam Block in Council Bluffs. He and his gang bilked over $5 million from people across the nation.

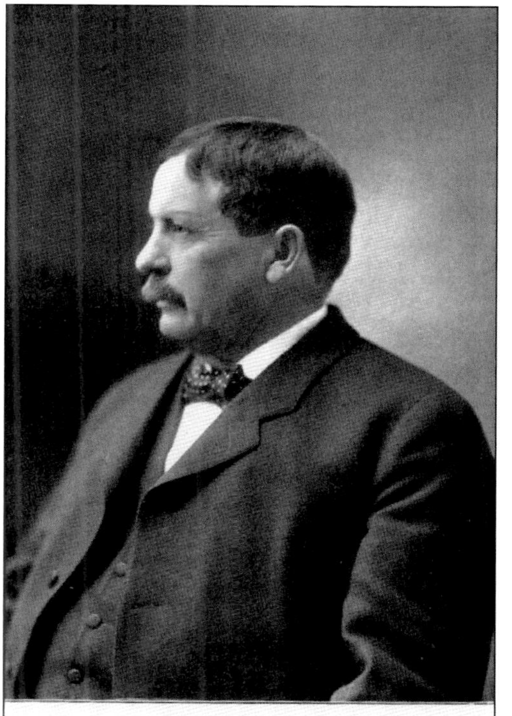

JUDGE SMITH McPHERSON.

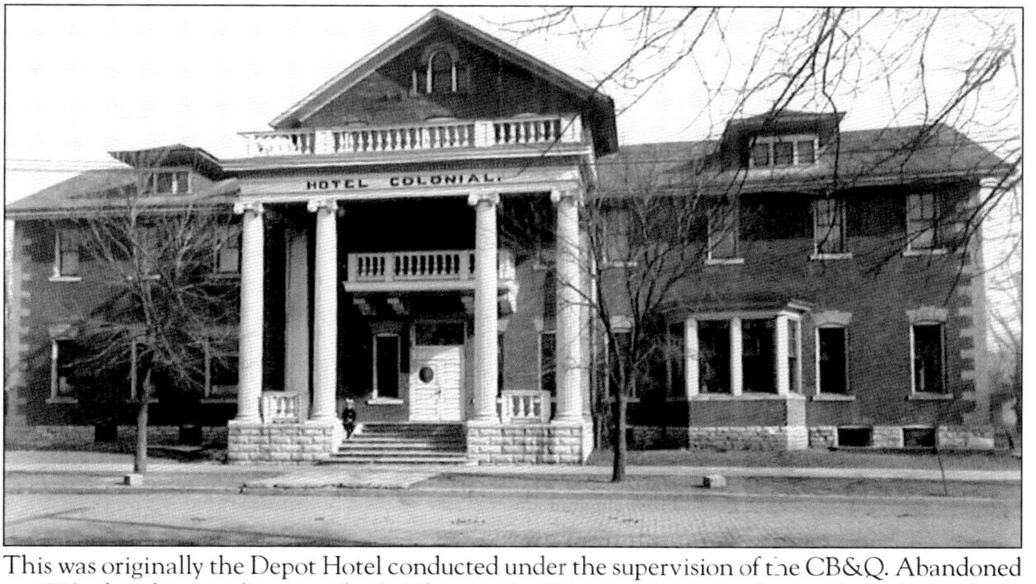

This was originally the Depot Hotel conducted under the supervision of the CB&Q. Abandoned in 1903 after the new depot was built, Thomas Griffith purchased it and moved it to Second and Market Streets where Laz Harding once had a hotel. He remodeled it with a brick veneer, classic columns, and added steam heat and electric lighting. He named it the Colonial Inn. It was known for an exceptionally fine restaurant. Mrs. Long remembered that the chicken chow mien was excellent. By 1931, this had become the Hotel Cooper, and it advertised that it operated on the European plan.

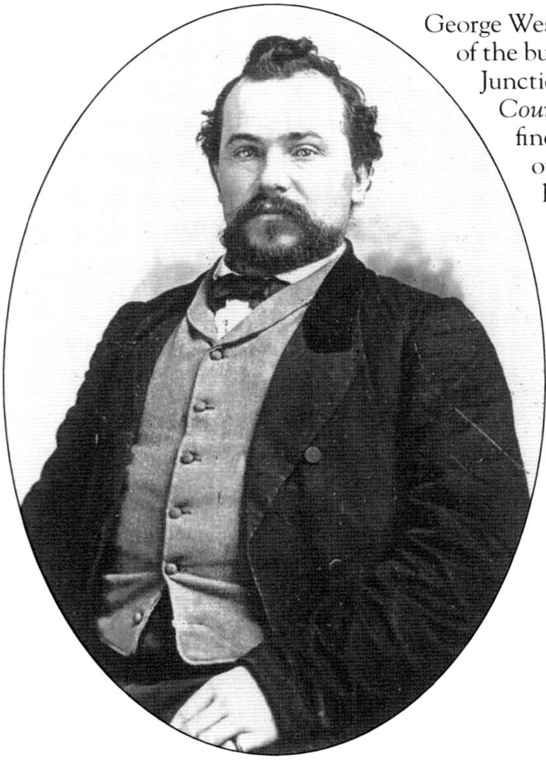

George West was a builder and architect who built many of the businesses, schools, and fine homes in Red Oak Junction. Merritt, in his *History of Montgomery County*, states that "Red Oak is said to have more fine residences and comfortable homes than any other town of its size in the state. Its business houses are substantial in appearance and are well kept; its merchants are progressive and up to date." This was the Red Oak George West helped to build. This photograph was taken in 1858.

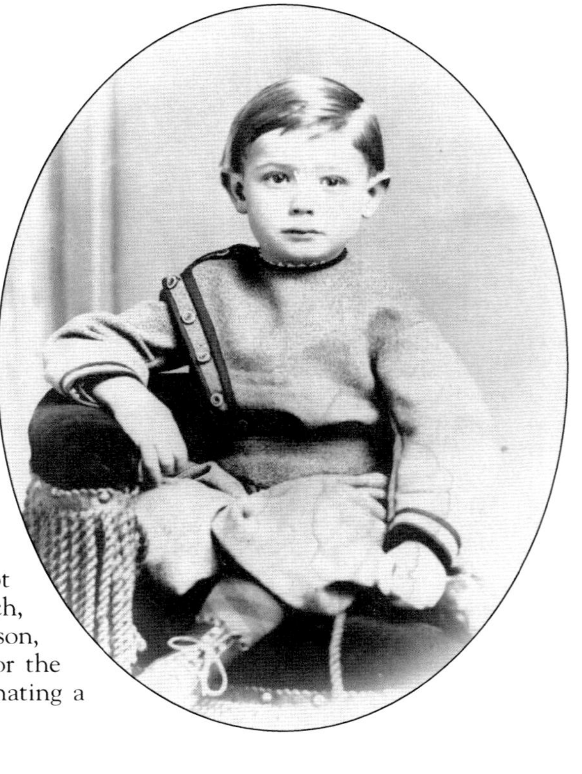

Henry Hebard West, son of George West, was born on January 23, 1872, in Red Oak. His middle name is in honor of Col. Alfred Hebard, whose house his father was building when he was born. In his later years, he wrote a memoir about growing up in Red Oak. Once when he got in trouble as a child, he knew he did not want to embarrass his family or his church, so he said his name was Smith McPherson, someone he admired. He was fined $1 for the mischief and another dollar for impersonating a federal court judge.

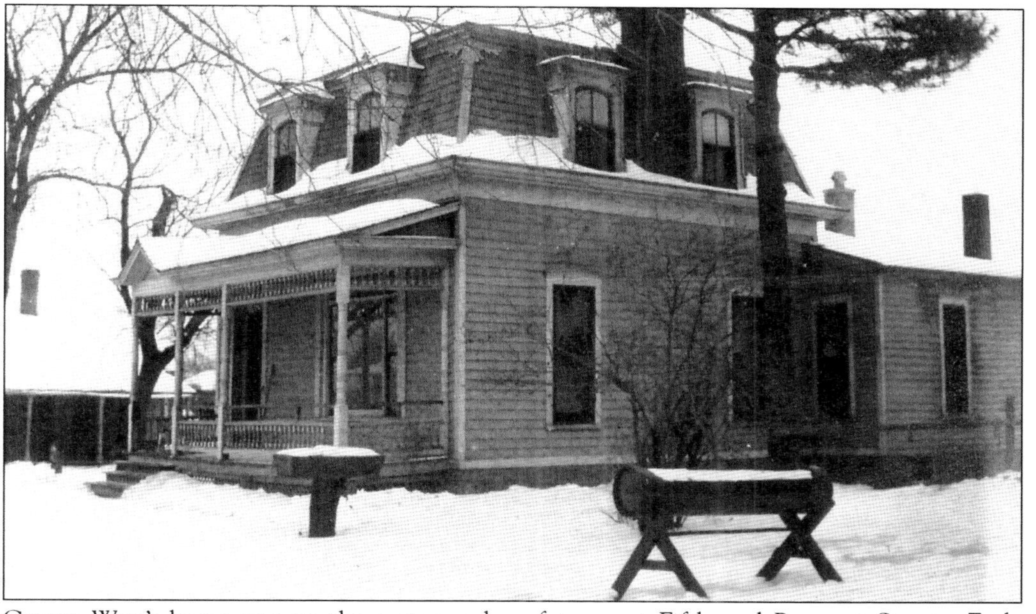

George West's home was on the eastern edge of town, at Fifth and Prospect Streets. Early one morning in 1882, West got a call demanding he come downtown. He was in the process of building the Masonic hall. He had instructed the workers to leave the scaffolding on the brick walls in place until the next day, when they would add the roof joists. They removed the scaffolding anyway. During the night, high winds had blown the front of the building apart. West braced the sidewalls that were out of line and brought the walls back into plumb with rods and bolts. They are still in place today.

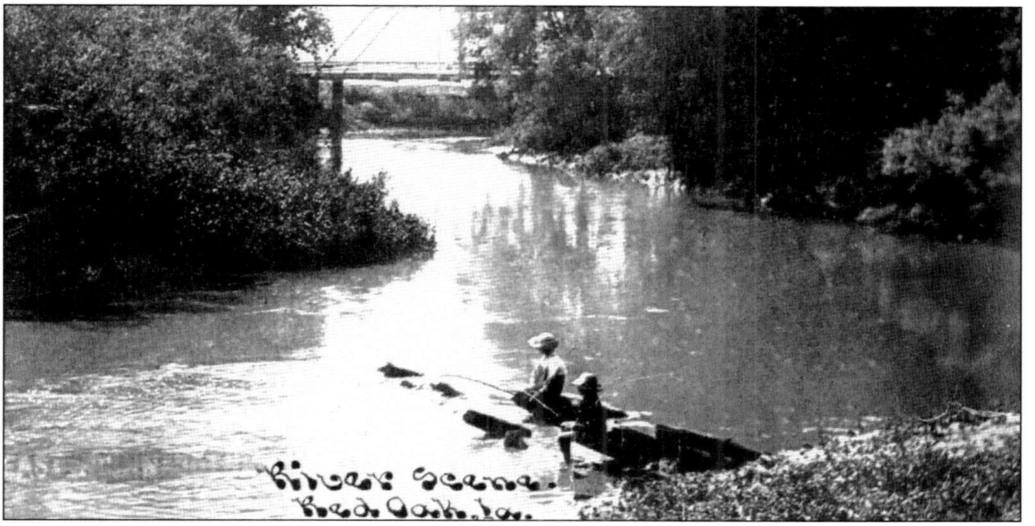

Henry Hebard West swam in the Nishnabotna River as a boy. He and his friends stripped off their clothes to swim just below the white bridge. After train passengers complained about the naked boys, constable Logan would walk down the tracks; as he approached, the boys would see him and slip into the woods. Once a boy lobbed a purloined apple at a passing train. The apple sailed through the cab window and hit the fireman. After that, the fireman would stand in the engine doorway, tossing coal to even the score—he never did.

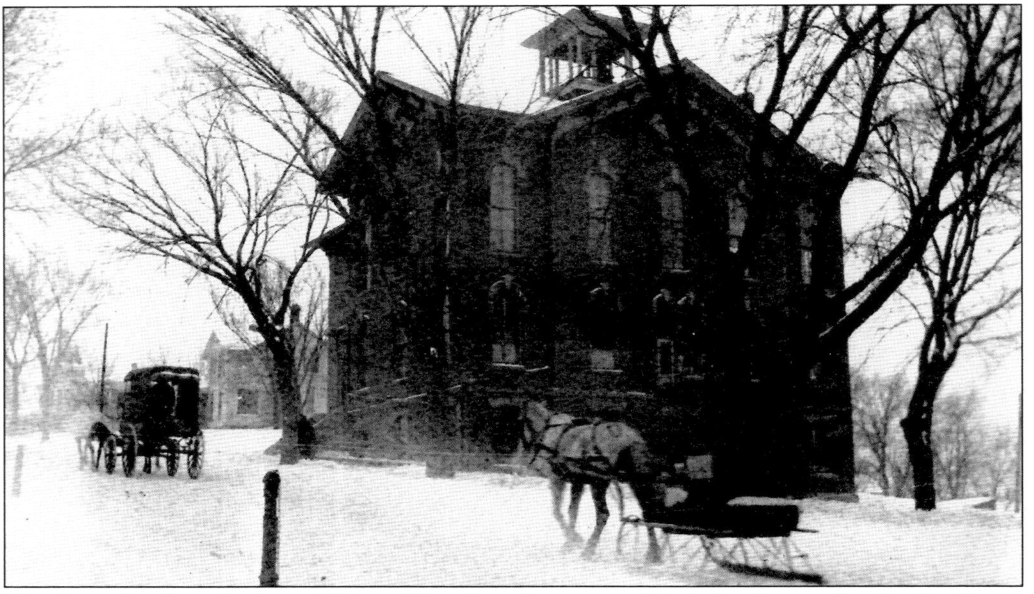

The first school was built in 1859 on West First Street near Nuckols of native lumber by Henry Campbell at a cost of about $250 to $300. In 1863, a second school was built of brick located on Corning Street. Kerrihard was the contractor and Bolt did the masonry. The East Ward School, pictured here, was built by George West in 1871. His son attended from first grade through high school in this school. It was later renamed Lincoln and was used up until 1952.

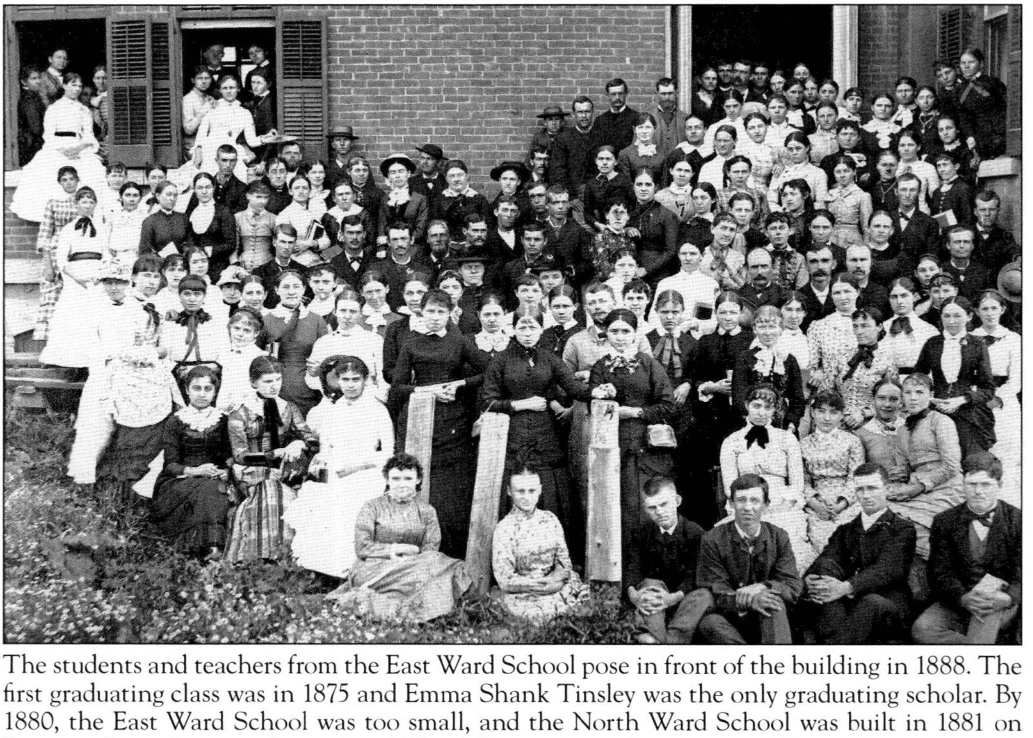

The students and teachers from the East Ward School pose in front of the building in 1888. The first graduating class was in 1875 and Emma Shank Tinsley was the only graduating scholar. By 1880, the East Ward School was too small, and the North Ward School was built in 1881 on Prospect Street between Second and Third Streets. It was later renamed Bancroft.

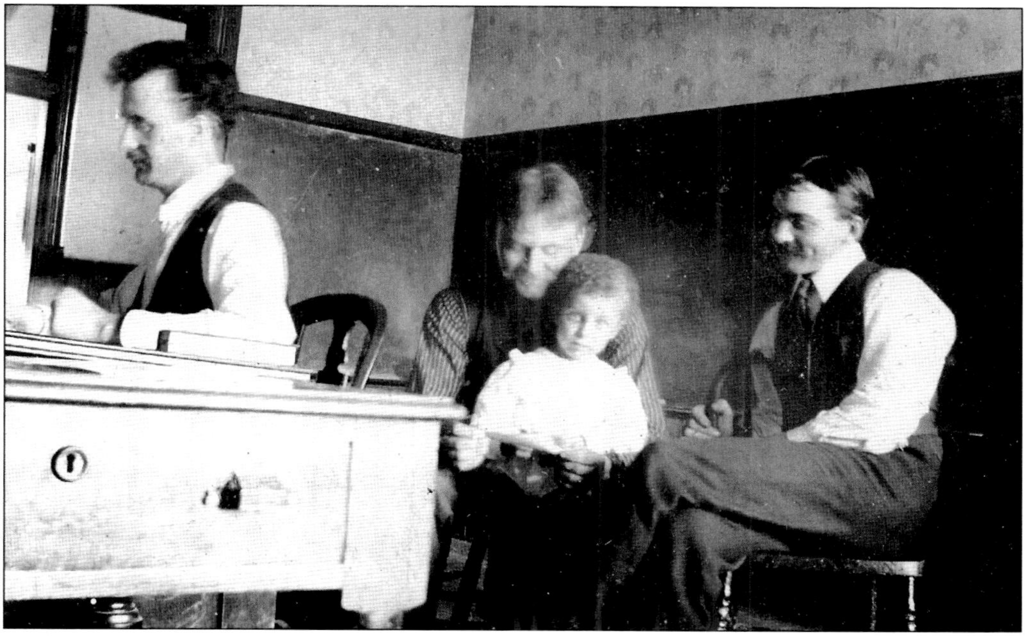

Prof. Ira Condit, at the desk; professor Rogers, holding the Condit child; and professor Nichols are pictured in a schoolroom around 1895. Red Oak was growing and the need for schools grew with the population. In 1885, South Ward School, later renamed Jefferson, was built on High between Second and Third Streets. Also built that same year was Webster on Broad Street between Joy and Valley Streets. In 1892, the West Ward School, Washington, was built at West First and Coolbaugh Street. The high school was built in 1916.

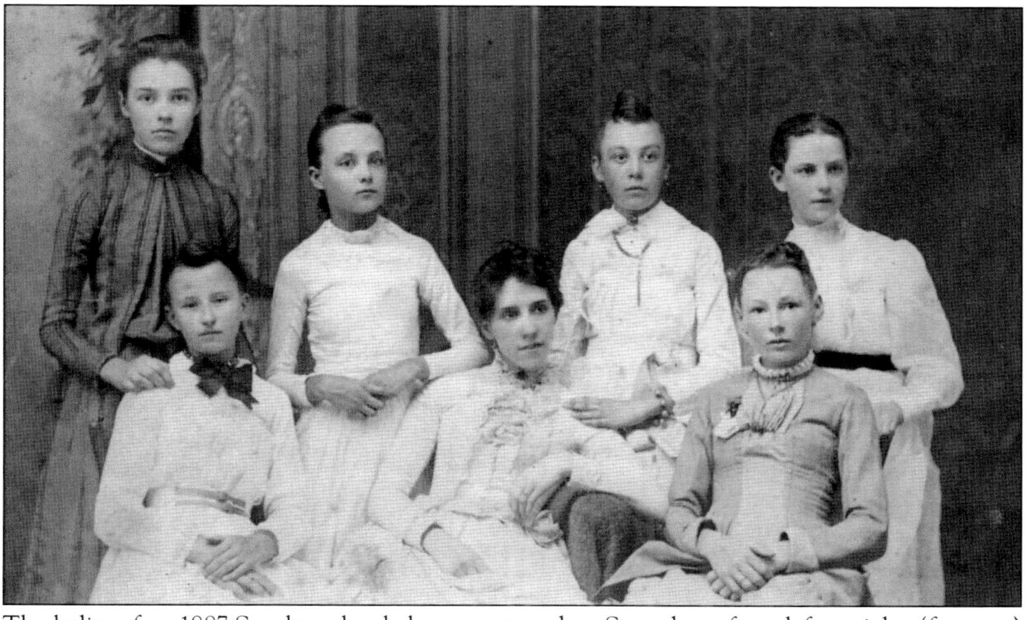

The ladies of an 1887 Sunday school class pose together. Seated are, from left to right, (first row) Rebecca Baker; Zoe Hopson, teacher; and Abbie Godfrey; (second row) Emma Binns; Leah Gassner; Lizzie Ashby; and Emma Manley.

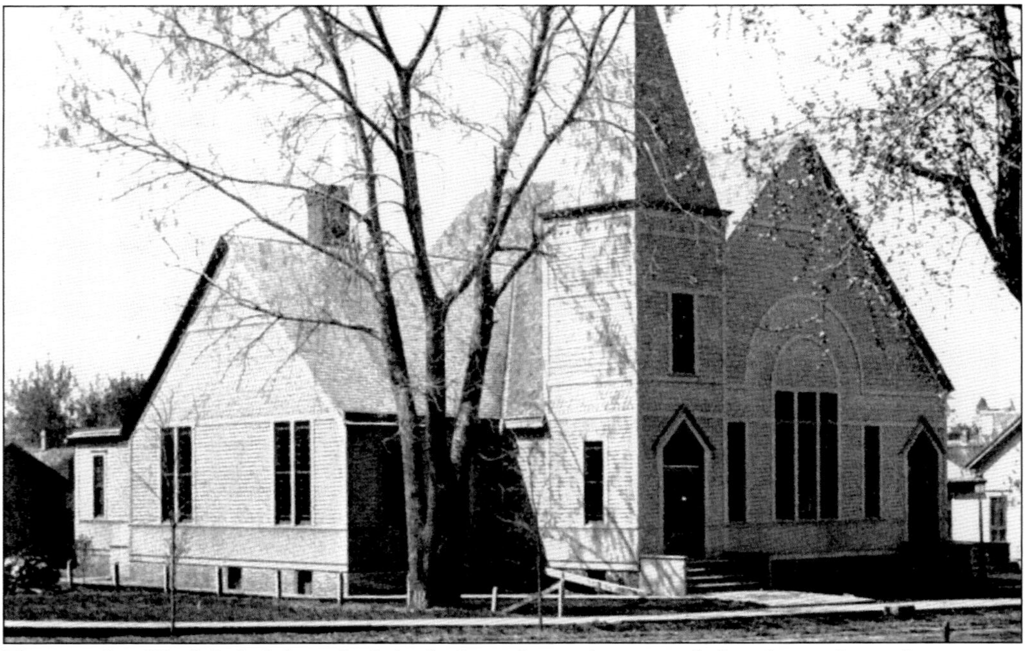

The people of Red Oak did not lack for faith or the traditions and churches to keep them strong in their devotion. The first church in the village of Red Oak was the Baptist church. It was organized on August 31, 1856.

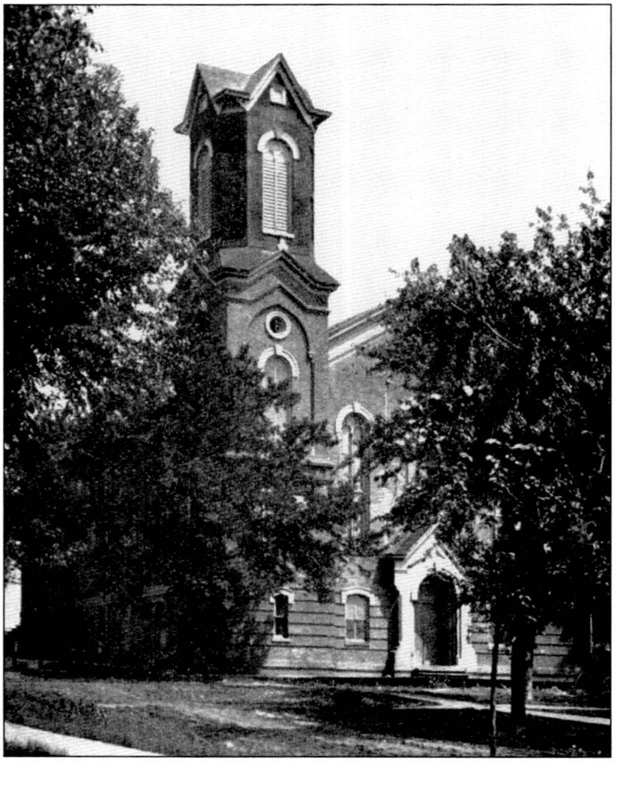

The first sermon preached in Montgomery County was by the Reverend Rand, a Methodist circuit rider from Adams County. Rev. Samuel Farlow had the honor of preaching the first Methodist sermon in the spring of 1857 in a log cabin on East Coolbaugh Street. Pastor Breeze was often seen with a rifle aimed at the steeple shooting woodpeckers. He did some fancy shooting. Pictured here is the Methodist Episcopal church around 1900.

The Presbyterian Church was organized on June 13, 1869. As a child, H. H. West remembered one Sunday morning at the Presbyterian church when preacher Chaffen, in the midst of a forcible exhortation, opened his mouth a little too wide and his false teeth flew out, shot over the pulpit, and landed on the floor below the platform.

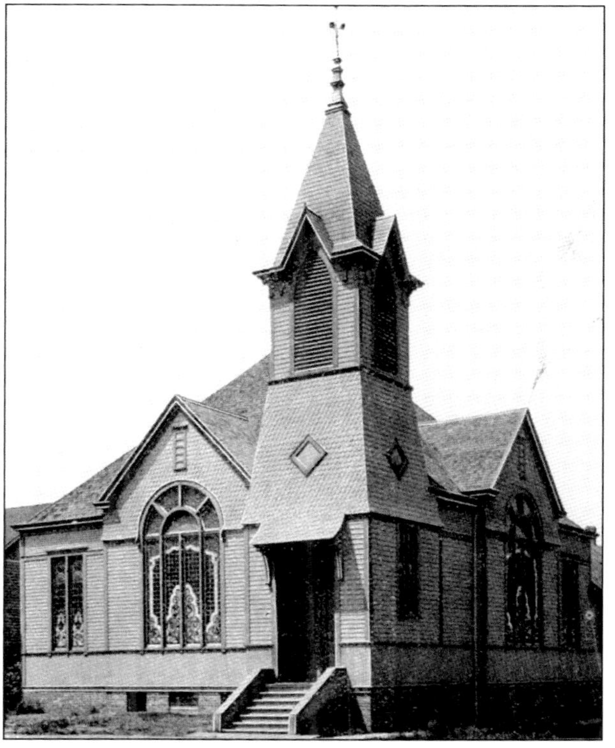

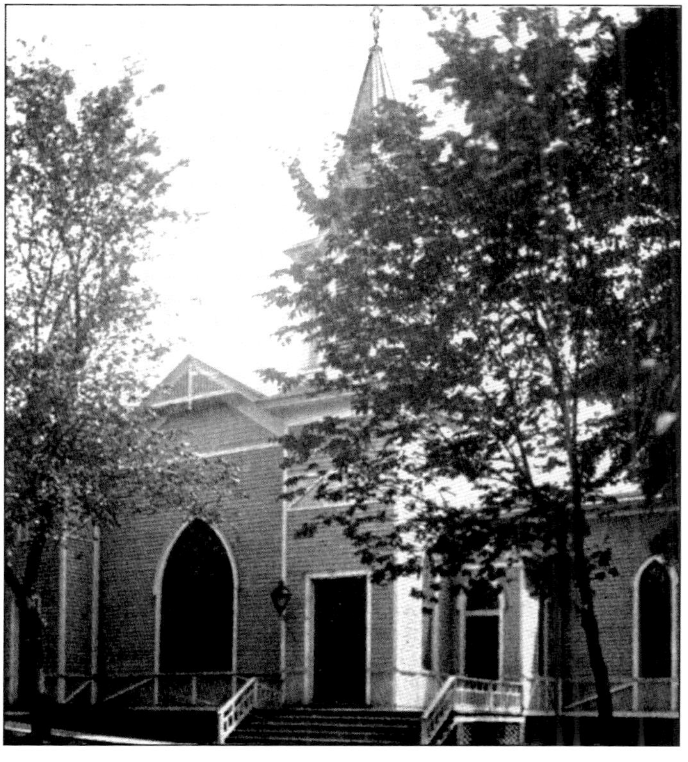

In 1869, John Todd called upon the Congregationalists. On August 8, 1870, they met in the Baptist church to organize their church. This church was built in 1873 by 24 members. One Christmas, Ike Brown, the superintendent, played Santa Claus. Brown reached into the tree, lit with colored candles, and his outfit caught fire. The men in the front row grabbed him and threw him out the window into the snow. They slapped him with snow until the fire was extinguished. He was badly burned on his face and arms.

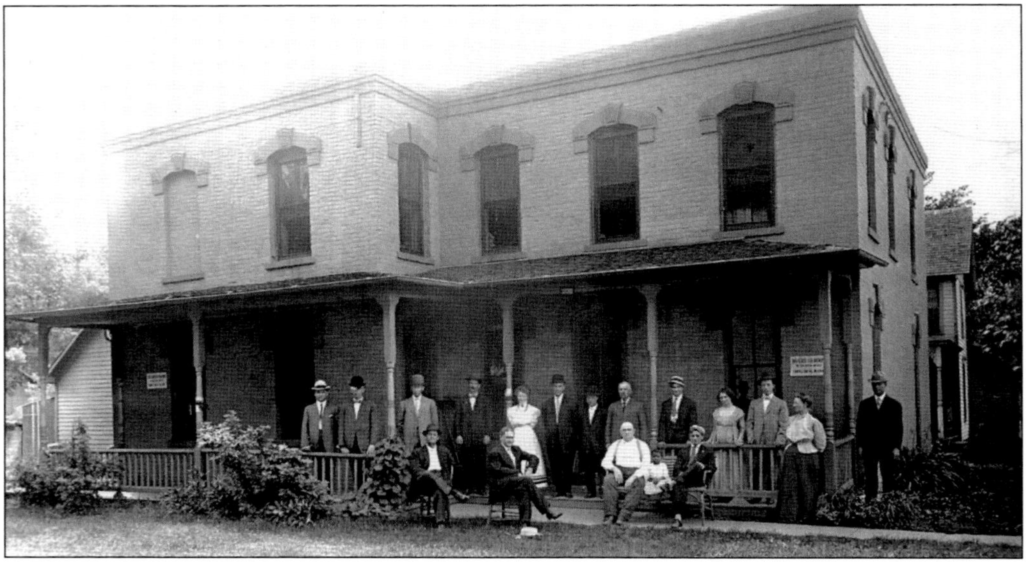

Before 1875, Montgomery County had no jail of its own. In January 1870, the county board joined with Red Oak to build a calaboose with an iron cell. There was not much crime, so the city used it to hold hobos or drunks. In the morning, they were taken to the Blue Front, given breakfast, and told to hit the road. Bolt, Crockett and Company were contracted to build a larger jail in 1875. It was brick and had two stories with six cells lined in boiler iron. There were rooms for the jailer and sheriff to be housed. A new jail was constructed in 1900. The old jail was sold and converted into a boardinghouse. The sign reads, "Rooms by the week or day—Mrs. George Barr." The man in the white shirt on the bench to the right is George Barr; Mrs. Barr is to the right standing on the porch. Mrs. Combs is dressed in white standing between eight unidentified men on the porch. Fen Moore is the man seated in the chair to the far left.

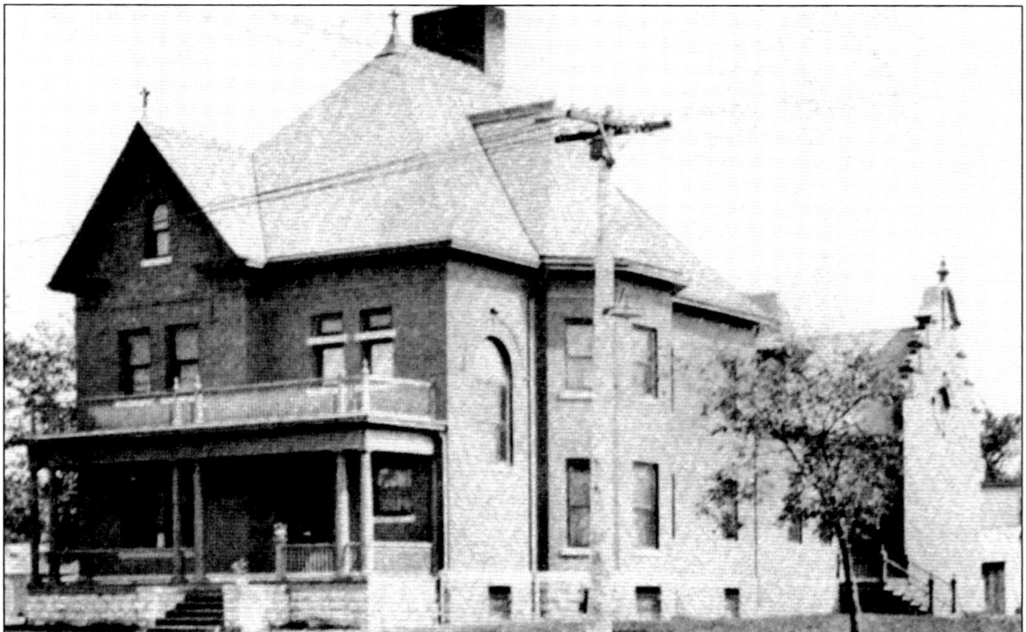

Early in 1889, the *Red Oak Independent* discussed building a new courthouse. Eight hundred people signed the petition for the board of supervisors to put it to a vote. It passed and $75,000 was allocated. On July 4, 1890, the cornerstone was laid. Richards and Company of Omaha was contracted to do the work, but it went out of business in July 1891, before the work was completed. The owner tried to sue the county for payment of work not completed but lost. Charles Bolt was contracted to complete the roof work.

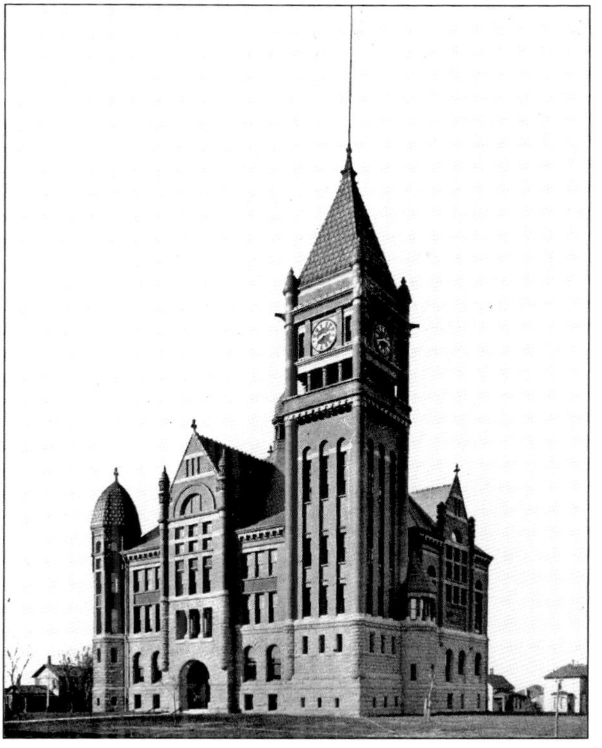

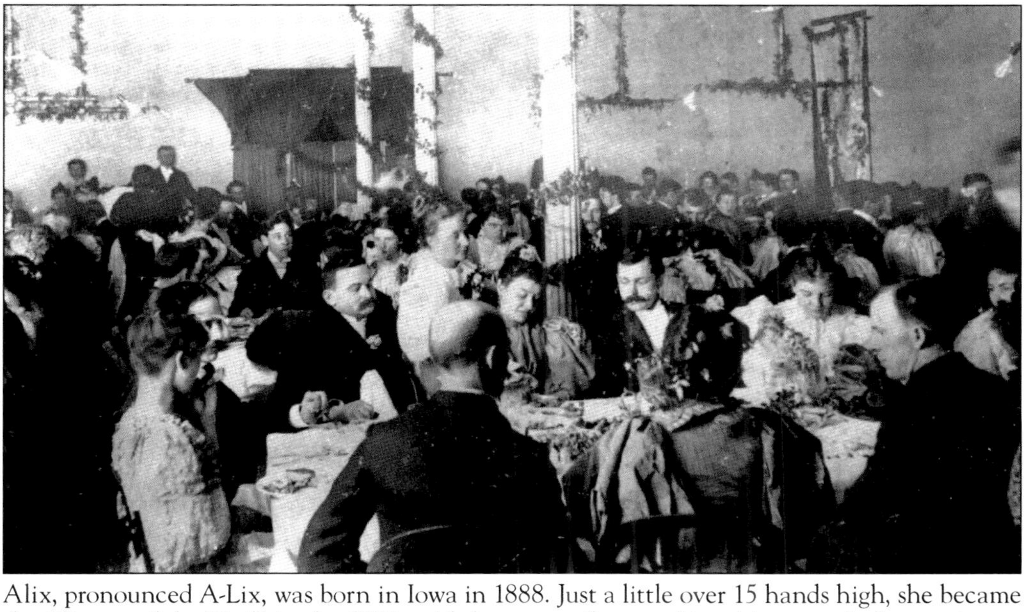

Alix, pronounced A-Lix, was born in Iowa in 1888. Just a little over 15 hands high, she became the "Queen of the Turf" in the 1890s with her one-mile-record-breaking speed of two minutes and three and three-quarters seconds. Carl Sandburg wrote a poem for sweet little Alix. Morris Jones and Red Oak investors built Pactolus Park. The race track was a failure from the beginning; it rained heavily turning the turf into a morass. Ironically the Pactolus was the river King Midas was told to bathe in to rid himself of the golden touch.

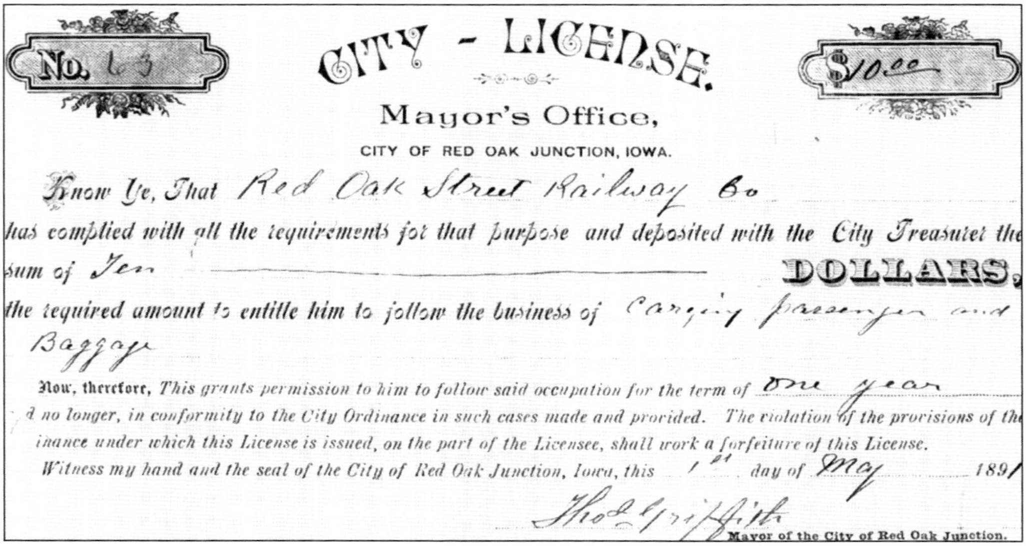

No. 63 — CITY - LICENSE. — $10.00

Mayor's Office,

CITY OF RED OAK JUNCTION, IOWA.

Know Ye, That Red Oak Street Railway Co

has complied with all the requirements for that purpose and deposited with the City Treasurer the sum of Ten DOLLARS, the required amount to entitle him to follow the business of Carrying passenger and Baggage

Now, therefore, This grants permission to him to follow said occupation for the term of One year and no longer, in conformity to the City Ordinance in such cases made and provided. The violation of the provisions of the ordinance under which this License is issued, on the part of the Licensee, shall work a forfeiture of this License.

Witness my hand and the seal of the City of Red Oak Junction, Iowa, this 1st day of May 1891

Thos Griffith
Mayor of the City of Red Oak Junction.

In November 1881, Johnson, Lockhart, Hinchman, Houghton, Hayes, West, Palmer, Whitaker, Byrkit, Fisher, Clarke, and the Wadsworths joined forces to create the Red Oak Street Railway. Johnson was named president, Whitaker as superintendent. It opened on April 1, 1882, with $10,000 in track and equipment. Two cars were pulled by either a horse or mule. The line traveled from Sixth and Prospect Streets, west on Reed Street, south on Fourth Street, and west on Coolbaugh Street to the Washington School and south to the Depot Hotel. The run took about 15 minutes and cost 5¢.

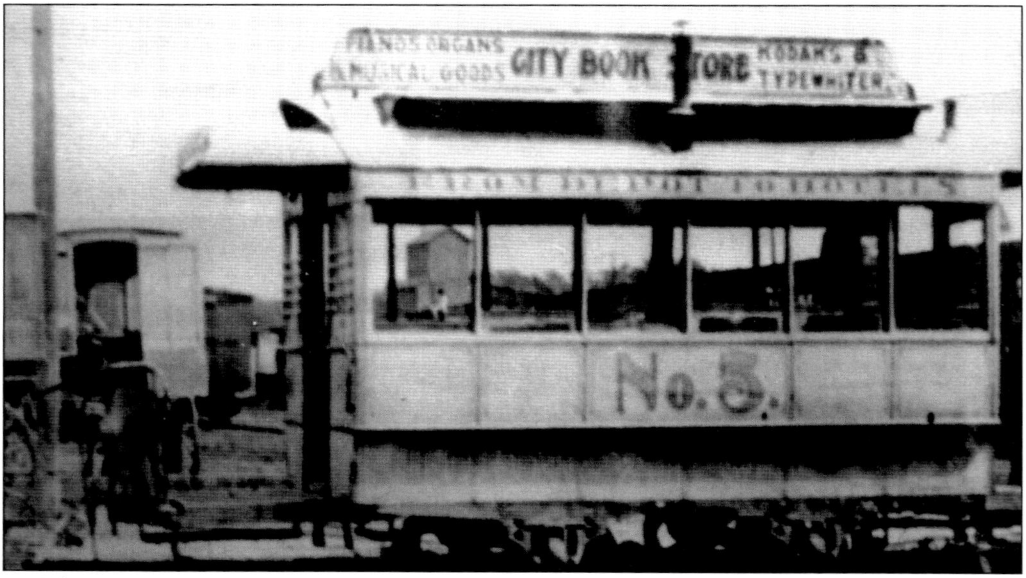

In February 1886, Marcus Bonham took control and ran the Red Oak Street Railway for the next 15 years. He made no attempt to keep to a time schedule, but always managed to make it on time to the trains. In 1901, it was sold to S. P. Wallace who kept it until 1902, when the city tore up the tracks to pave the streets. Wallace had no money for paving between the tracks, and made no effort to improve them. He tried to sue but was unsuccessful against Mayor Thomas Griffith and the city council.

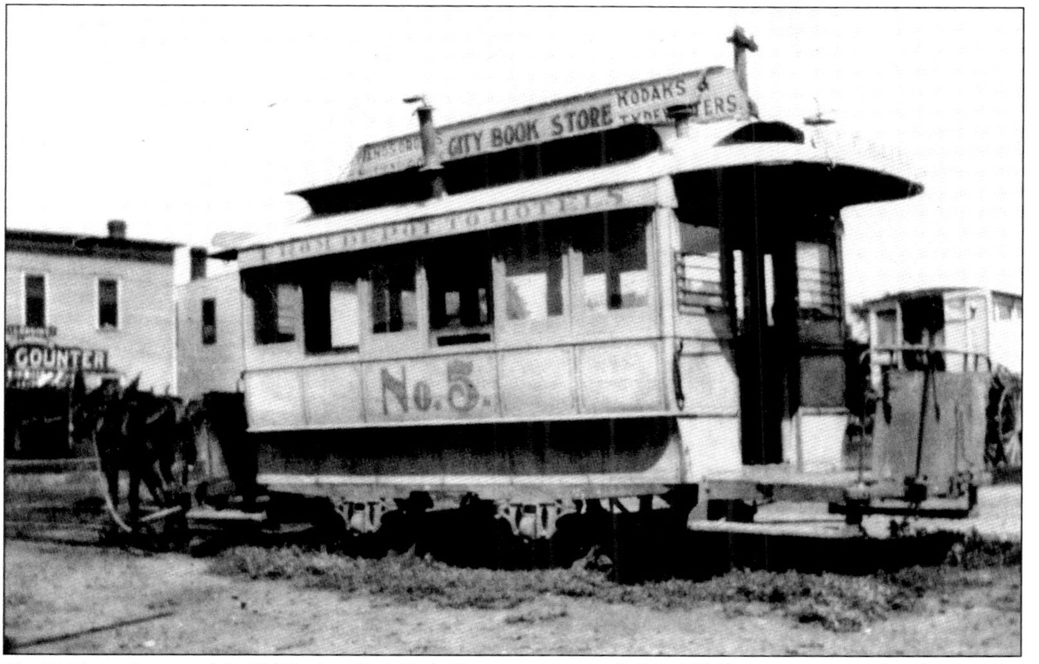

On Friday, August 15, 1902, the *Red Oak Express* reported that Wallace attempted to lay tracks after the city had taken them up for paving. He threatened the paving contractor; a warrant was sworn out for his arrest. At about 5:00 a.m., officer Damuth noticed water running down Coolbaugh Street and discovered the fire plug was opened. Water flooded the area where the paving was to be done, but was turned off before it could damage the cement. When workmen arrived, Wallace made such a scene that he was placed under arrest. He called his wife to bail him out. When she arrived, officer Doris disarmed her of her revolver.

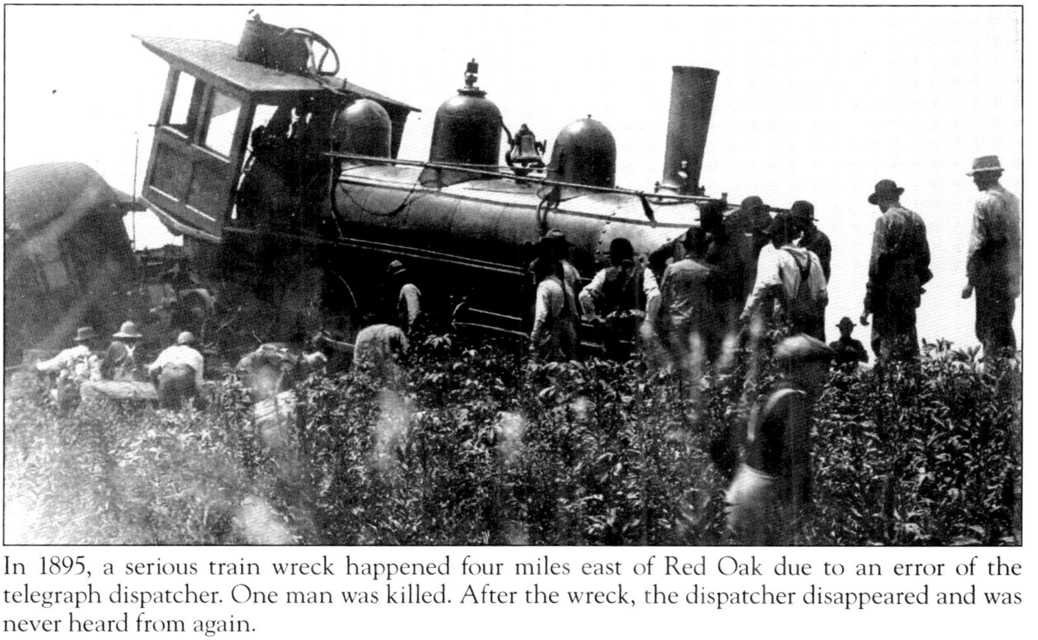

In 1895, a serious train wreck happened four miles east of Red Oak due to an error of the telegraph dispatcher. One man was killed. After the wreck, the dispatcher disappeared and was never heard from again.

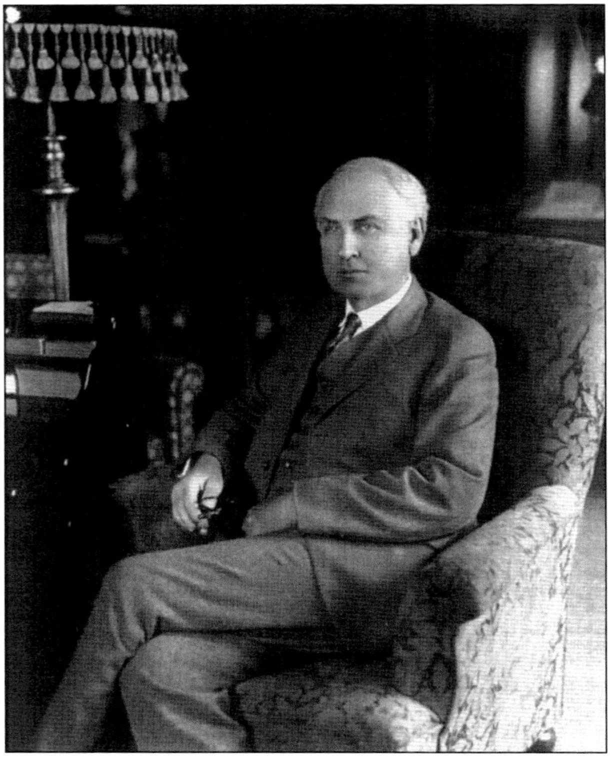

One of the most influential people to come to Red Oak was Thomas Dowler Murphy. In 1888, he graduated from Simpson College. His classmate Edmond Osborne convinced him to join him in purchasing the *Red Oak Independent*, one of three newspapers in town. In 1890, the Osborne and Murphy Company commissioned a woodcut of the new courthouse. The artwork cost more than they had anticipated. To offset the cost, they sold advertisements to surround the woodcut, placed a calendar pad at the bottom, and an industry was born: the art calendar.

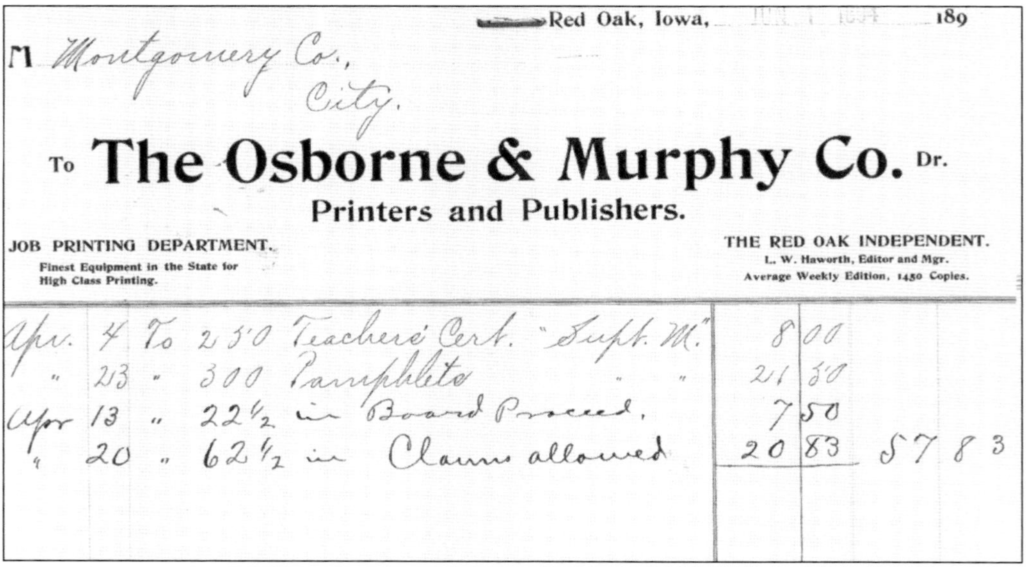

Red Oak, Iowa, JUN 1 1894 189

M Montgomery Co.,
City.

To **The Osborne & Murphy Co.** Dr.

Printers and Publishers.

JOB PRINTING DEPARTMENT.
Finest Equipment in the State for High Class Printing.

THE RED OAK INDEPENDENT.
L. W. Haworth, Editor and Mgr.
Average Weekly Edition, 1450 Copies.

Apr.	4	To 250 Teachers' Cert. "Supt. M."	8	00	
"	23	" 300 Pamphlets " "	21	50	
Apr	13	" 22½ in Board Proceed.	7	50	
"	20	" 62½ in Claims allowed	20	83	57 83

This bill to Montgomery County for printing from the Osborne and Murphy Company is dated June 1, 1894. Osborne and Murphy were successful in their endeavors, and incorporated in 1891. Osborne was in charge of sales and Murphy handled the manufacturing and business interests. In 1895, Osborne and Murphy were not in total agreement on things; Murphy sold his interests to Osborne, but retained the newspaper. The partnership dissolved and in 1899, Osborne moved his business to Newark, New Jersey.

Three

A New Century

At the dawn of the 20th century, Red Oak experienced a great surge of growth and prosperity. Fire, grasshoppers, and flood could not keep Red Oak from growing. As with any city, the lives, loves, ambitions, and business interests of a strong group of leaders interweave into a tapestry that becomes the fabric of a city and its history. Red Oak has been fortunate in its leaders as they worked to make Red Oak a shade better than it had been in the past.

Great strides had been made in keeping Red Oak Junction up to date and modern. The waterworks was established in 1880. The first telephones were installed in 1881. By 1882, gas service had begun, and a local street car provided service from 1882 to 1902. In 1892, Red Oak Electric Company, as agent for Westinghouse, began service. The railroad was redesigned, and a new depot was built. The streets around the square were paved, sidewalks were laid in concrete instead of wooden boards, and steam heat from the power plant was piped to businesses though an innovative underground system around the square.

On June 13, 1901, the word *junction* officially dropped from the name. Red Oak had grown from a small cluster of four houses and Charles H. Lane's mercantile to a thriving city ready to face the new century with hope, pride, and an indomitable spirit.

What lay ahead no one could predict. They had come through the pioneer days, and with fierce determination were ready for what lay ahead. The world was changing, and Red Oak was ready to keep up, change, and grow. The lives, loves, hopes, and dreams of the citizens of Red Oak continued to weave together creating the fabric of its history. People like Thomas Murphy and Charles Wilson would weave their threads into this tapestry and would made Red Oak known throughout the nation and the world.

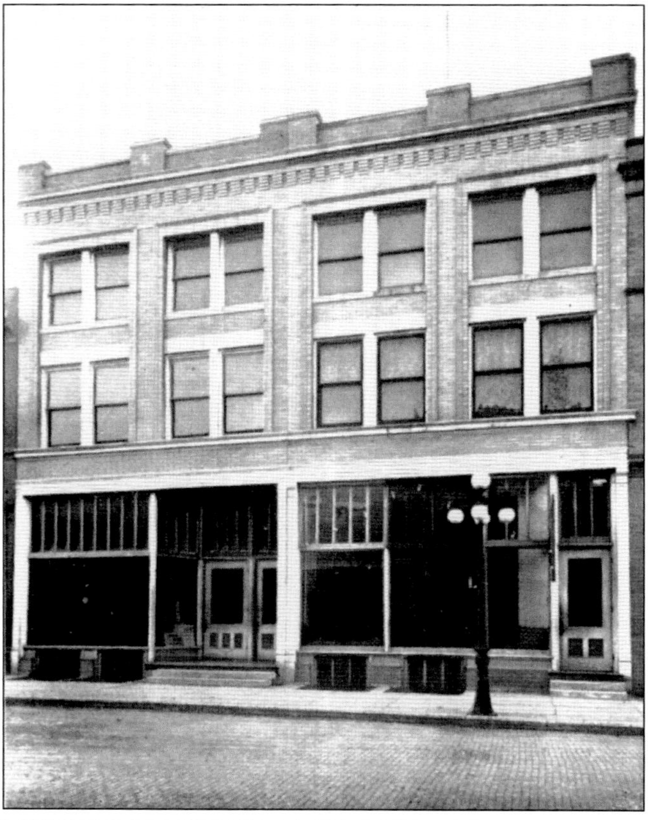

Thomas Murphy remained in Red Oak and established the Thomas D. Murphy Company. He purchased the *Red Oak Express*. Murphy gained a statewide reputation for his pungent editorial style. In 1900, the Murphy Company's first factory building was located on Coolbaugh Street just east of the square. Later it became the Red Oak Express offices. Murphy's business was growing quickly, he needed more and more space. At one point, seven buildings were utilized for the growing calendar company.

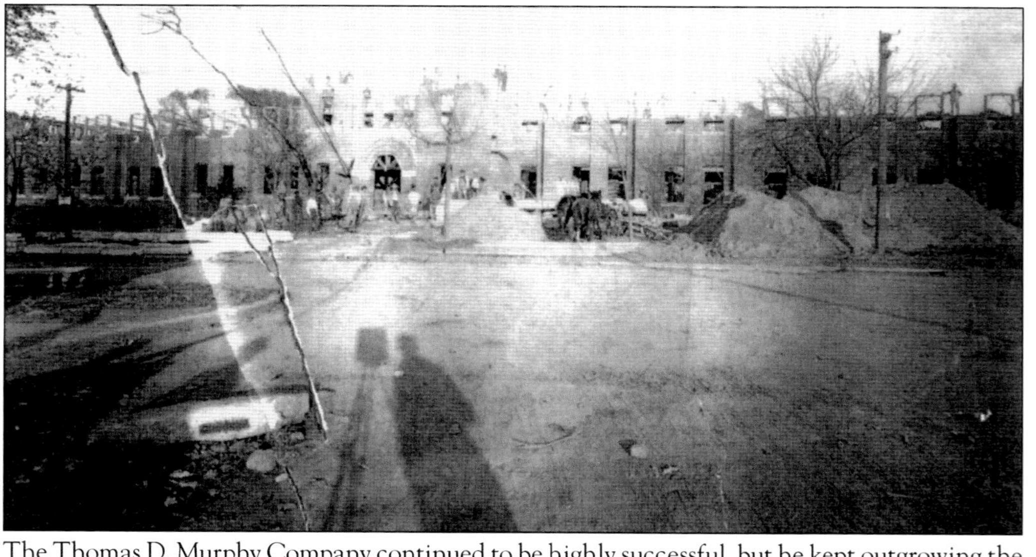

The Thomas D. Murphy Company continued to be highly successful, but he kept outgrowing the buildings that housed his company. Murphy decided to build his own plant at 214 South Second Street. By 1904, there were seven buildings in use, and offices in London with 30 salesmen. On a late afternoon in 1904, three men, George Vannausdale, Mr. Marcum, and W. A. Butenkoff, stand in front of the Murphy Company building as it is being constructed.

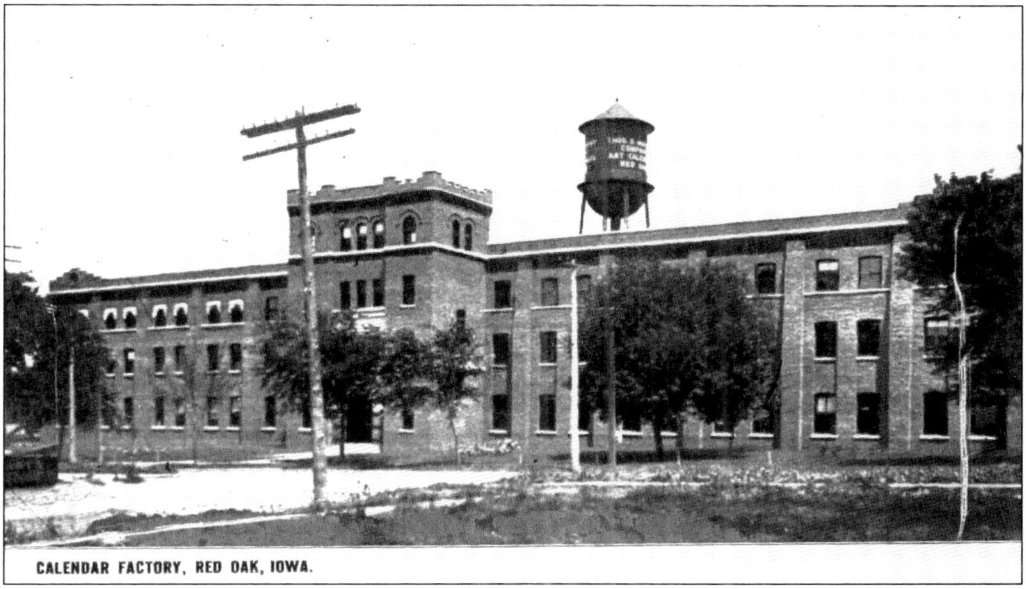

This postal card displays the newly completed T. D. Murphy Calendar Company. The business continued to grow, by 1906 there were 300 employees in Red Oak. Murphy had to expand again. He enlarged this factory.

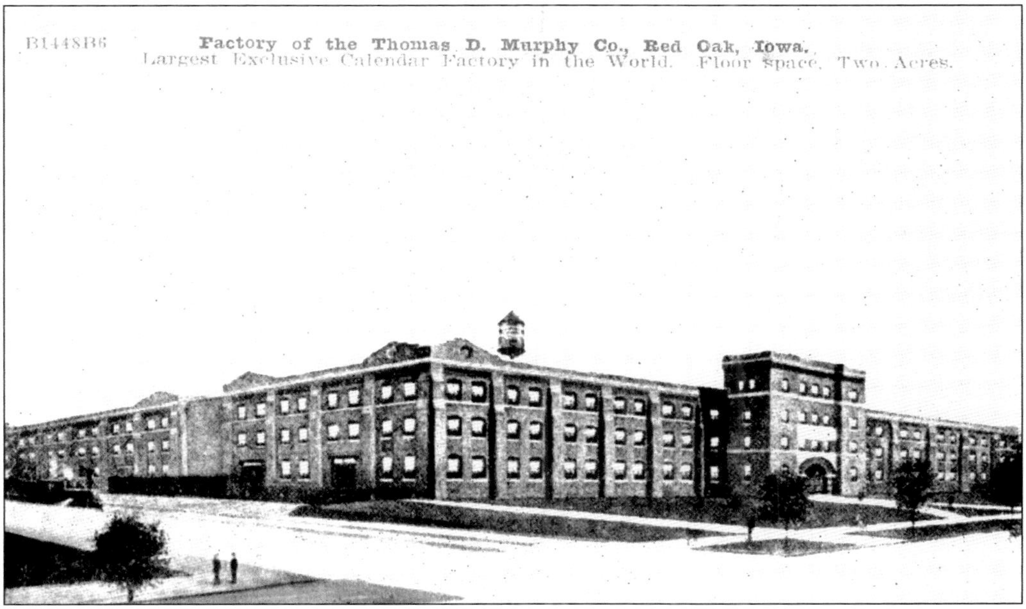

This postal card from about 1915 boasts that the factory is the largest exclusive calendar factory in the world with floor space of two acres. The plant had its own power plant to provide steam heat to the entire building, an automatic sprinkler system in case of fire, and a railroad spur line.

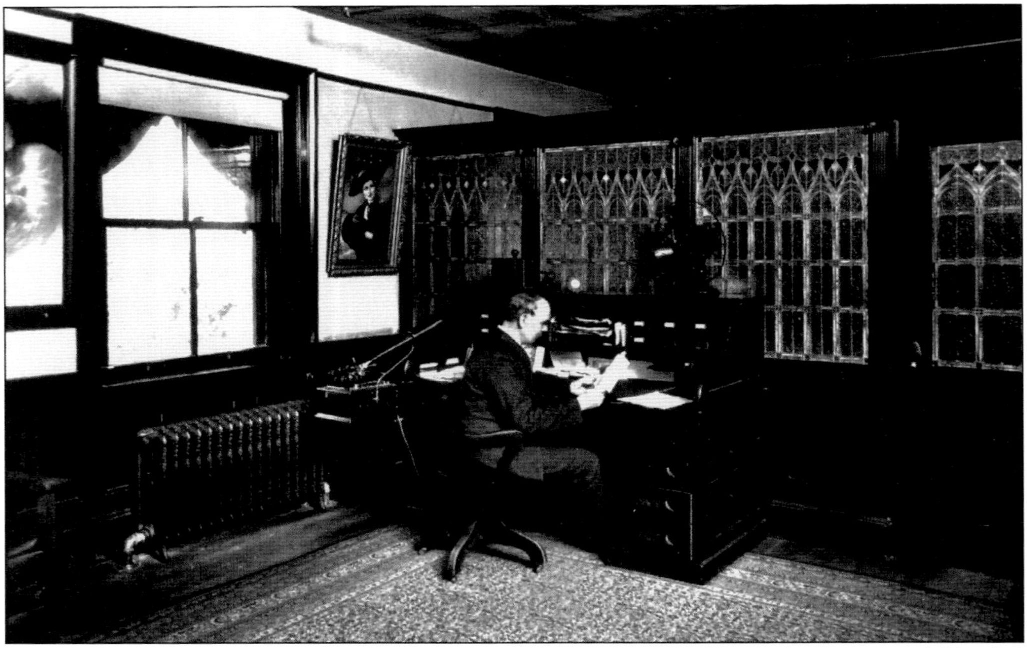

Pictured here is the office of the president of the Thomas D. Murphy Company. Beautiful leaded windows partitioned the room, some of the artwork that was not displayed in the art gallery hung on his wall. Note the up-to-date dictation system, an Edison record-making machine on the table below the painting, and the latest in air-conditioning, an electric fan on the desktop.

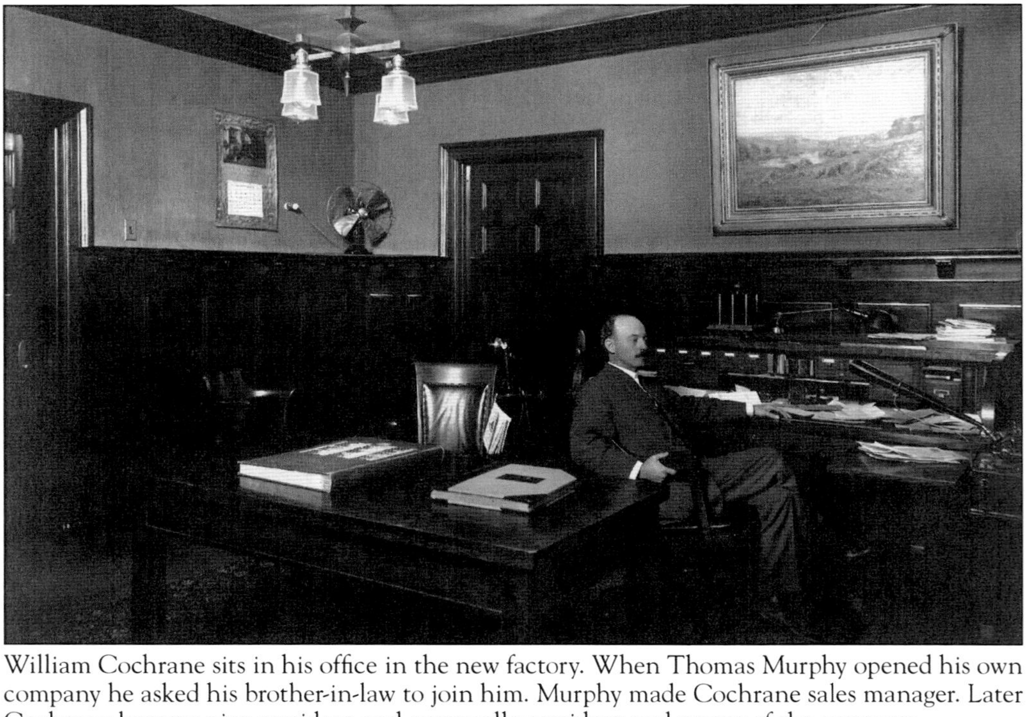

William Cochrane sits in his office in the new factory. When Thomas Murphy opened his own company he asked his brother-in-law to join him. Murphy made Cochrane sales manager. Later Cochrane became vice president and eventually president and owner of the company.

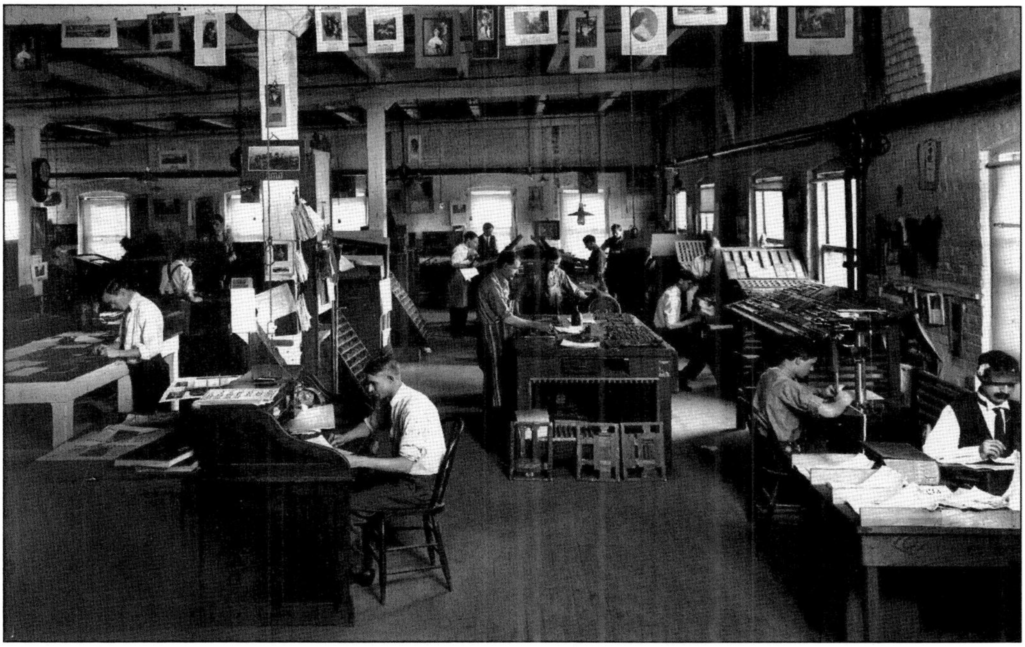

This is the composing room, where typesetters set the type by hand, creating the plates that would print the calendars. Artwork hangs from the beams overhead. Murphy commissioned artists to create beautiful works of art for the calendar illustrations. Many of these were then framed and displayed in the gallery.

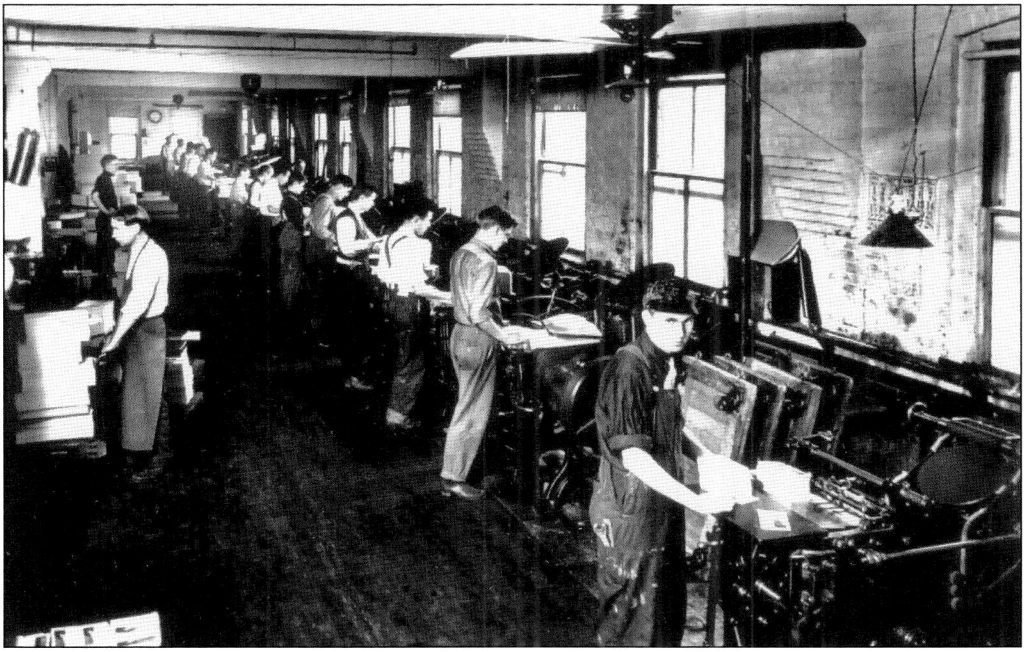

This row of Gordon presses has plenty of men to run them. The Murphy Company employed hundreds of people in order to turn out the volume of calendars ordered by businesses throughout the nation and in the world wherever English was spoken.

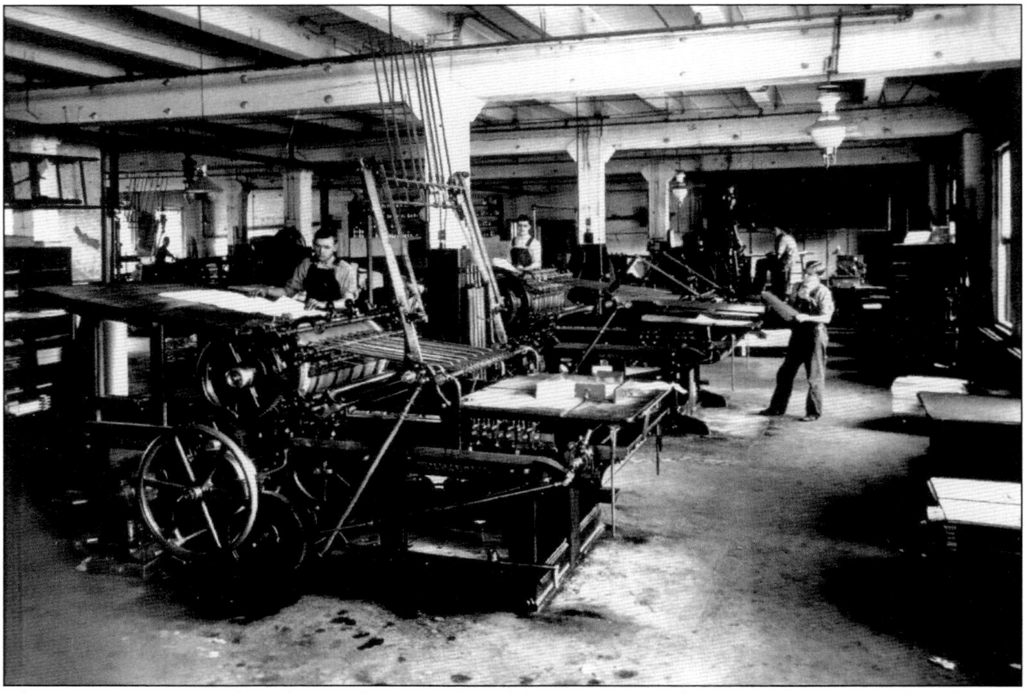

The pressrooms were kept busy. Photographs, old paintings, and artwork were reproduced using the halftone process.

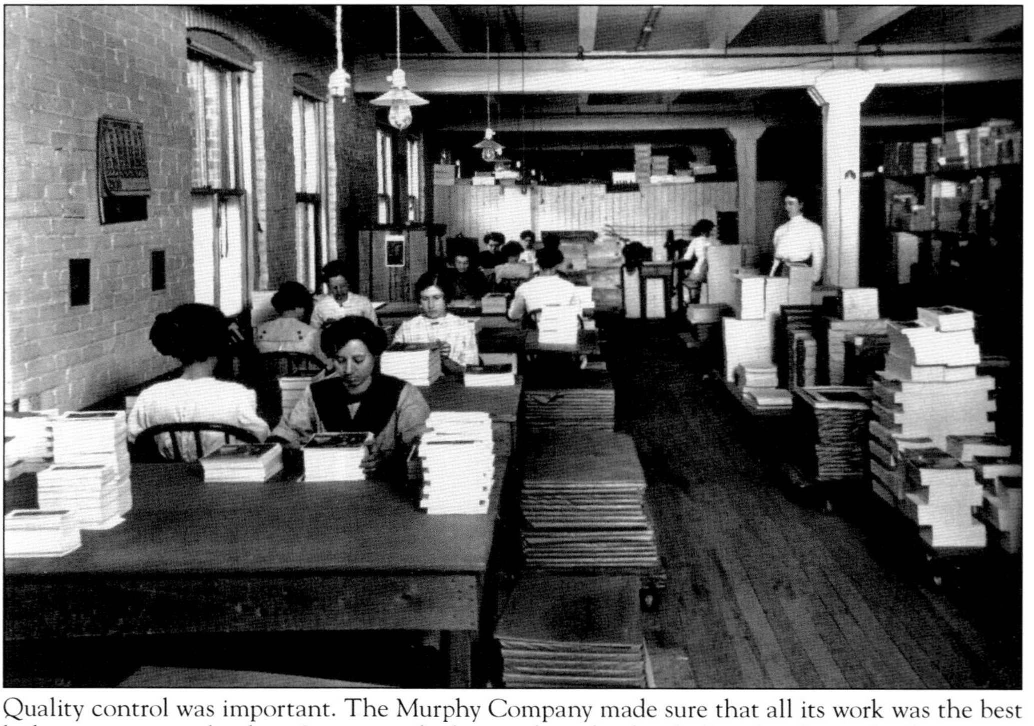

Quality control was important. The Murphy Company made sure that all its work was the best before it went out the door. Inspectors look over the calendars before they leave the factory.

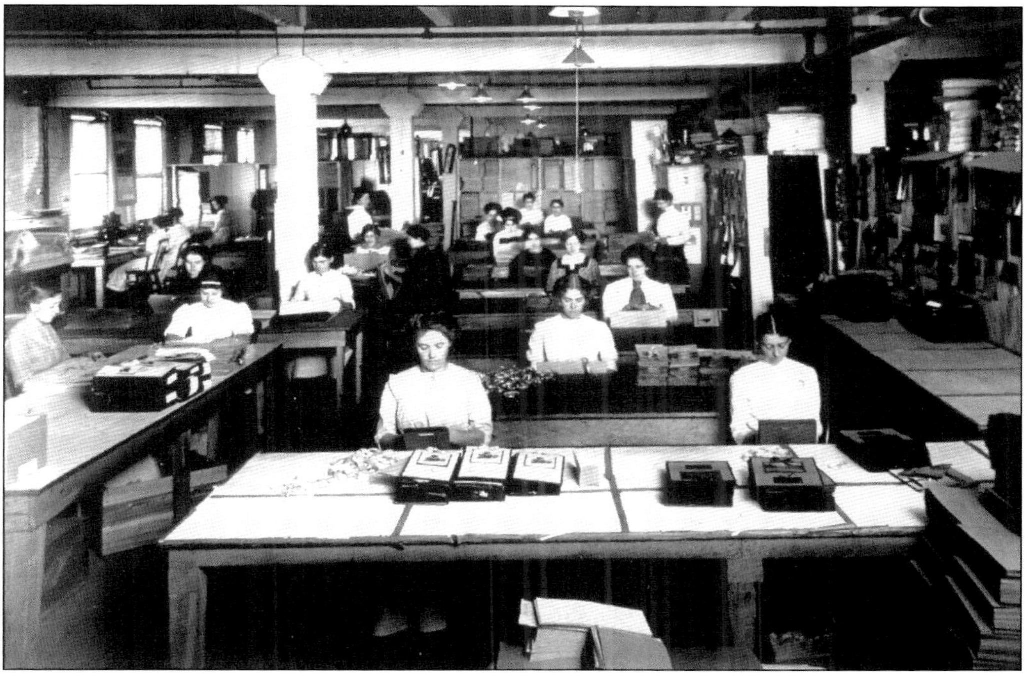

The Murphy Company employed a great many people. These ladies are doing the small handwork of hand tying ribbon bows onto each of the calendars. It was an extravagance to some, but it was one of the little quality touches that made a Murphy Calendar better than any other.

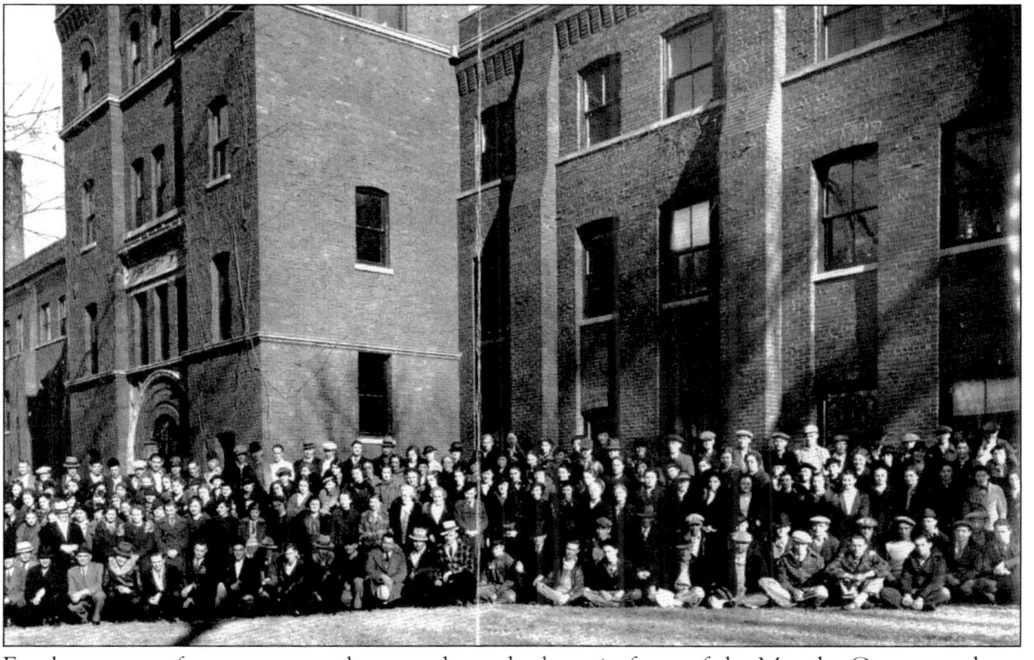

Employees pose for a company photograph on the lawn in front of the Murphy Company about 1937. For many of those who worked there it was like a family, and once someone was hired, they usually kept their job until they retired.

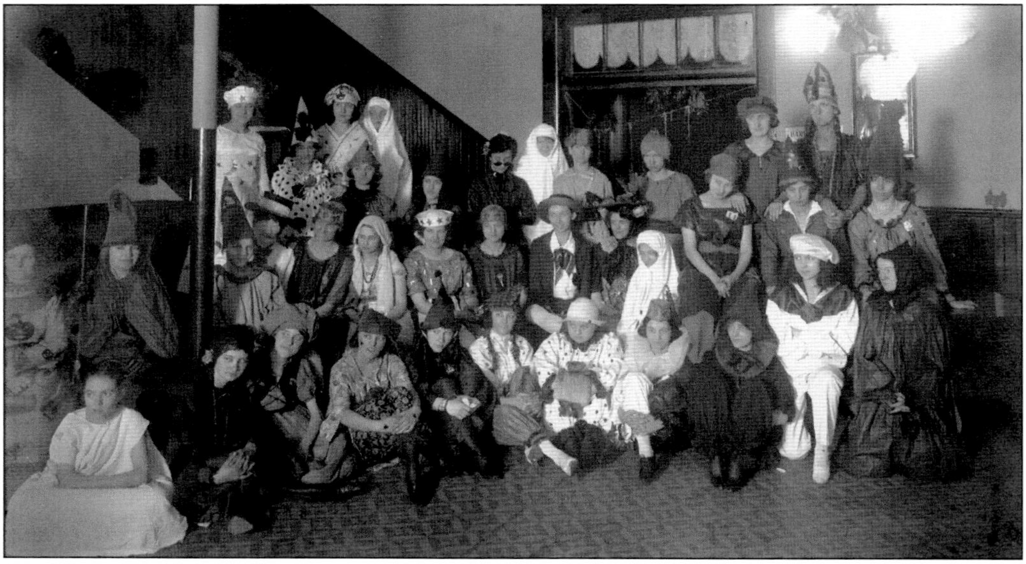

Employees of the Murphy Company pose in costume for the Halloween party on October 30, 1920, held in Murphy Hall at the Colonial Hotel. Laura Evans won the best-dressed-person award. See here are Laura Hayes, Mabel Bishop, Gladys McGreer, Jennie Walton, Bessie O'Rourke, Leona Hayes, Mariel Leas, Dorothy Hill, Estelle Priest, Frances O'Rourke, Kate Trapnell, Mabel Johnson, Mary Kernen, Ruth Wyckoff, Florence Binns, Mabelle Lundquist, Beulah Wadell, Verna Lundgren, Eunice Van Cleve-Johnnie, Laura Evans, Mona Rapp, Crystal Lamb, Floss Combs, Mrs. Shanver, Alice Peterson, Ruth Wilson, Vera Waldrum, Lorene Wells, Edith Crawford, Hazel Dean Jackson, Edith Malhoih, Lena Ashstrand, Doris Clement, Viola Heilman, Gladys Burdick, and Nell Stoneman.

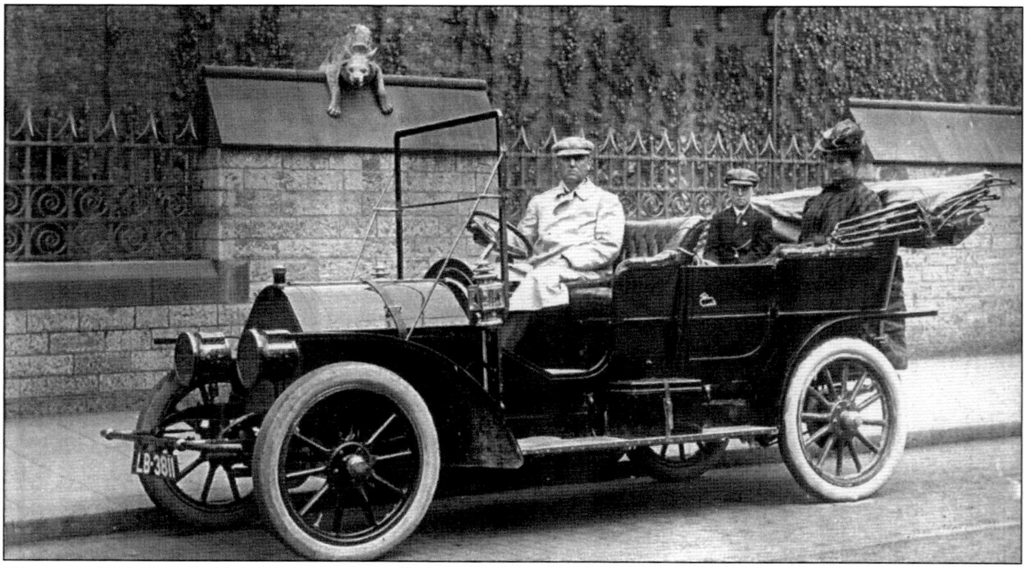

Thomas D. Murphy loved to tour in his car and traveled extensively. He is seen here in Wales in 1910 with his son, Thomas C., and his wife, Ina. He wrote and published a series of books as a result of his travels in America and Europe. Each is illustrated in the same exquisite manor as his calendars.

Thomas Draper owned the first car in Red Oak. His daughters pose in the new horseless carriage in about 1902. Blanche Draper Brayton holds the steering wand, next to her is her sister Nell Draper Northrup. Thomas Draper took Thomas Murphy for his first ride in an automobile. Mr. Spencer ordered a car from Des Moines in 1902. It came on a railcar flat. Murphy still had horses and would pass Spencer going up Coolbaugh Street. He would lean over and say, "Better get some horses Mr. Spencer."

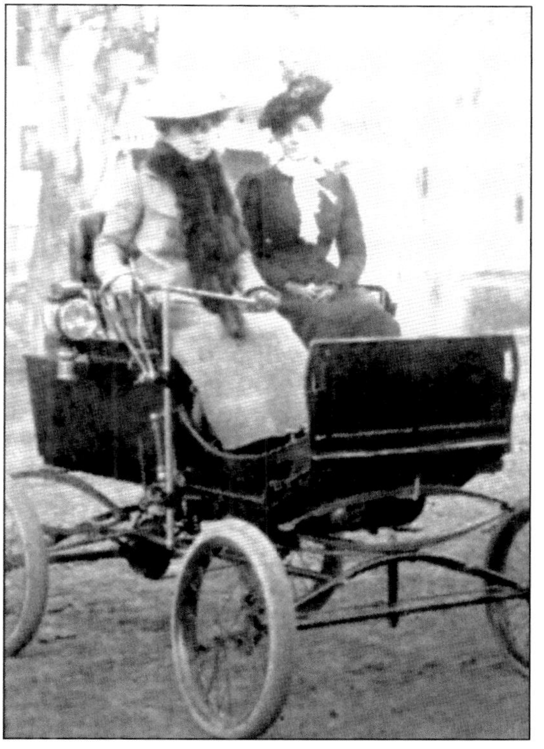

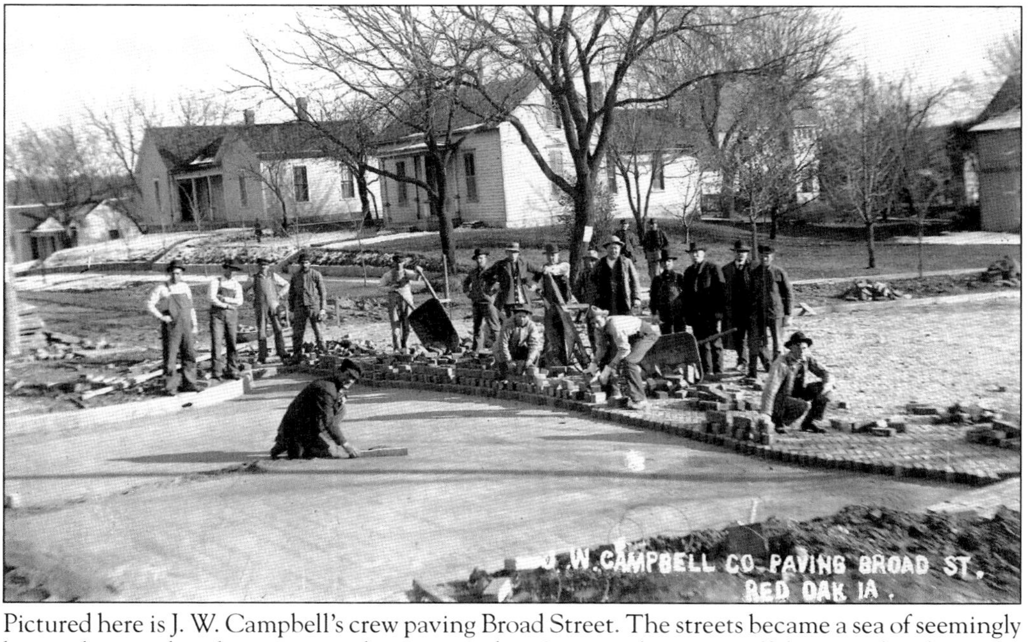

Pictured here is J. W. Campbell's crew paving Broad Street. The streets became a sea of seemingly bottomless mud and manure in the wet weather. Mayor Thomas Griffith pressed to have the streets around the square paved. Finally in 1902, the city council approved the idea, and paving began around the square. By 1903, paving began in the residential districts on the east hill. An ordinance passed in 1903 that mandated the replacement of boardwalks with cement walks.

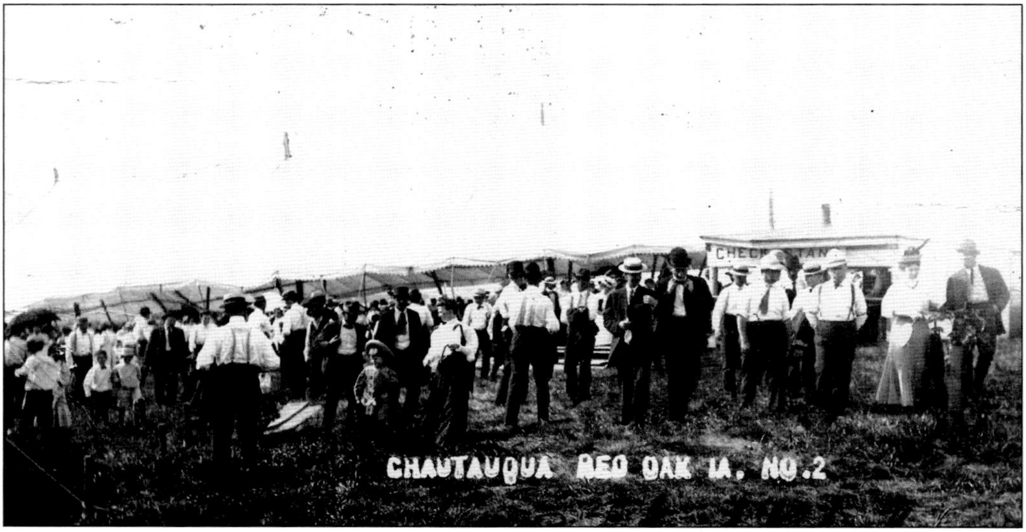

In August 1874, in western New York State on Lake Chautauqua, an event that was simply meant to better educate Sunday school teachers in the Methodist church kicked off a movement that spread across the county like wildfire. It was so successful that other educational opportunities were offered, and even correspondence degree programs were established. Many people who traveled west on wagon trains discovered others in their train were taking the same study courses and would sit and discuss what they were learning when they broke for camp along their way. Ralph Waldo Emerson and Henry David Thoreau went on lecture tours, usually in the winter months.

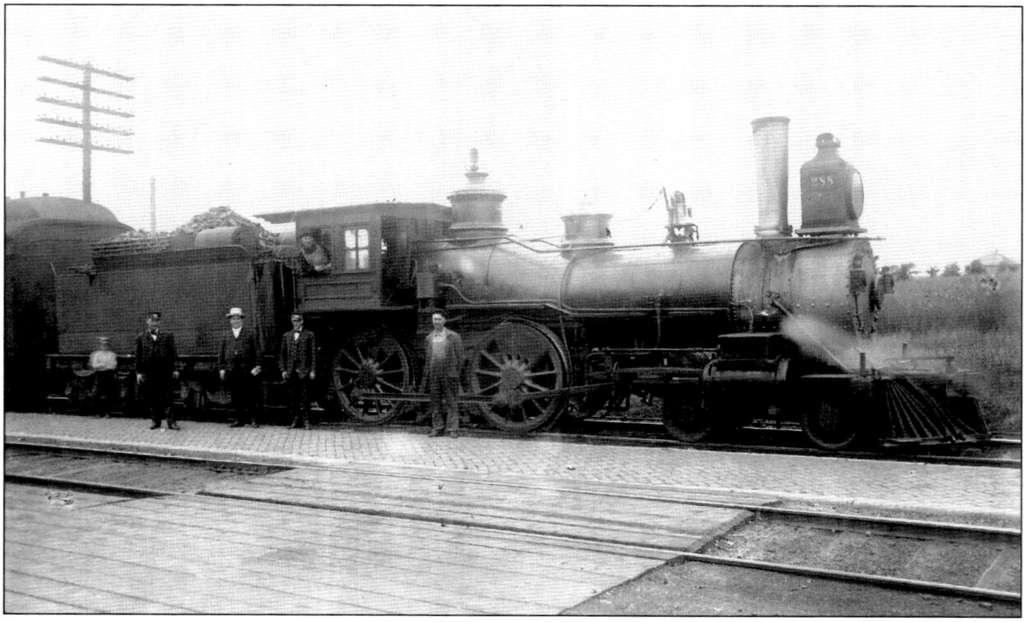

On June 29, 1905, the steam train hisses as William Jennings Bryan, second from the left, arrives in Red Oak for the gala opening of the chautauqua where he is the featured speaker. Bryan made three unsuccessful bids for the presidency in 1896, 1900, and 1908. The engineer is M. E. Combs.

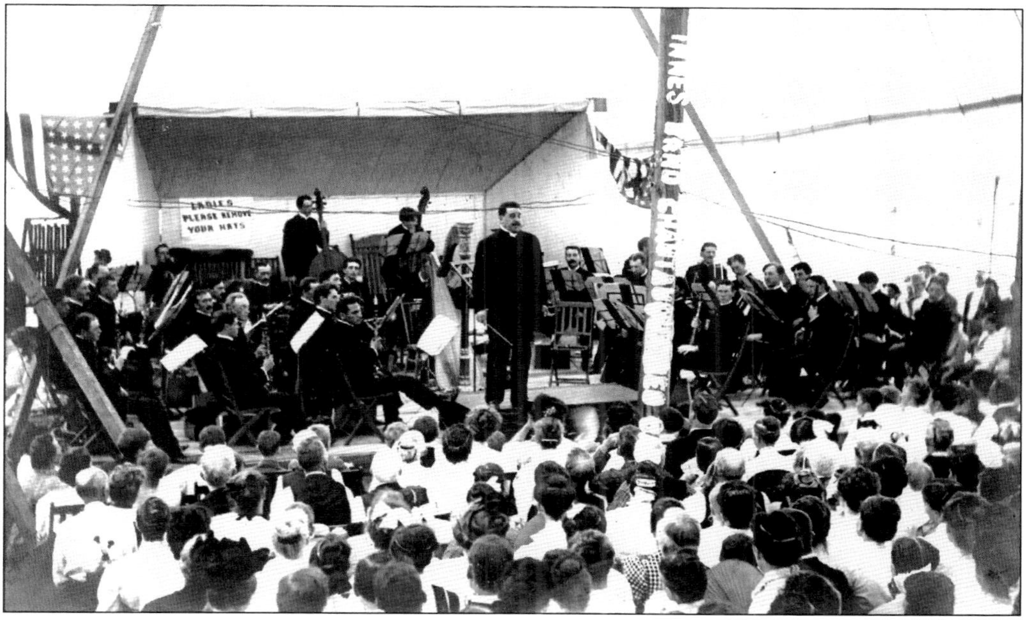

The first season of the Red Oak Chautauqua movement was held from June 29 through July 6, 1905, in a tent with a capacity for 3,000 people. On the program were William Jennings Bryan, attorney and a veteran presidential candidate and famous speaker; Jane Addams, the world famous founder of the settlement house in Chicago; Edith Henry Wallace; and Gov. Robert Lafollotte of Wisconsin. The Innes Band provided musical entertainment.

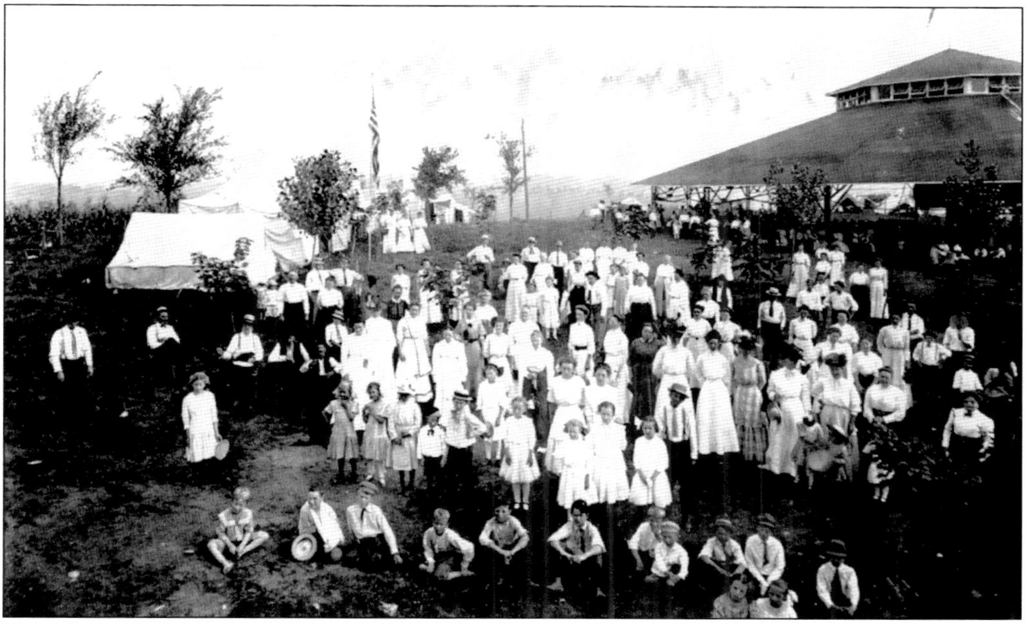

Electric lights illuminated the tent and grounds. Season tickets sold for $1.50 and $2. Accommodations were available on the grounds for 25¢ per night, tents and lots rented between $2.50 and $6. Even the railroad offered special rates from points up to 150 miles from Red Oak. The tent sessions continued until 1907, when a tent collapsed in a high wind injuring a spectator.

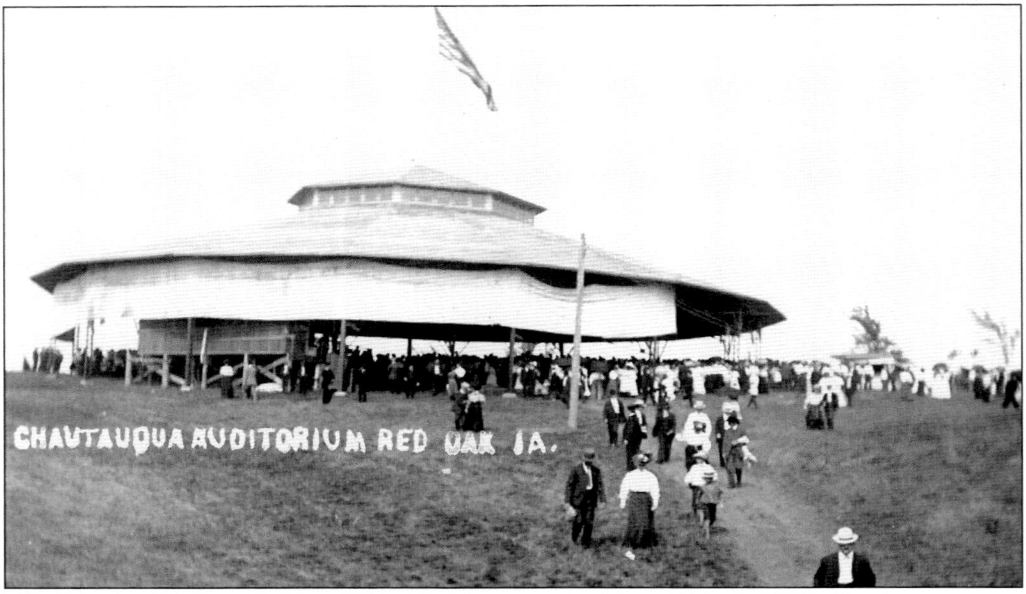

In 1908, the land was purchased by the Chautauqua Association for $750. Fund-raisers were held to raise $5,700 to build a permanent structure, volunteers worked right along with laborers to finish the roof and meet the deadline of opening day. The permanent pavilion would hold up to 5,000 people. In 1921, the city purchased the pavilion and grounds for $1,000, with the agreement that they would maintain it and allow the Chautauqua Association the use of it for 10 days out of the year. Eventually the movement faded, and attendance dwindled, and by the early 1930s, it was hardly used at all.

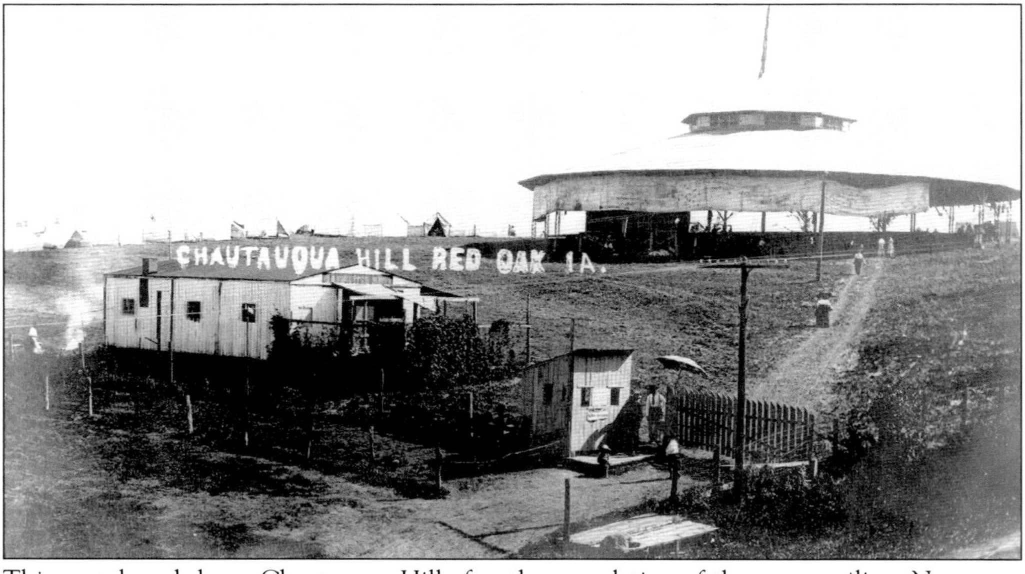

This postal card shows Chautauqua Hill after the completion of the new pavilion. Numerous tents are seen up the hillside, there is fabric draped about the building as a sun shade. The gate keeper's shack is pictured on the left. It is still morning, and not much is happening. Some men and children hang about the ticket booth; an umbrella offers shade to the ticket taker later in the day.

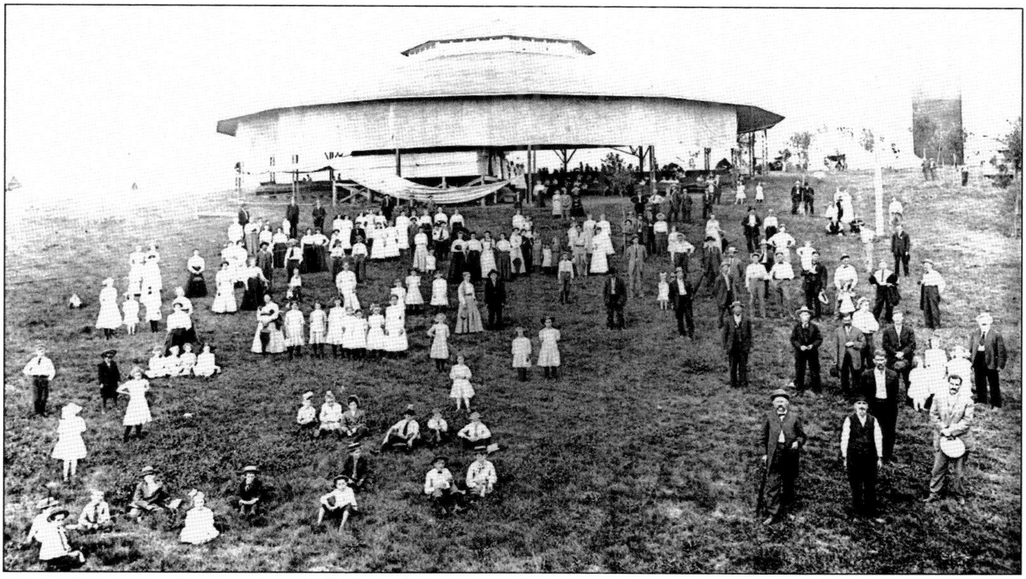

Over the years, the pavilion fell into disrepair. The roof leaked and the podium and seats rotted. In 1968, the roof was in such poor condition that the park board had to decide to raze it or repair it. A contractor offered to buy it for salvage. This prompted the formation of the Chautauqua Restoration Committee. They listed the pavilion on the National Register of Historic Places and in 1972 were able to obtain funds to save the pavilion. Today it is one of the few remaining chautauqua pavilions in the nation.

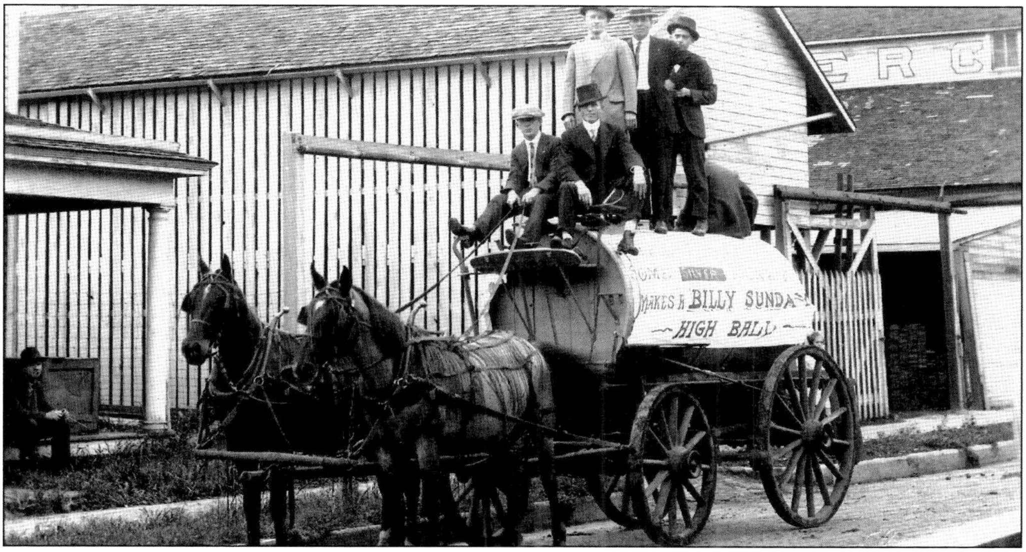

A group of men had some fun when Billy Sunday came to speak about the evils of alcohol, gambling, and dancing at the Chautauqua Pavilion in Red Oak. William Ashley Sunday was born in 1862 in Ames. From 1883 to 1891, he played baseball for Philadelphia, Pittsburg, and Chicago. He became famous when he played right field for the Chicago White Stockings. He retired from baseball and held his first revival in Garner in 1897. The sign on the barrel reads, "A glass of this and some silver money makes a Billy Sunday High Ball." The barrel contained water to spray on streets to minimize the dust.

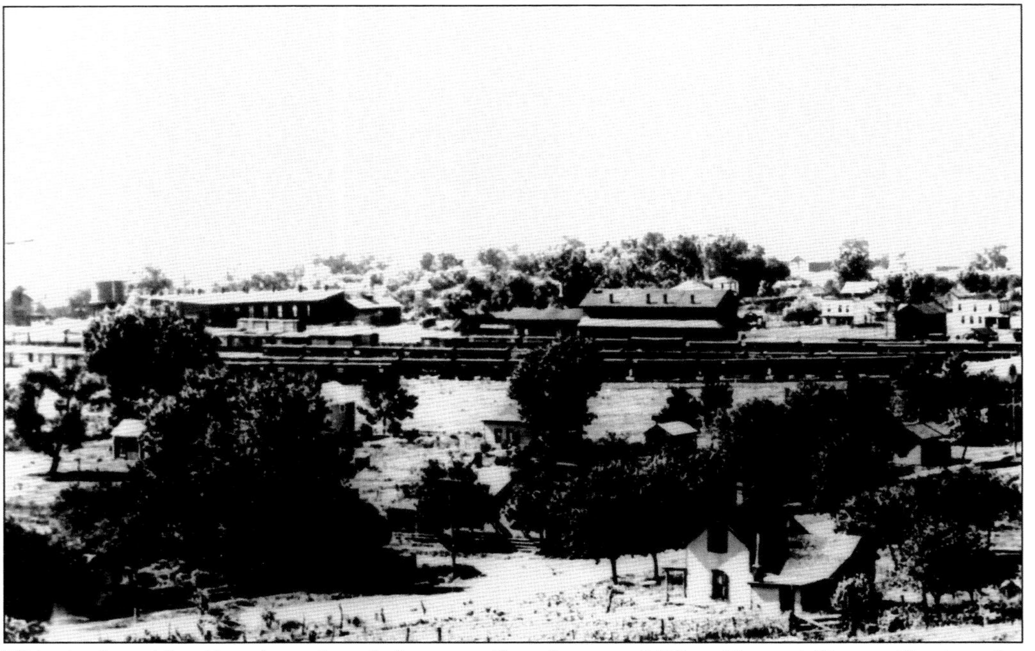

This is the old railroad yard and depot at Broadway and West Second Street. During the Depression there was a hobo camp west of the railroad freight house. "Hair-breath Harry" was the most well known of those that came through town. The hobos would meet in this camp, cook a good meal, then move on after a few days. There was a coded language of symbols that they used to let other hobos know where there might be work, a good meal in exchange for some labor, where the police were likely to get after them, and where there was danger.

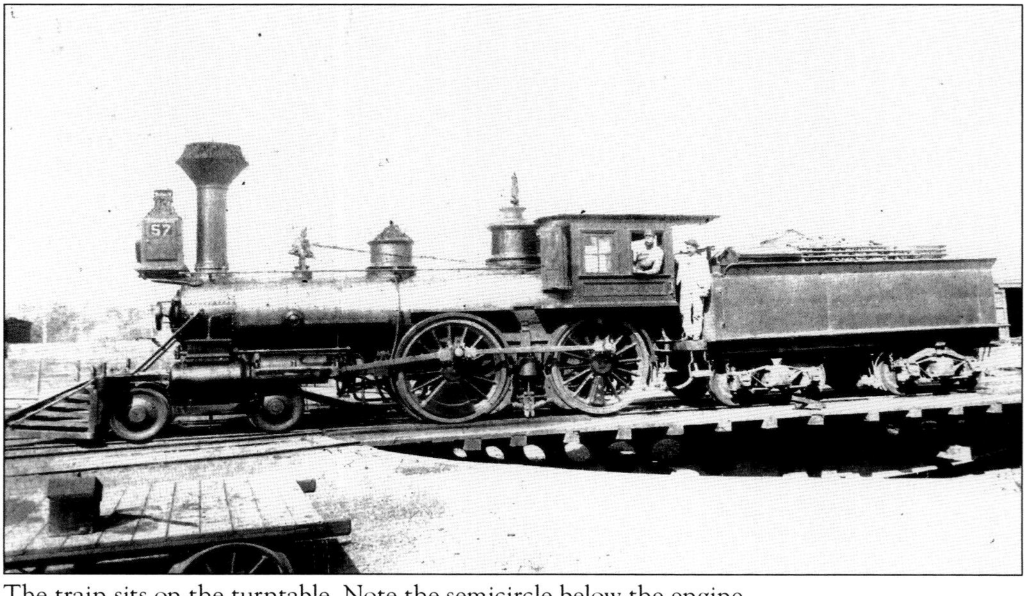

The train sits on the turntable. Note the semicircle below the engine.

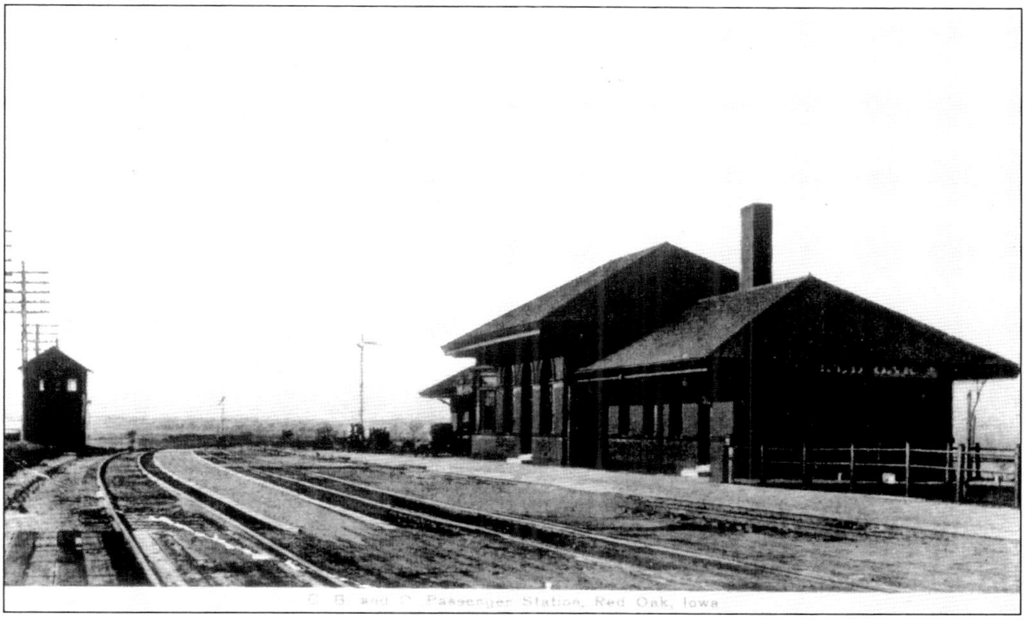

The new CB&Q depot at the south end of East Second Street is pictured here. In its heyday, there were 14 passenger trains and 3 mail trains that came through Red Oak. The mail trains were painted white, they did not stop, so there were catchers to throw the mail for delivery and catch the outgoing mail.

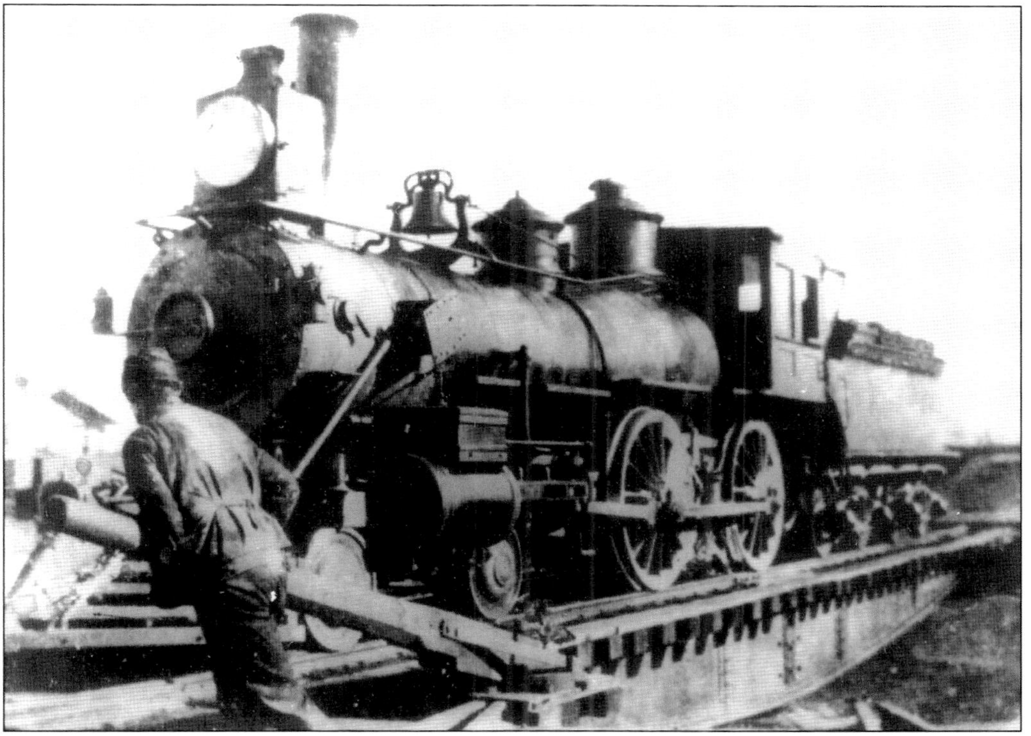

The workman is turning the train on the turntable manually.

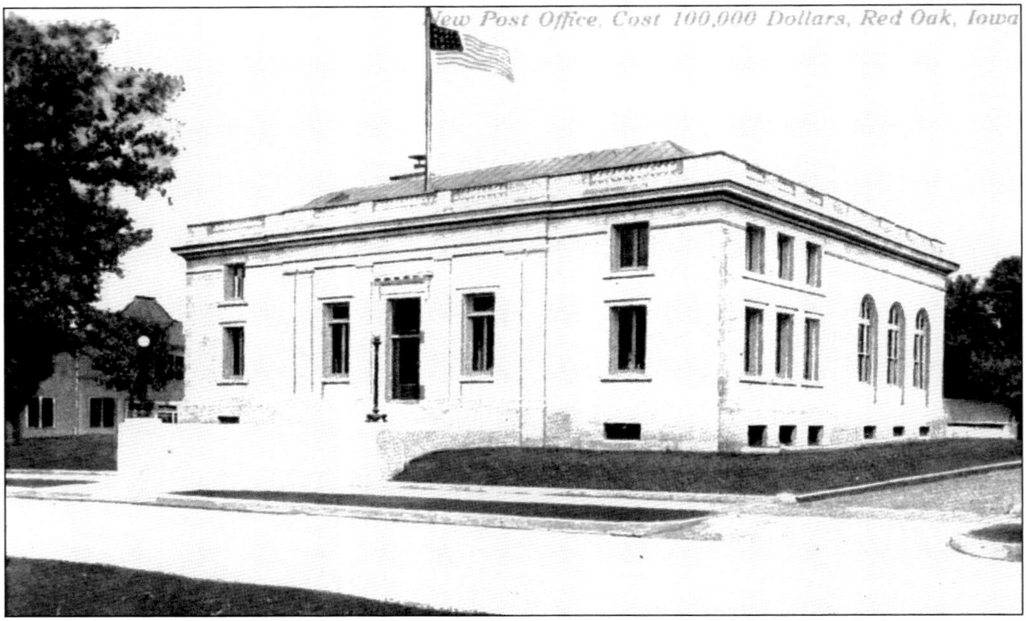

New postal offices were built where an old carriage factory and residences had been previously. This building cost $100,000 to build. Many years later, when the post office wanted to build a new building, the people of Red Oak declined as they loved their historic postal office.

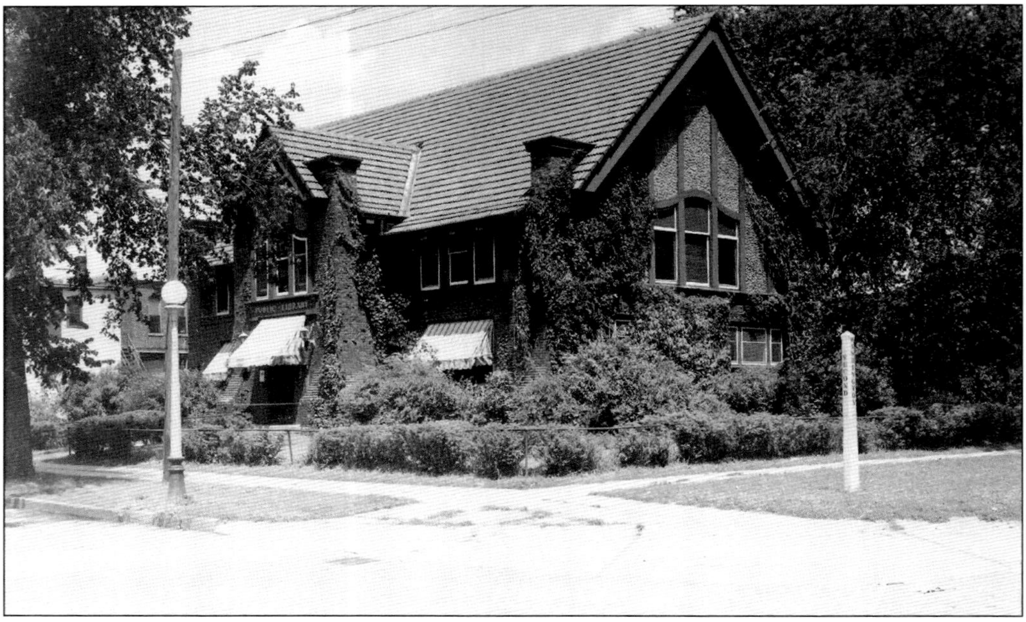

Red Oak was fortunate enough to receive a Carnegie library, thanks to the efforts of Judge Horace Deemer. Around 1905, Patton and Miller, a Chicago architectural firm, received a commission from Red Oak to build a library funded by a Carnegie Library Grant of $12,500. The design was Elizabethan English, with strong influences of the arts and crafts movement and utilized rough textured clinker bricks. It was built in 1909, and in 1923, an addition was added that was designed by the successor firm of Holmes and Flynn.

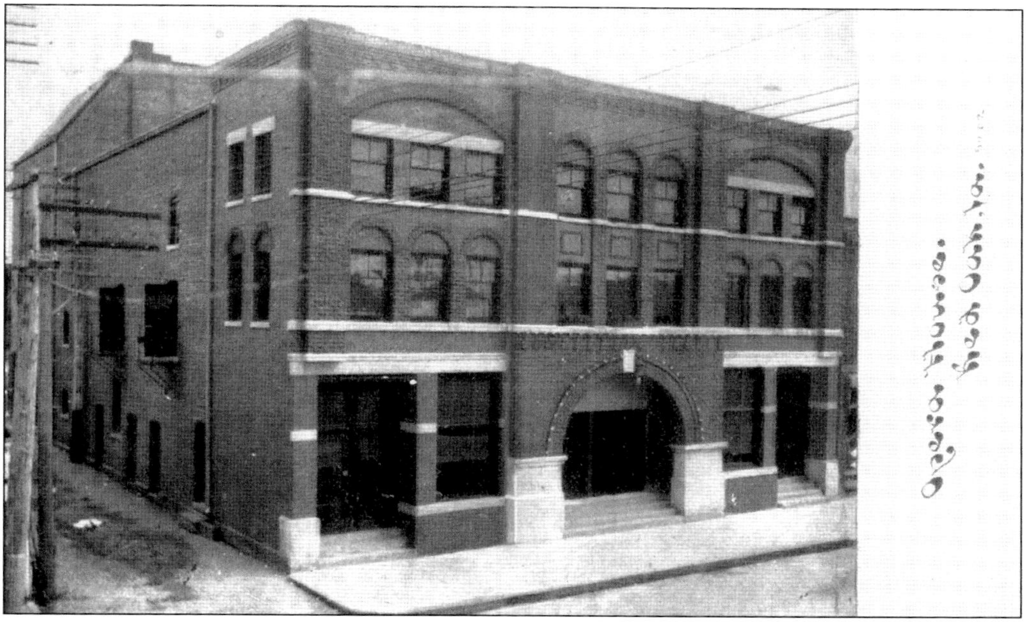

The Beardsley Opera House was built in 1909, one-half block south of the square on Third Street, and cost $40,000 to build. Many high school graduations held their commencements in the theater. In 1932, there was a fire in the building. They were about to install a new RCA sound system. It sat empty for many years before it was torn down.

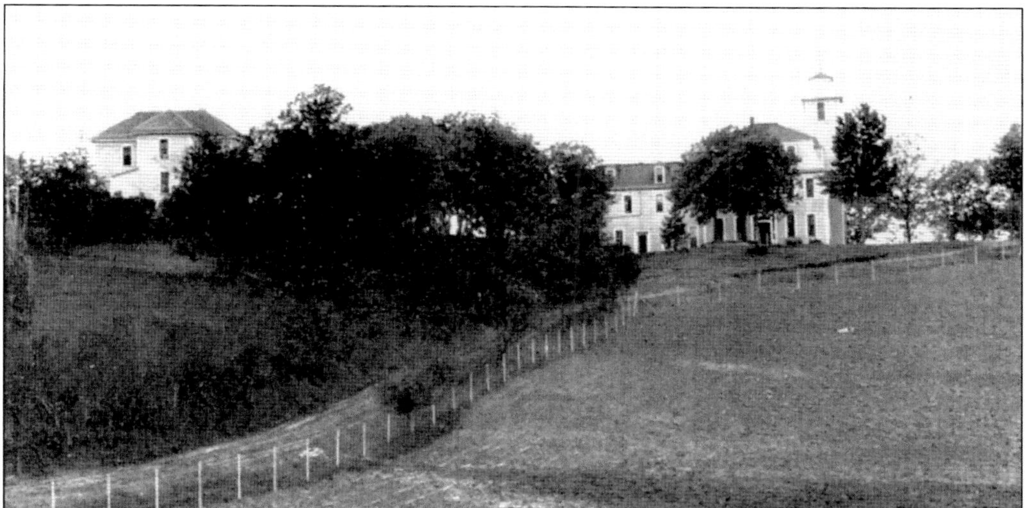

Hamilton White's failed Sanitarium Hotel was just what Dr. Francis Powell, superintendent of the Glenwood Institute for the Feeble Minded, was looking for. In about 1903, he purchased the building and extensive grounds in order to fulfill his dream of a school for "backwards and mentally handicapped children." He named it Oak Hill. Before he could realize his dream he died, and his daughter Dr. Velura Powell and his widow opened the school. It became known as the Powell School and continued under Dr. Velura Powell's care until the Riley Nelson family took over in the 1940s. They were forced to close by 1978 because of many government regulations.

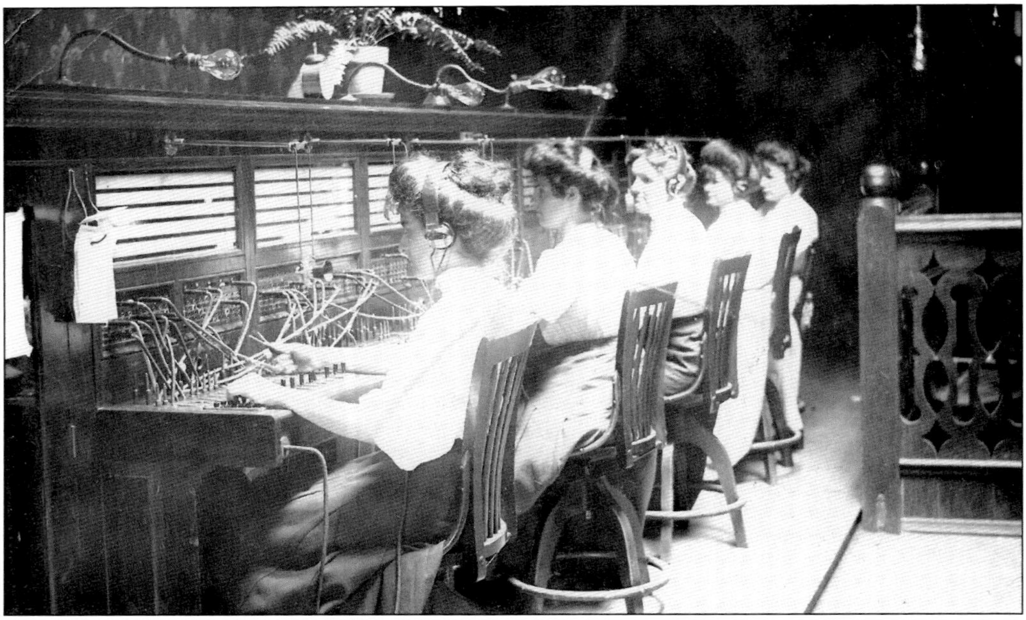

Telephone service first came to Red Oak in 1881. The Montgomery County Telephone Company was headquartered in Red Oak; the central office address was 319 Reed Street. A group of ladies in 1902 work the manual switchboards in the telephone offices in the First National Bank Building.

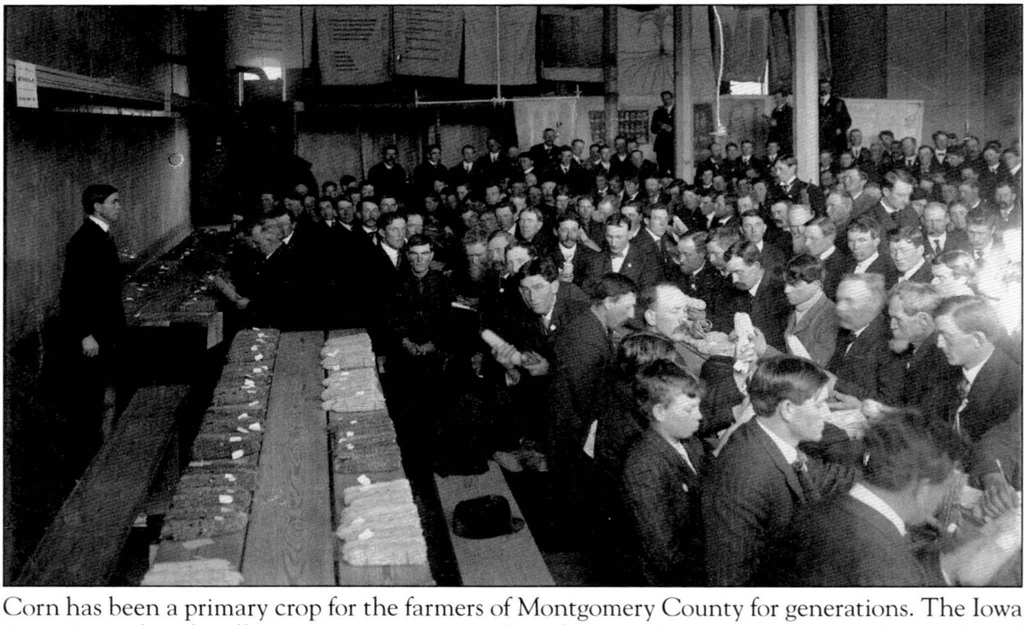

Corn has been a primary crop for the farmers of Montgomery County for generations. The Iowa State Agricultural College gave instruction in the selection of seeds, preparation of the soil, and rotation of crops all with the promise of increased annual yield. This photograph is of the first "corn school" that was held in Red Oak around 1904. In 1905, the Seed Corn Gospel Train, sponsored by the Iowa State Agricultural College, traveled all over the state to spread the word about the latest improvements to seed corn.

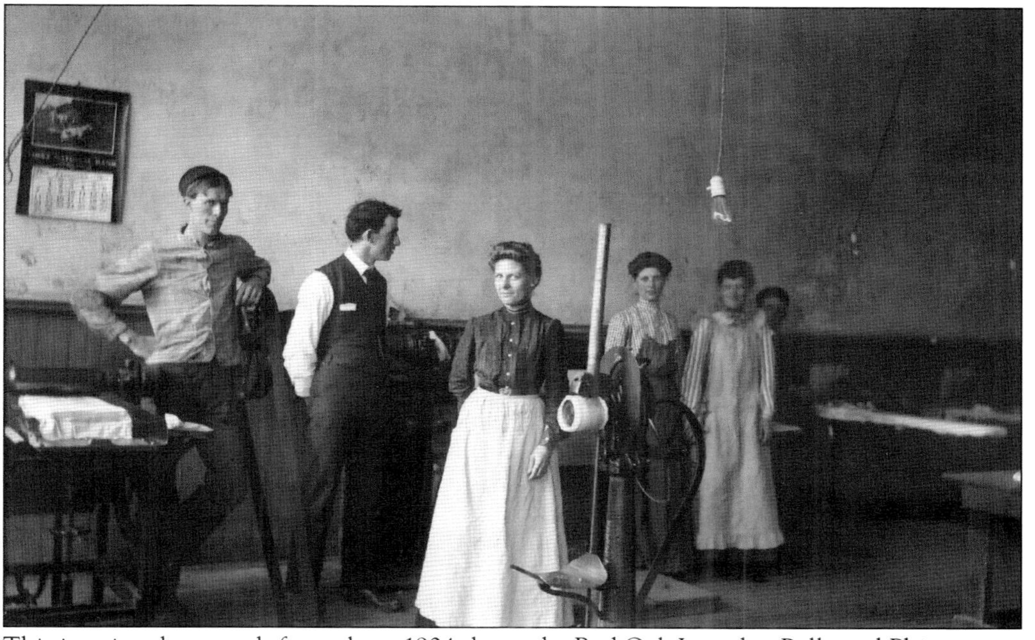

This interior photograph from about 1904 shows the Red Oak Laundry. Pully and Phipen were the proprietors, and it was located at 204 Coolbaugh Street.

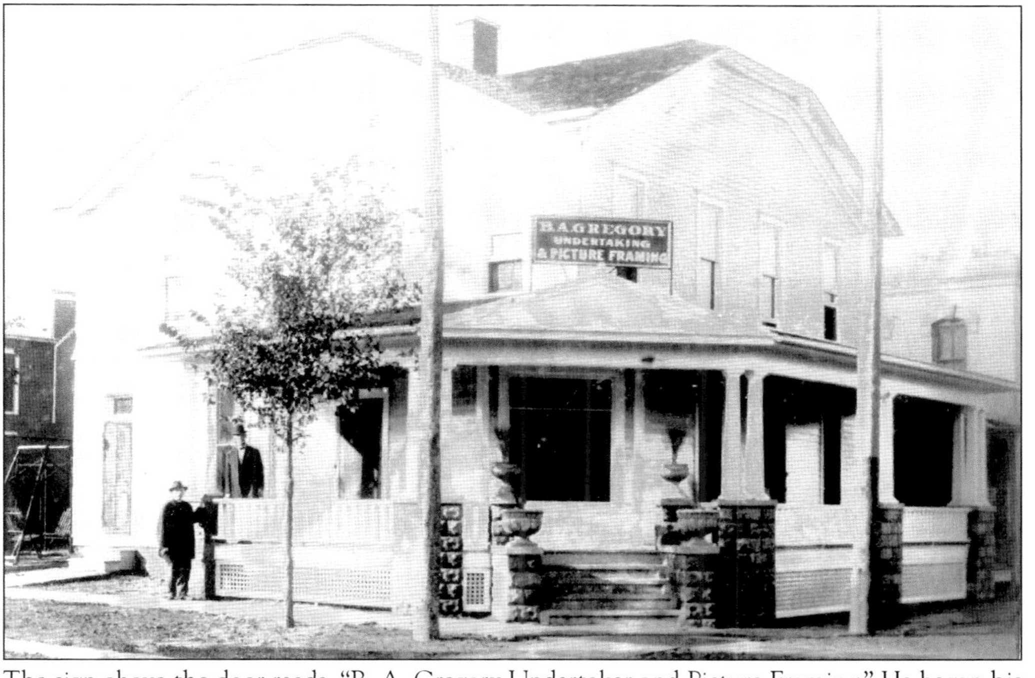

The sign above the door reads, "B. A. Gregory Undertaker and Picture Framing." He began his business about 1909 in his home before he moved to a location downtown. His furniture store was at 220 Coolbaugh Street and his undertaking rooms were at 210 Washington Avenue. One could say that picture framing was a side business, because as an undertaker, he was not always doing a stiff business.

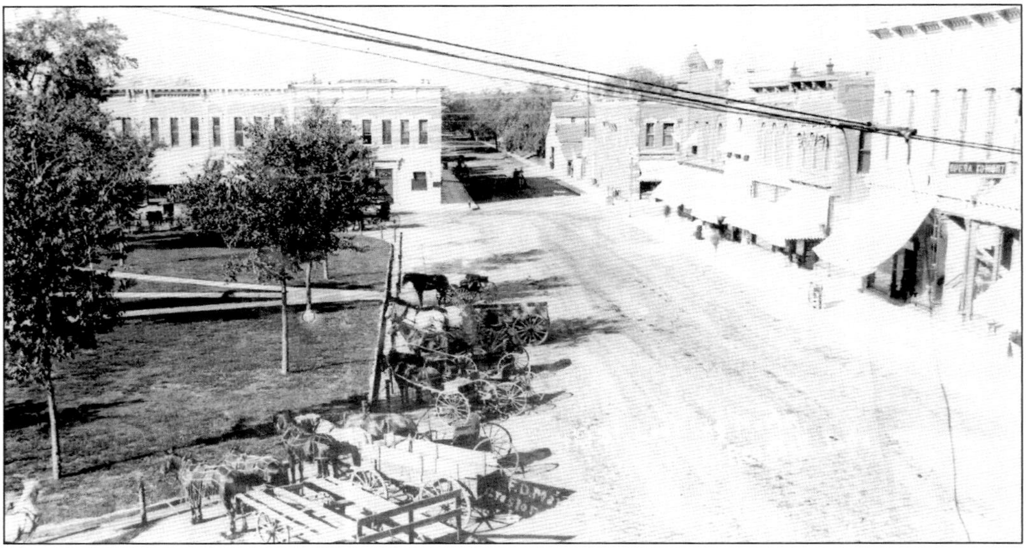

The square is seen here before 1909 looking north on Fourth Street. Red Oak National Band is in the upper center at the corner, at the lower right a sign announces that there will be an opera tonight at the Rynearson Opera House. Bryson and Son built the opera house in 1876, and on December 25, 1876, a centennial ball was held, celebrating 100 years of America. Two hundred people attended. When the Beardsley Opera House opened in 1909, the Rynearson closed. The square has been planted with trees, and walkways cross the grass.

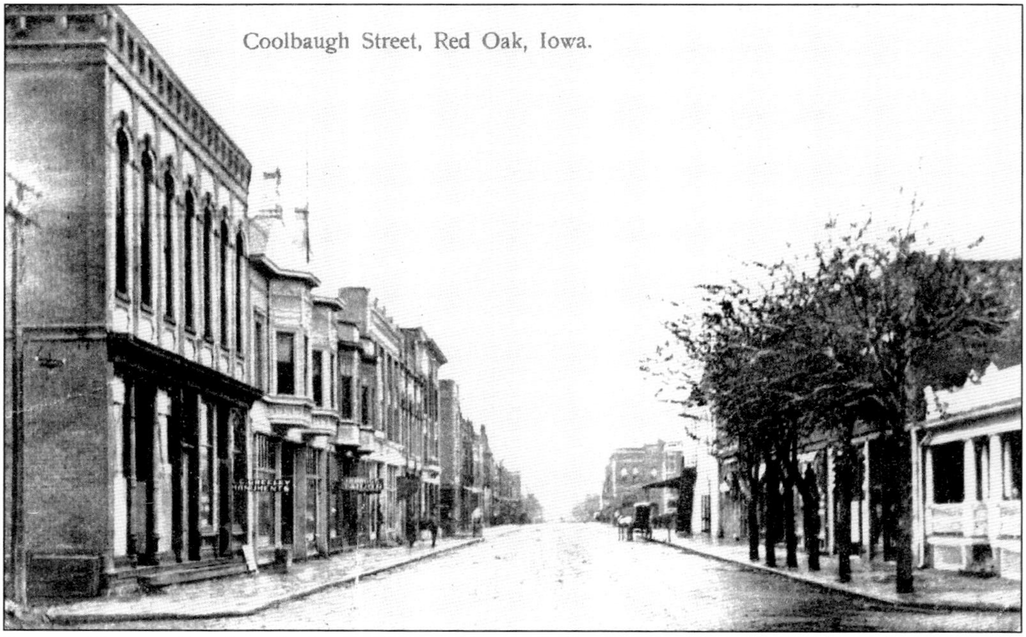

Pictured here is Coolbaugh Street about 1909. L. C. Greeley Monuments is the first sign on the left, and the one beyond that is for the tailor shop.

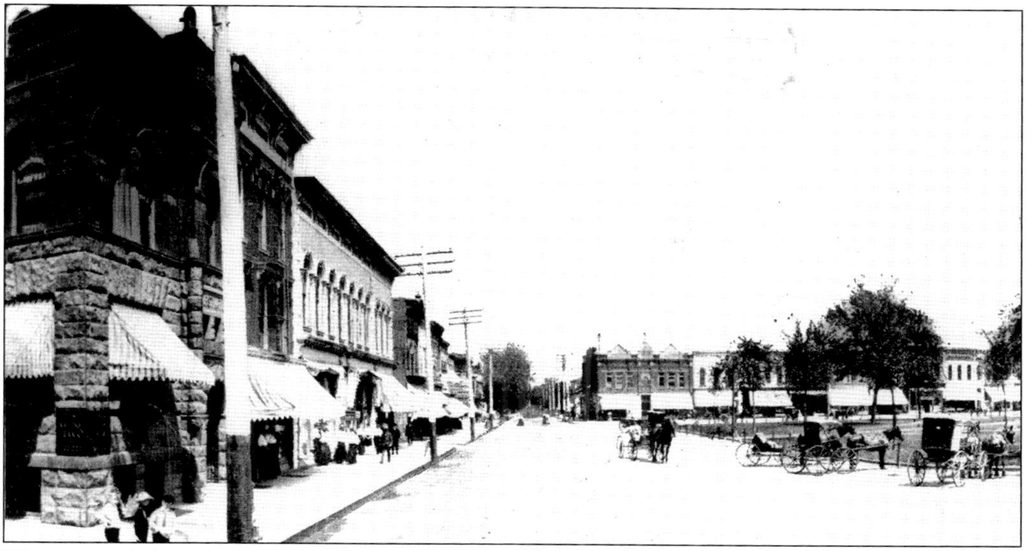

The view of the square, from about 1900, was taken from Coolbaugh Street looking north at the west end of the square. This was the site of the first business opened by Charles Lane in 1856. By the 1870s, this block consisted of, from left to right, the First National Bank, E. M. Corey's Grocery House (known as the Farmers Store, then Charles Lane Dry Good Emporium, and then George Powers Dry Goods), Evans Jewelers, Lane Impliments, a photographer, and Koehler Grocery.

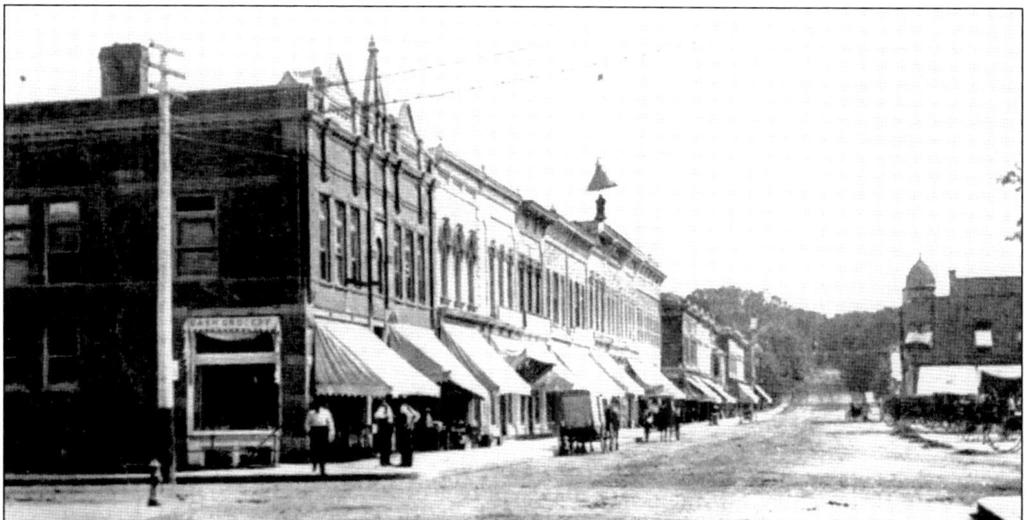

This view from Reed Street looking east shows an awning that reads "Cash Grocery" on the corner shop.

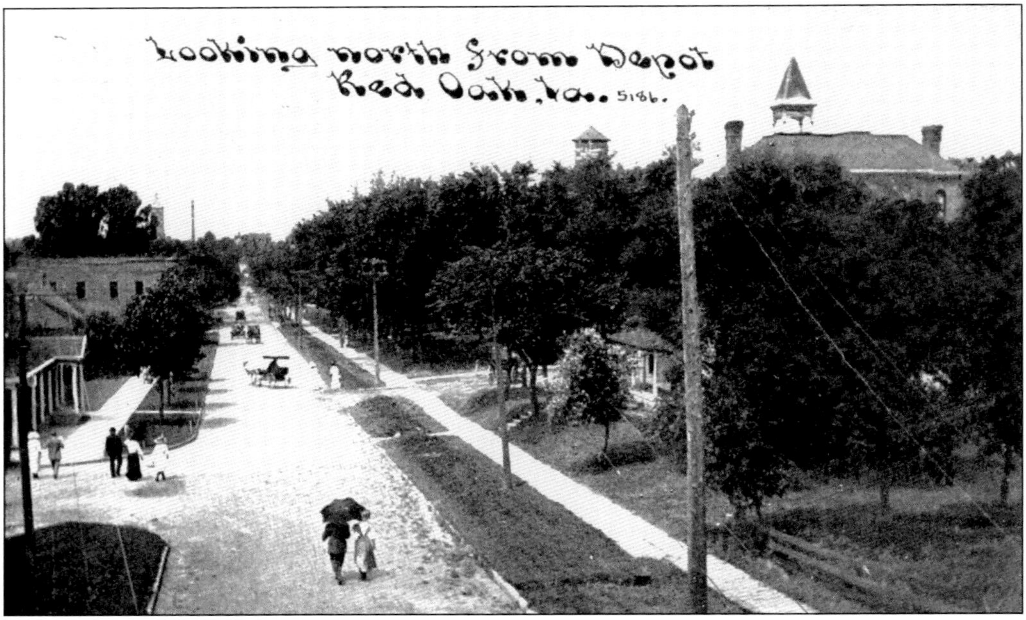

This postal card reads, "Looking north from the Depot." The Evans House, a hotel built for the traveling salesmen and the railroad men, is to the left and a school is on the right. The Murphy Company water tower is beyond the school. People are walking and plenty of rigs are out for a day's driving.

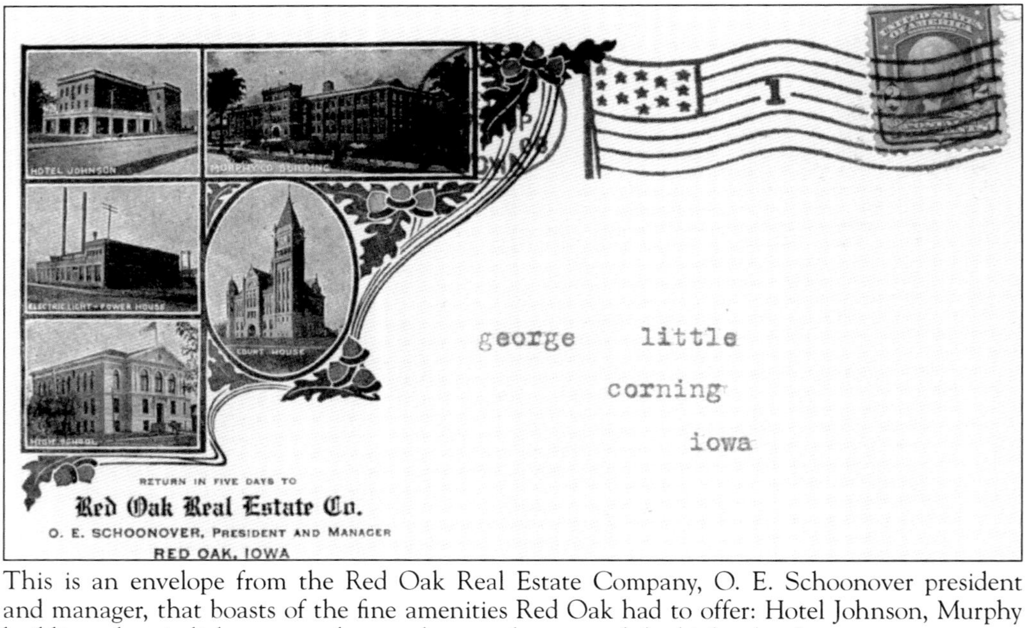

This is an envelope from the Red Oak Real Estate Company, O. E. Schoonover president and manager, that boasts of the fine amenities Red Oak had to offer: Hotel Johnson, Murphy building, electric light—power house, the courthouse, and the high school.

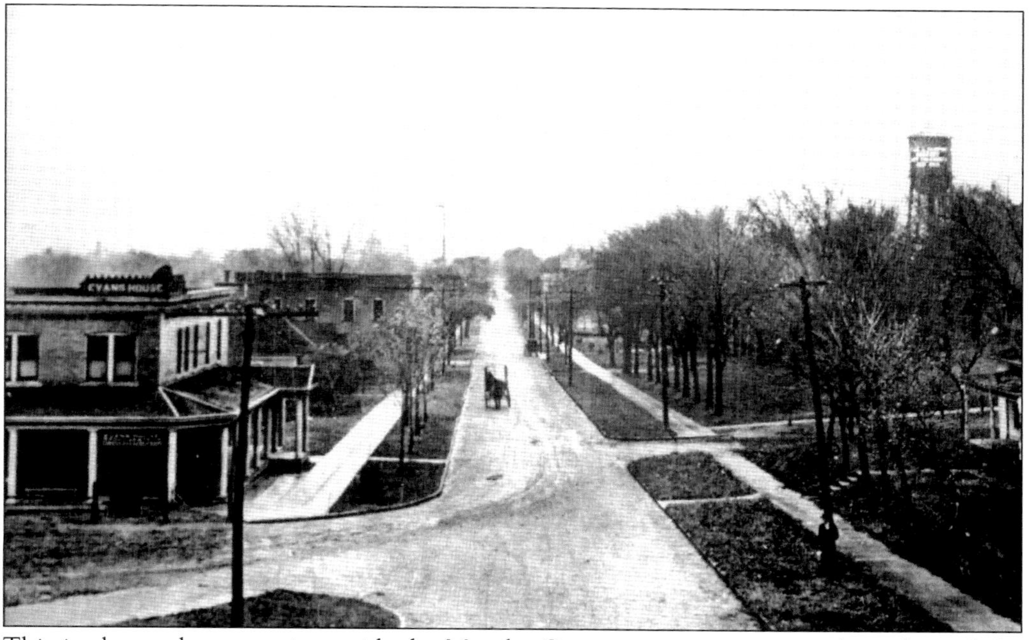

This is almost the same view, with the Murphy Company water tower on the right and the Evans House on the left. There is a tall smokestack in the distance. Red Oak had many hotels. In 1874, a complete breakfast at the Hotel Exchange consisted of pancakes, applesauce, ham or bacon, any style eggs, pork chops, country-style fried potatoes, fried apples, coffee, and apple pie, all for 35¢.

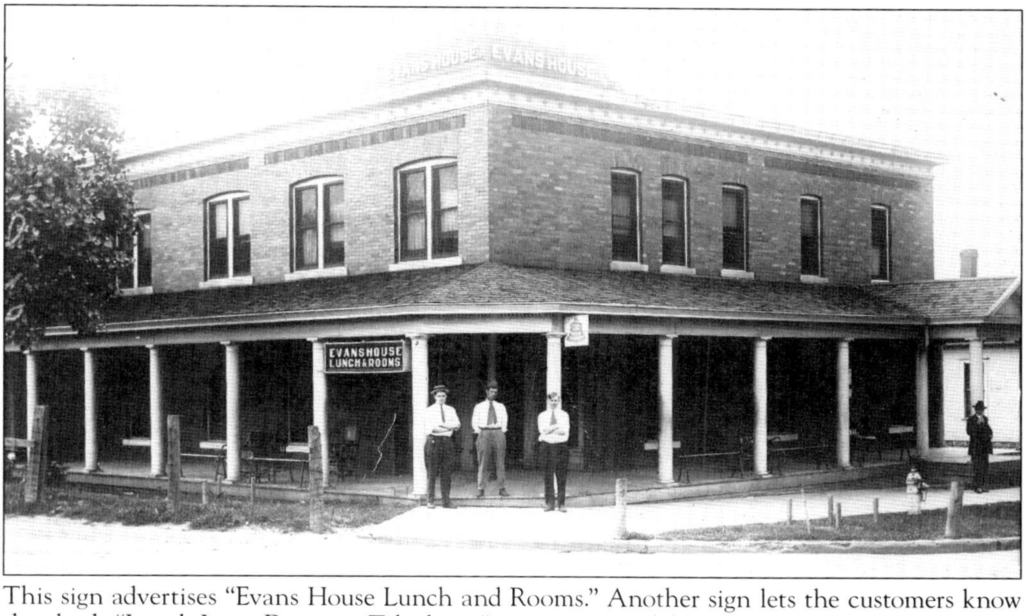

This sign advertises "Evans House Lunch and Rooms." Another sign lets the customers know that both "Local, Long Distance Telephone" service is available. Wooden chairs are lined up on the porch. Iron hitches line the edge of the porch for horses. Evans House was on Second Street at the foot of the new depot driveway. Today the porches are gone, and this is now an apartment building.

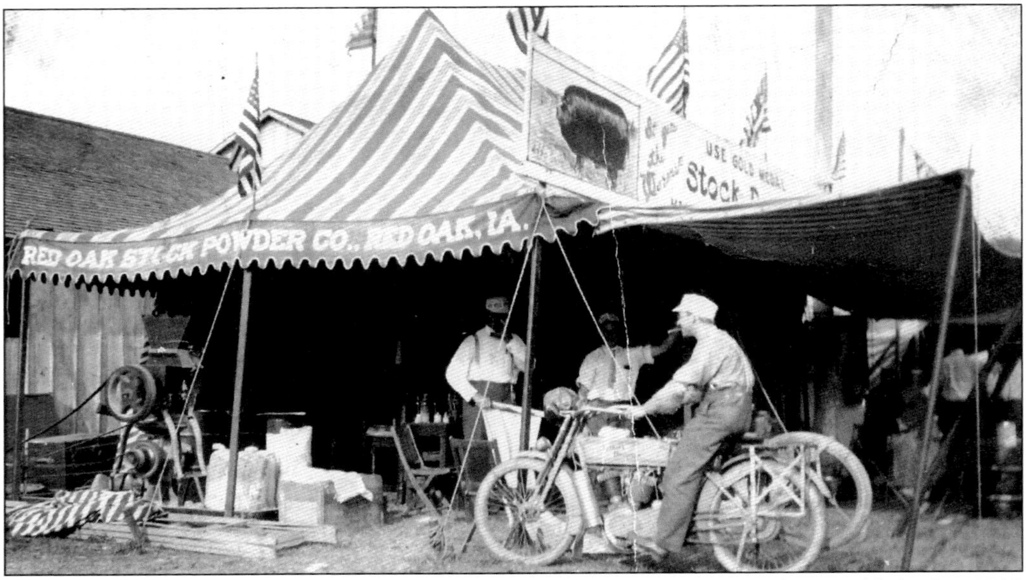

This is the Red Oak Stock and Powder Company's tent at the fair. It was first established in 1899 in Shenandoah by F. W. Dixon and his son, Ross. Their business grew and they moved to Red Oak in 1906, taking over the first floor and basement of the IOOF building. An advertisement in 1915 promised that their powders, Santonin Worm Powder, Gold Medal Regulator, and Gold Medal Stock Powder, were all high grade for any kind of stock, horses, cattle, sheep, and hogs, in fighting disease.

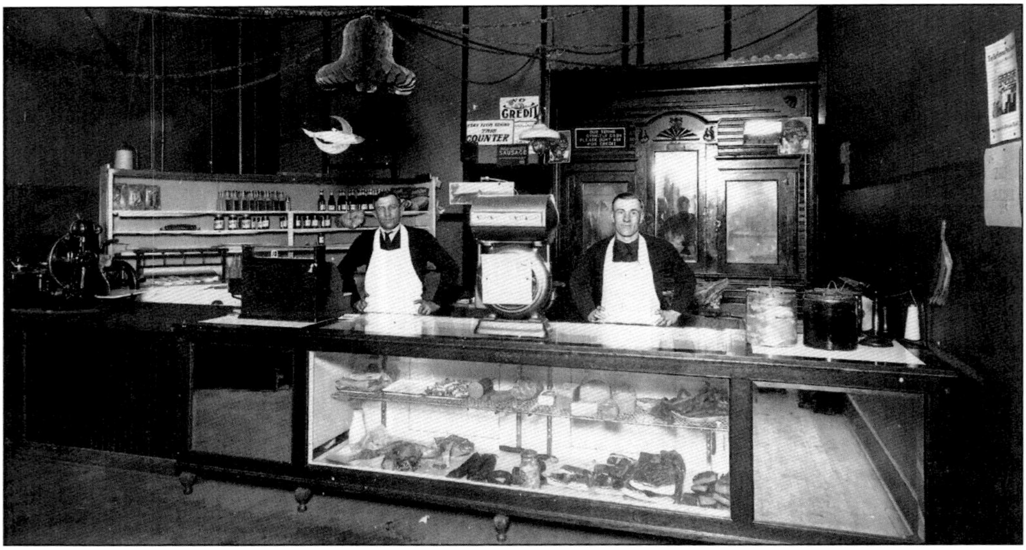

Campbell's Grocery Store is decked out for Christmas. The best quality meats, hams, bacon, and sausages, are displayed in the case. The signs on the wall convey warnings: "Stay from behind this counter," "No credit," and "Our terms strictly cash, please don't ask for credit." Another sign advertises that they carry Polish quality sausage. There is a beautiful refrigerator unit in the back, they use no springs, honest weight scales. Also available to the consumer are Booth's fish products and a variety of sauces, honey, and pickles. A candlestick telephone is on the counter at the right.

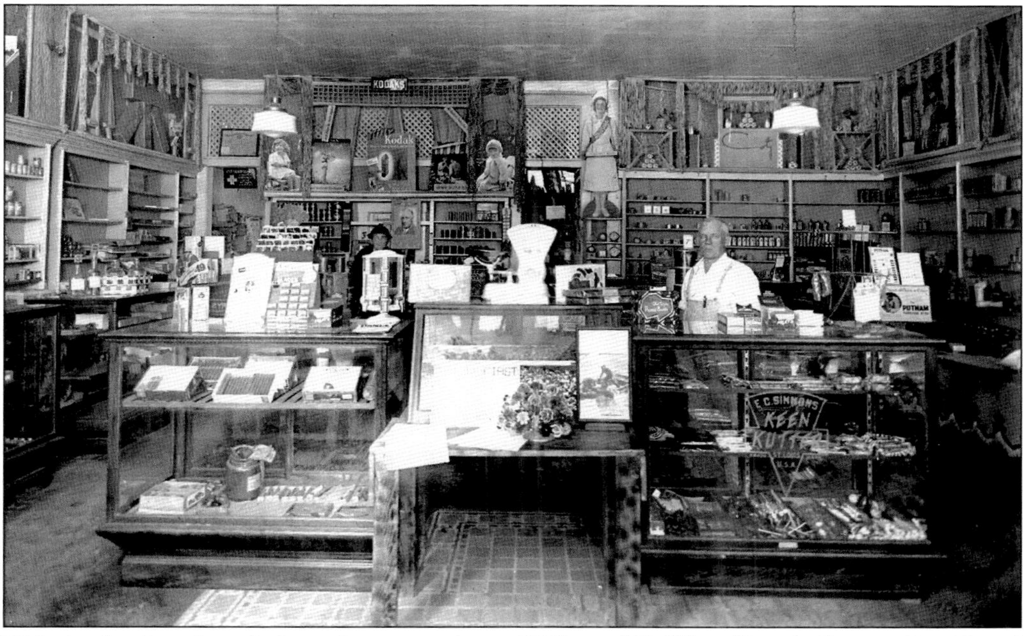

This is the interior of Artz drugstore about 1915, at 510 West Fourth Street. David and Petty Artz came to Red Oak in 1889. Their home was at 901 Sixth Street. Mrs. Hamilton of 1000 Coolbaugh Street had a gift for being able to tell people where to find lost things. David Artz lost a gold watch. She read her tea leaves and told him he could find the watch under some hay. He went to the basement and found the watch under a shipment packed in excelsior, a common packing material of his day.

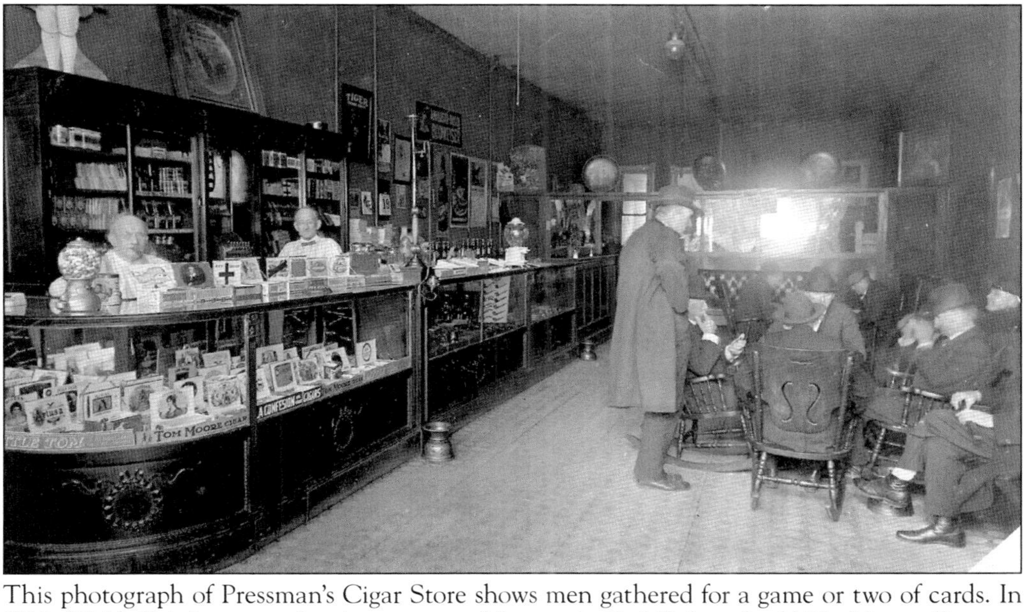

This photograph of Pressman's Cigar Store shows men gathered for a game or two of cards. In 1912, W. H. Shinley opened a cigar store and factory in Red Oak and sold Big Moose, Rummy, and Little Rose cigars. They made 150,000 cigars annually and did $15,000 a year in receipts. In 1923, Roy Wester bought a cigar store that was open 24 hours a day.

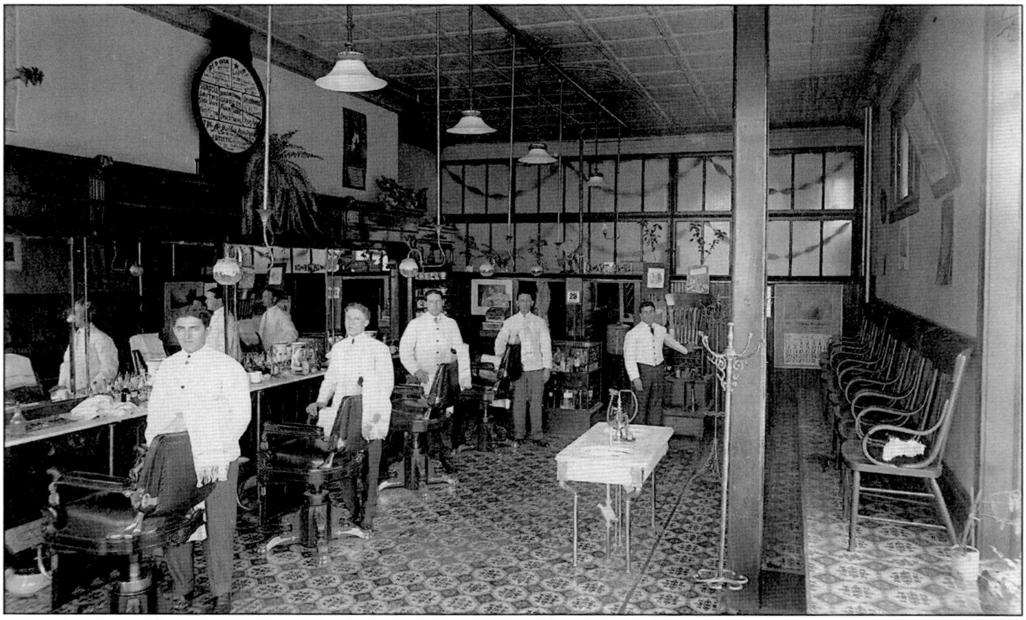

Seen here is the Frank Langford Barber Shop in the Houghton building in 1910. From left to right are Cecil Wright, Burt Parmer, Ed McMullen, Frank Langford, and the porter, Scotty. The sign on the wall above them advertises other Red Oak businesses: Sundell and Smith's Shoes, Star Laundry, McMillen artistic photography, Boylen Thomas carpets and furniture, and insurance.

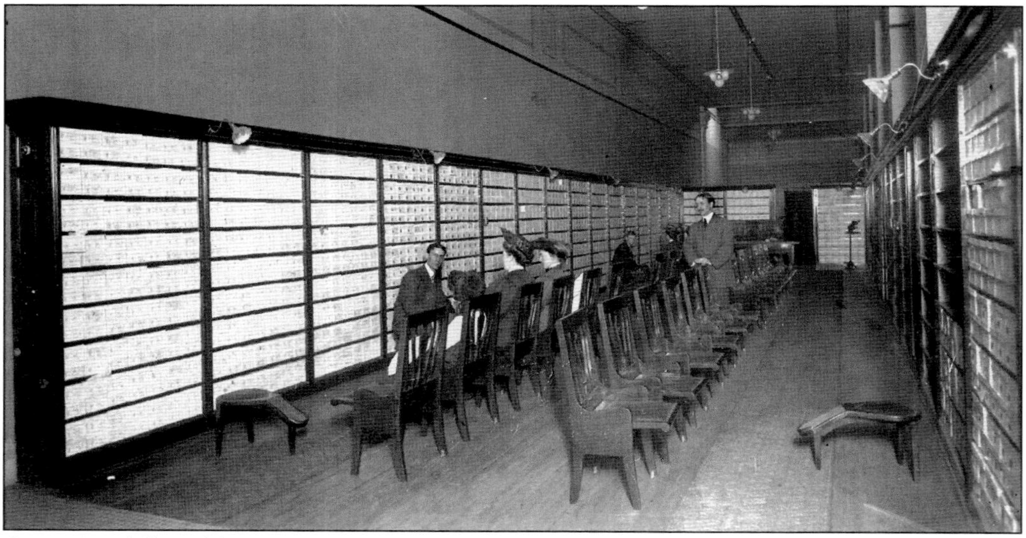

Oscar Sundell and his son Paul help the ladies select shoes about 1912. Oscar was born in Sweden in 1854. In the spring of 1880 he emigrated from Sweden. At that time, a shoe store was unknown in Sweden, and all the work was done by hand, traveling from home to home. He worked in Omaha for 17 years, then joined with a Mr. Newman in 1897 in Red Oak. He partnered with Joe Smith for nine years, then bought out Nelson's shoe shop until 1914. He continued to do business as Sundell's Shoes at 418 Coolbaugh Street until he moved to 503 Third Street in 1929.

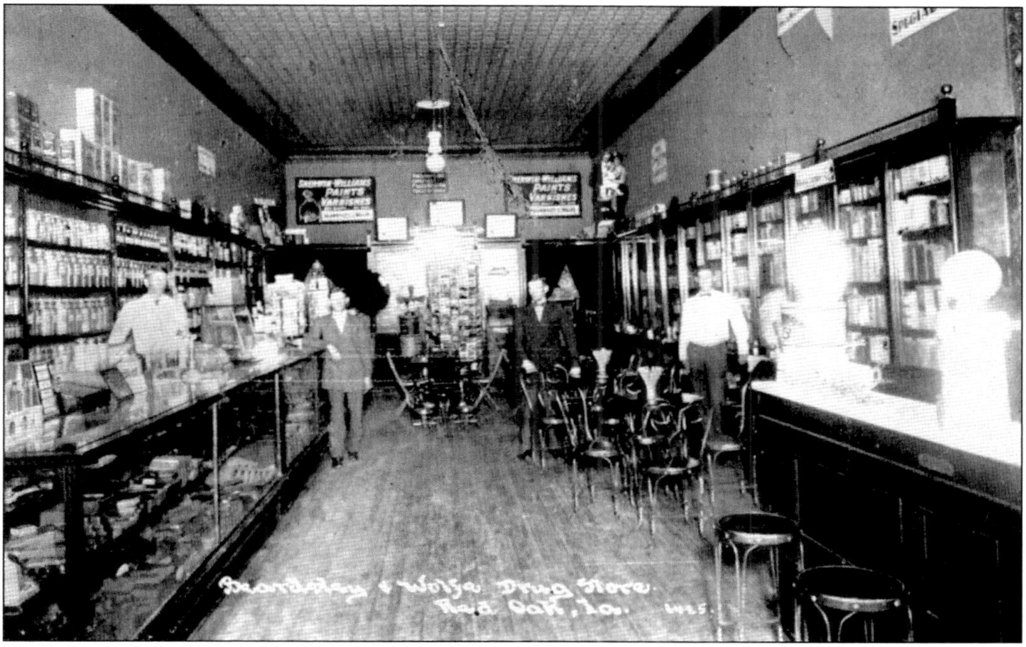

This is the interior of Beardsley and Wolfe Drug Store. It carried a full line of Sherwin Williams paints and had a soda fountain. Henry Hebard West recalls that the best soda water was at Hinchman's Drug Store and the best ice cream and peanuts were at Renkin's.

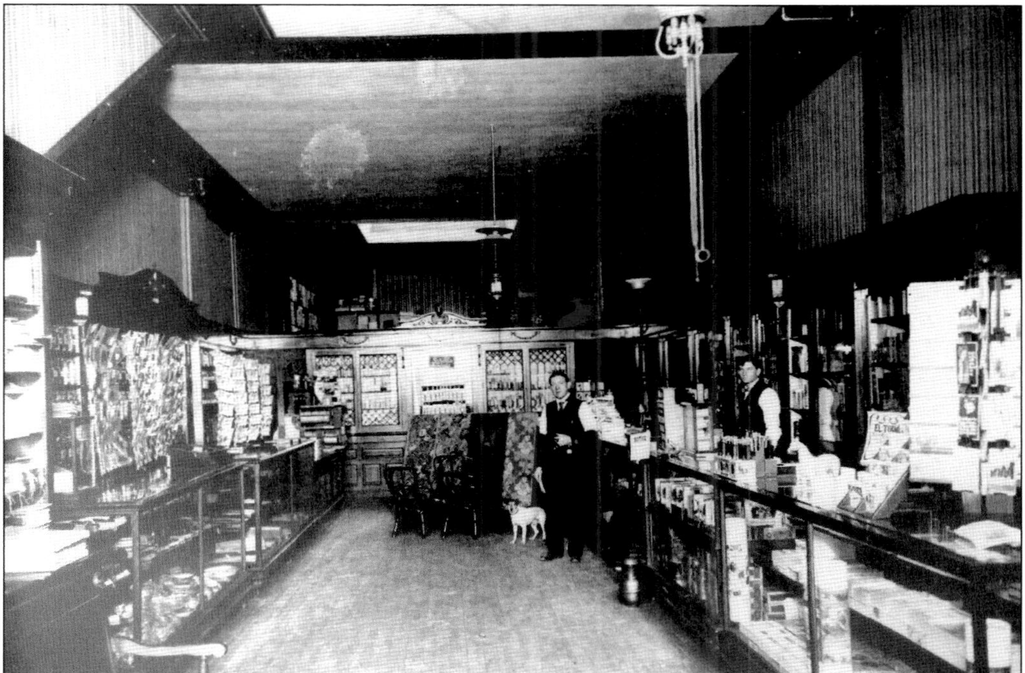

This is an early interior photograph of the Red Cross Drug Store. This store sat on the place on the square where the first house in Red Oak was built.

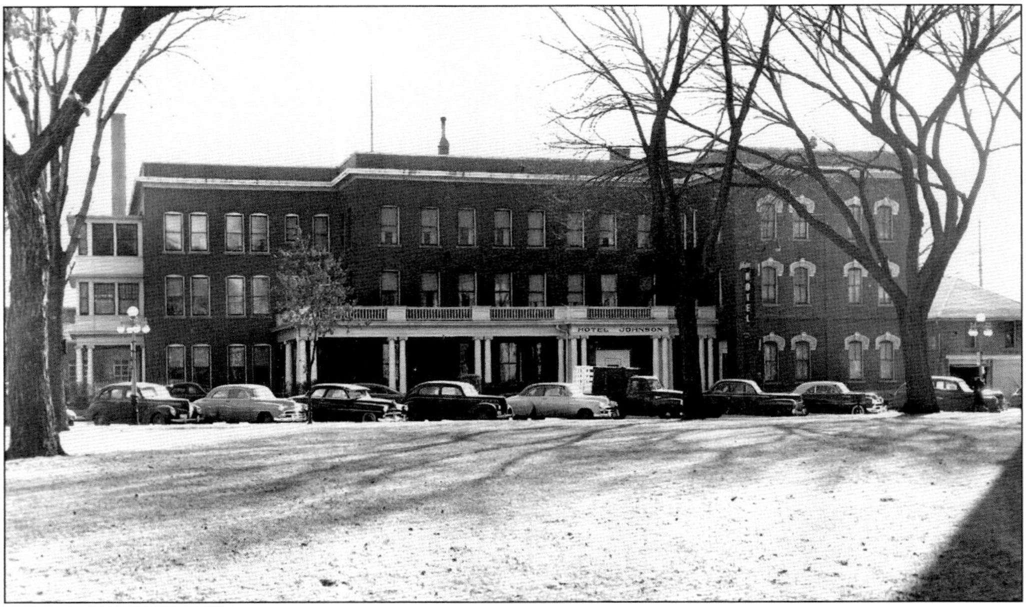

In 1880, the Judkins brothers built a hotel at 106 Coolbaugh Street. There were seven hotels at the time that were already well established. Judkins House was a three-story hotel that cost $16,000 to build and had 60 rooms. In 1885, it was purchased by P. P. Johnson and renamed Johnson House. Johnson swapped the property with Mary Walker in the 1890s. Her brother Mr. Trimble ran it for a while, then abruptly disappeared. Ben and Henry Heckert took over the management. Samuel Payne leased the hotel in 1901 and purchased it in 1904. Everything was refitted with the aim of being a first-class hotel. By 1906, the Hotel Johnson was rated one of the finest in Iowa. Some of the famous guests were William Jennings Bryan, Chief Justice Howard Taft, Adm. Richard E. Byrd, and Julian Street. Below is an interior photograph of the dining room from about 1938.

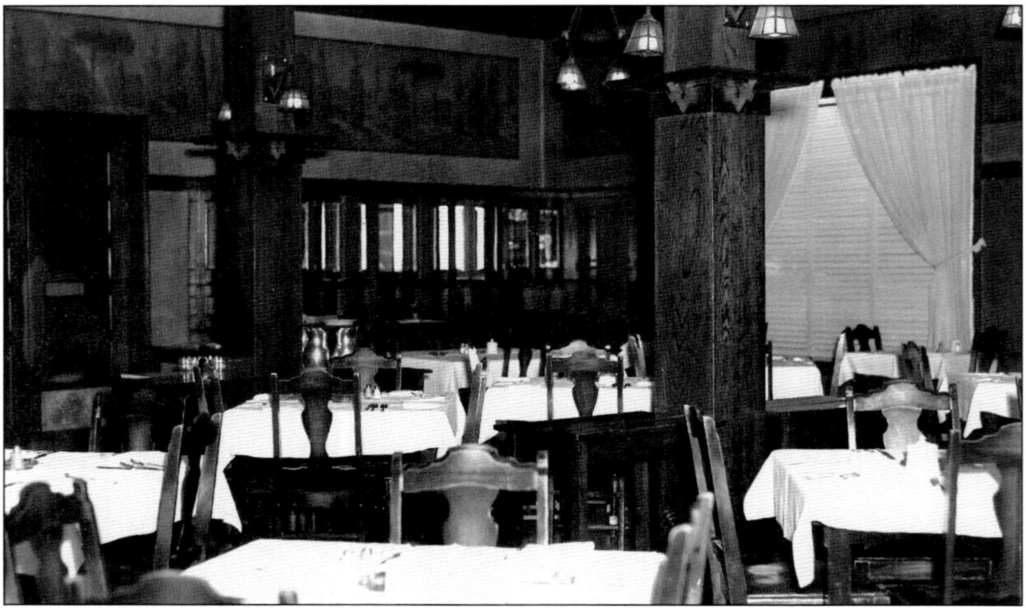

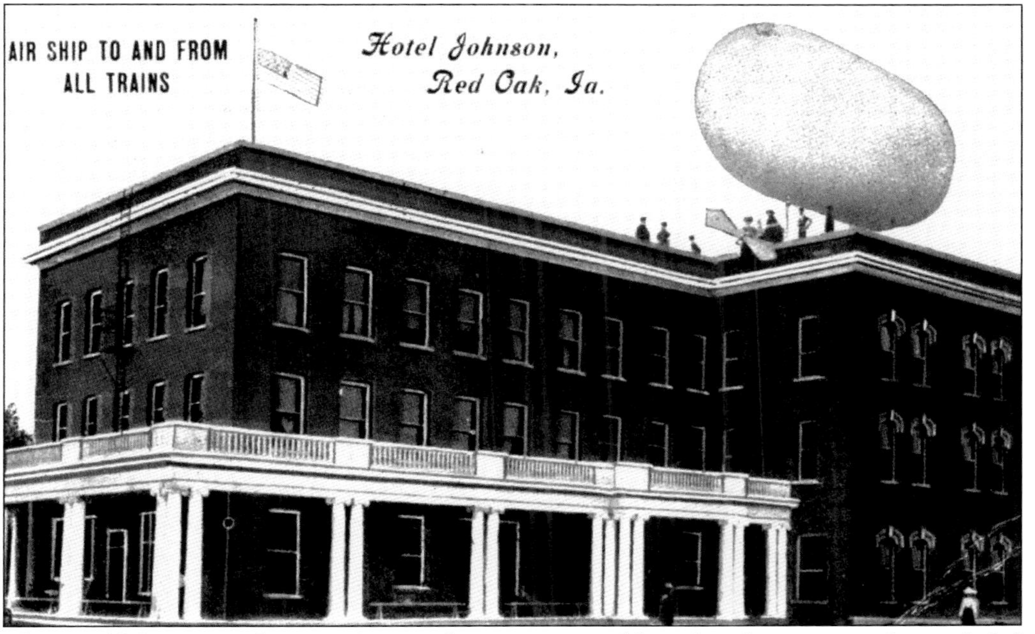

The Hotel Johnson tried to provide everything a guest would need, and at one time that included air-ship transport to and from all trains. In 1909, rates were $2 for a room and $2.50 for a room with a bath. There were 82 guest rooms, 40 of those had their own private bath, and there were 5 apartments. In 1951, 10 tile shower units were installed. A barbershop, bus depot, and Western Union all had offices in the hotel.

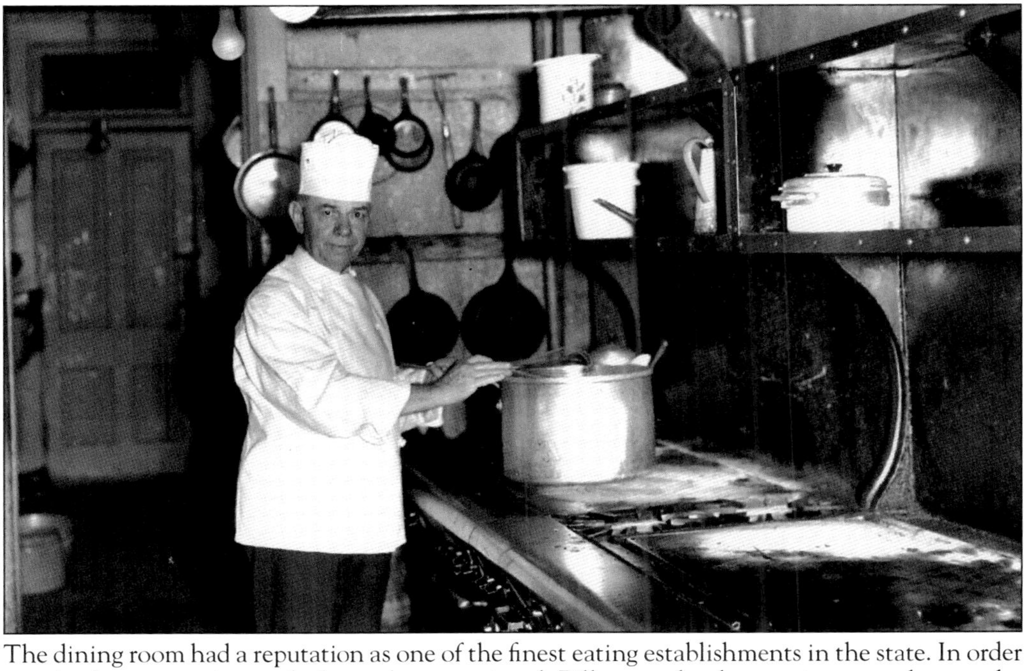

The dining room had a reputation as one of the finest eating establishments in the state. In order to gain that reputation, a chef must be exceptional. Billy poses by the massive stove, he was the cook for the Hotel Johnson in 1938. The kitchen was in the oldest part of the hotel.

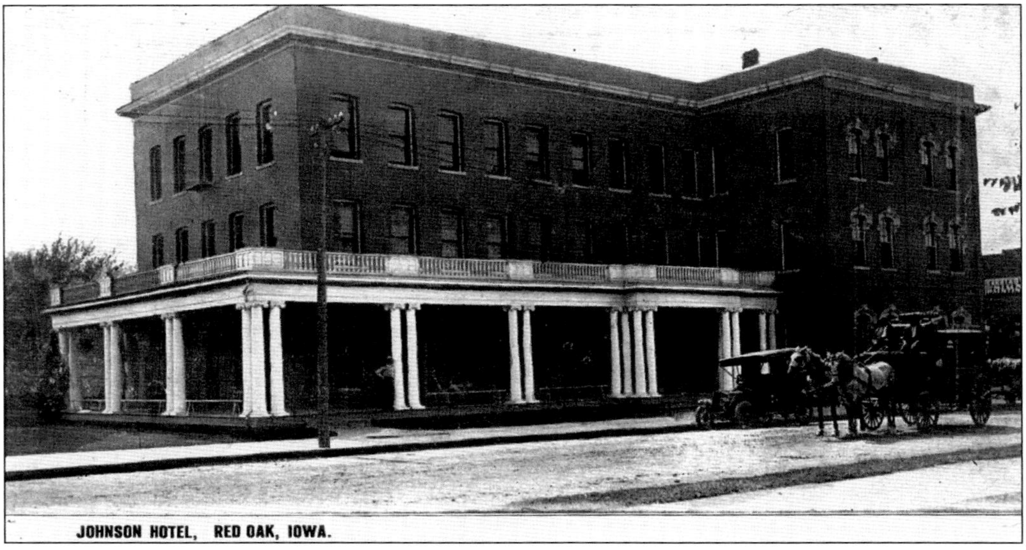

This postal card shows the Hotel Johnson before 1917. For weeks, the *Express* had published articles about Thomas Edison and his invention of the electric light. Henry Hebard West remembered the first display of electricity in Red Oak in about 1886. Next door to the Hotel Johnson was Brown's Foundry. Inside a huge dynamo was set up, and wires ran from Brown's to the hotel. Out of a second-story window a two-by-four had a big arc light hanging at the end of it, and as the light of day faded, the dynamo was charged, and the first electric light was displayed in Red Oak. West remembered hearing the buzz of the dynamo as the arc light illuminated the twilight.

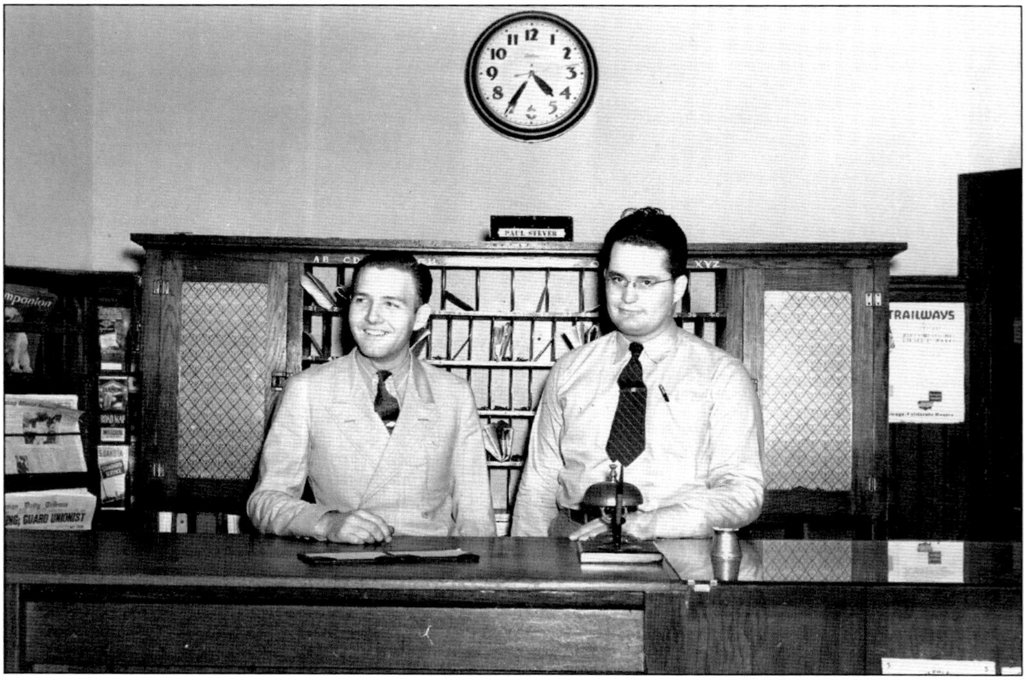

Desk clerks at the Hotel Johnson in 1938 stand at the ready.

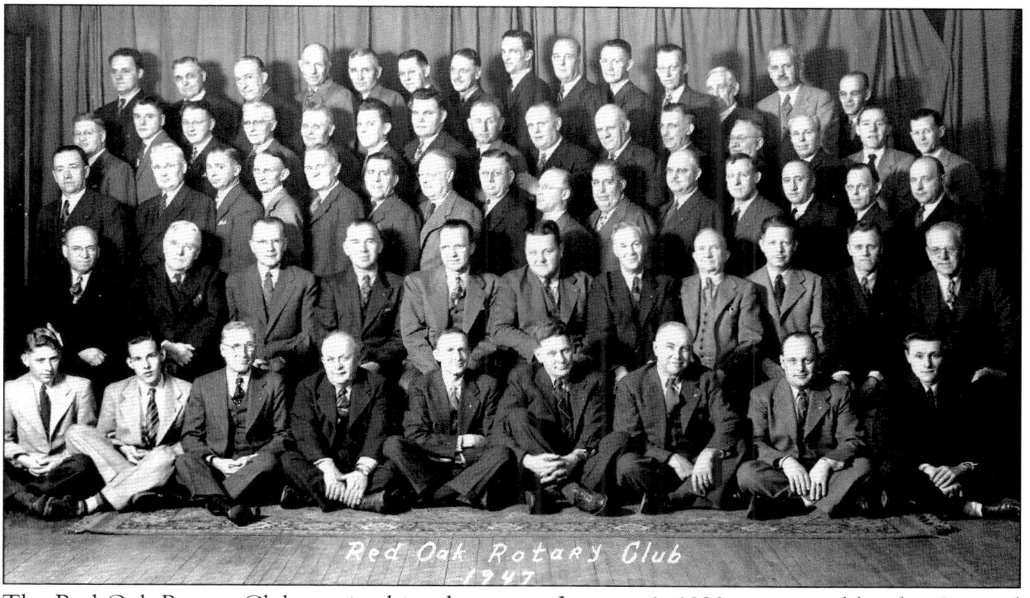

The Red Oak Rotary Club received its charter on January 1, 1920, sponsored by the Council Bluffs club. Glendon Fischer was elected the first president. Other charter members were F. F. Baker, Charles Carey, William Cochrane, F. E. Crandell, Charles Finley, Edward Frum, Ozra Givson, Dr. Gilmore, Gordon Hayes, H. C. Houghton Jr., George Kerrihard, Frank Limbach, John Loomis, Harry Petty, Paul Richards, Dr. Roy Morris, Archer Payne, Earl Robinson, and Dr. Seabloom. The men of the Red Oak Rotary Club are seen in 1947.

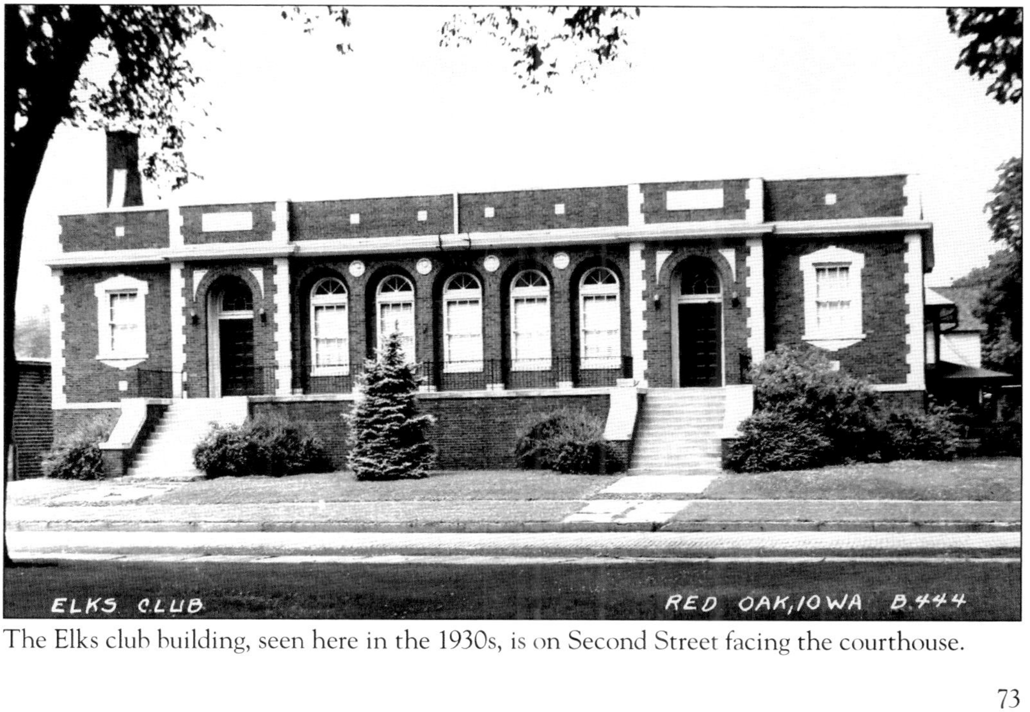

The Elks club building, seen here in the 1930s, is on Second Street facing the courthouse.

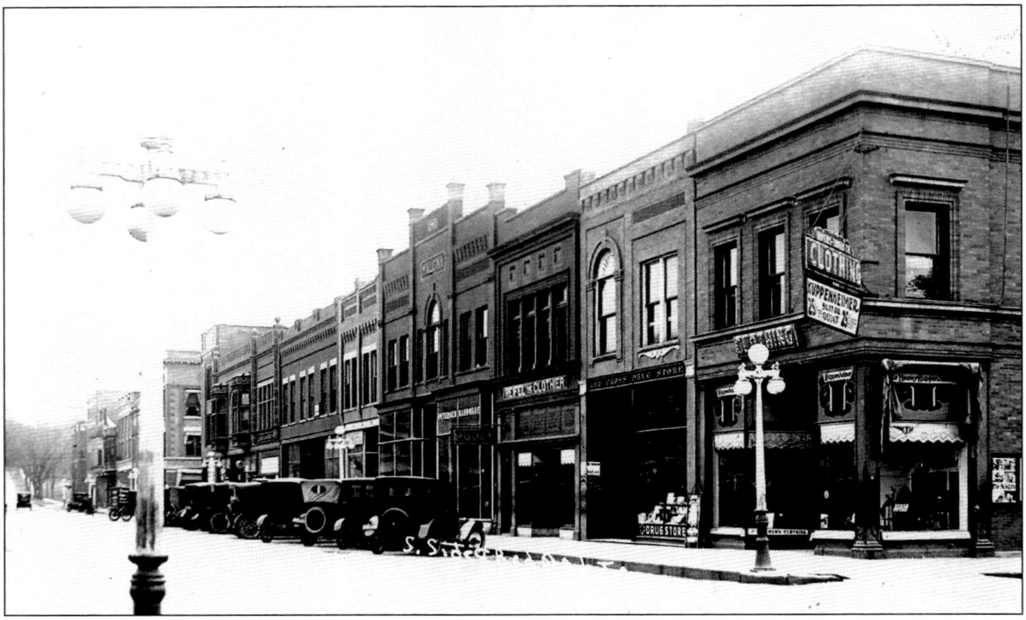

The scene on this busy winter day in Red Oak shows that a Kuppenheimer suit or coat was 25 percent off in the clothing store. Next door was the Red Cross Drug Store, before expansion, then Reifel the Clothier with a pool hall on another level, and Petersen Hardware in the Maloney building.

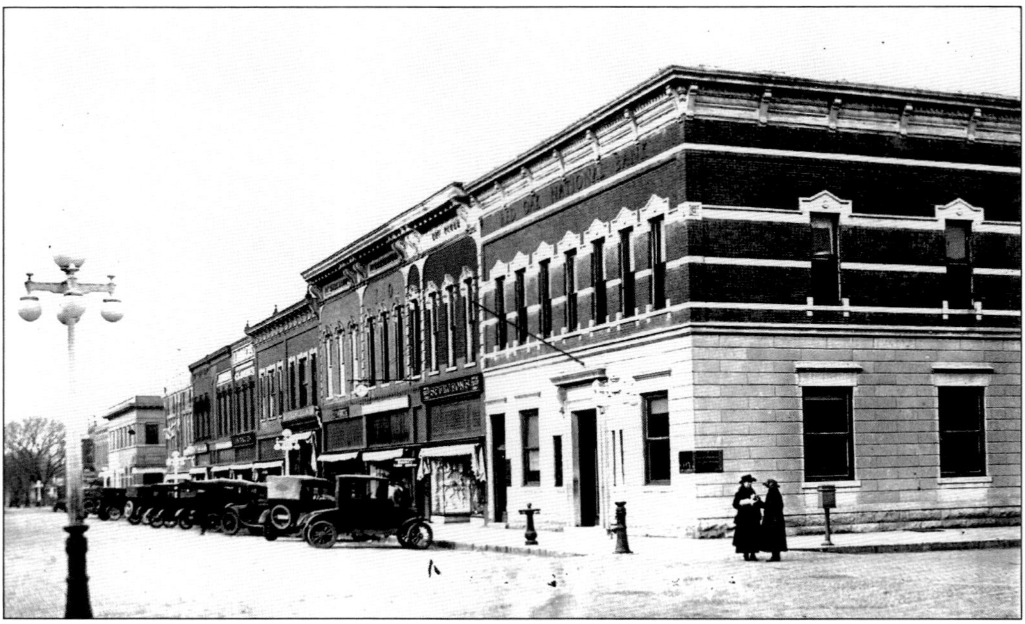

Two women visit on the corner outside of the Red Oak National Bank Building about 1917.

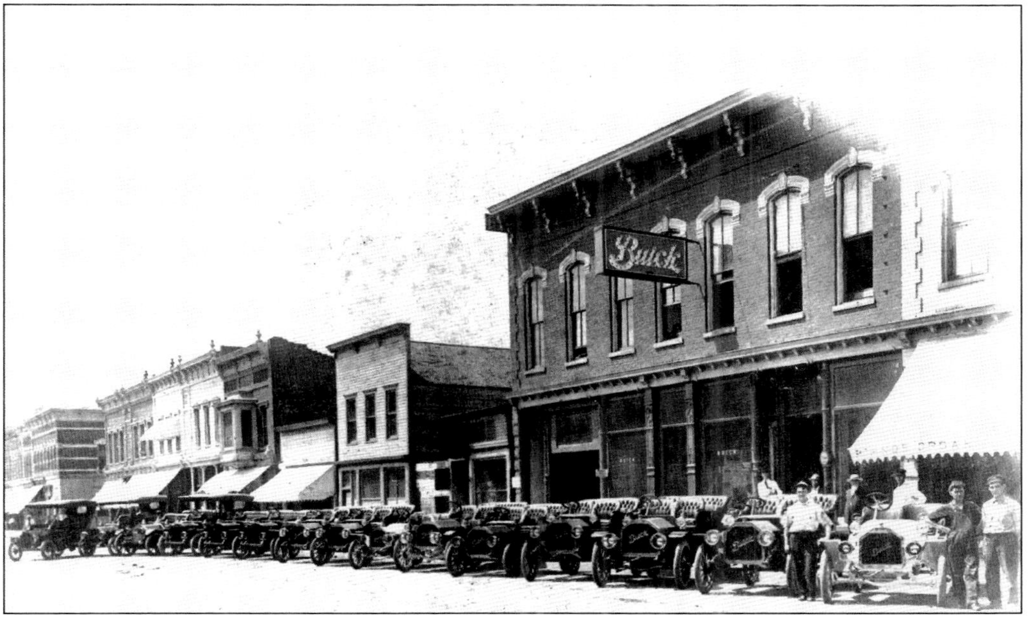

Pianos and organs are for sale next door to the Buick dealership that proudly displays the latest models on the square. Automobile dealerships began to open in the 1920s. When the concrete highways were built, demand for automobiles increased. Old Highway 34 was paved from 1928 through 1930, Highway 71 in 1928, and Highway 48 was paved in 1931.

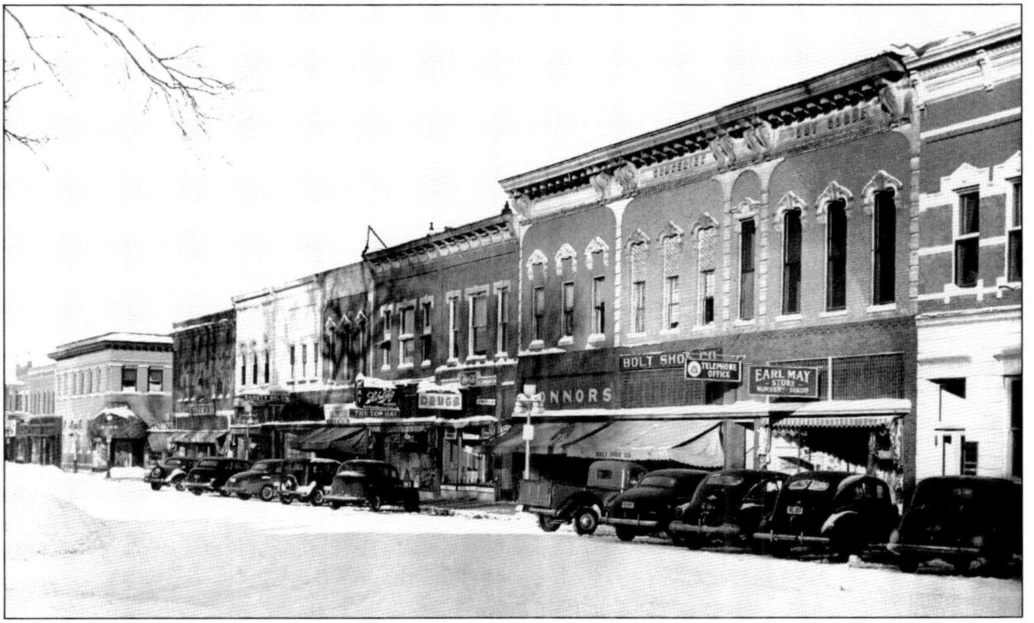

Reed Street on the square is seen here, looking west on a snowy winters day. The business seen are, from right to left, Earl May Store, with a full stock of seeds and nursery plants and supplies; the Bell Telephone offices upstairs; the Bolt Shoe Company; Connors; farm loans on the second floor; a drugstore; the Top Hat bar and grill; the Gamble store; the Robison Beauty Salon; and Safeway.

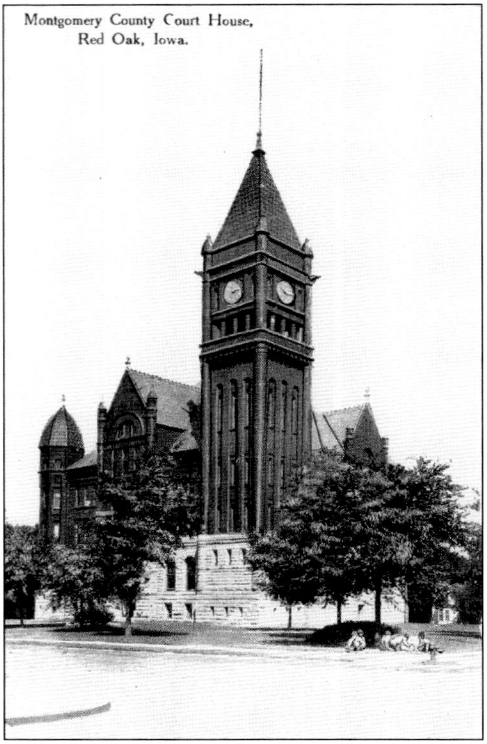

Judge Smith McPherson helped lay the cornerstone of the new courthouse in 1890. Corn, wine, and oil were sprinkled on the stone to symbolize nourishment, refreshment, and joy. McPherson was toastmaster for a large party across the street in the Hotel Johnson. Once it was completed, the view from the tower in the courthouse provided another perspective on the growing city of Red Oak.

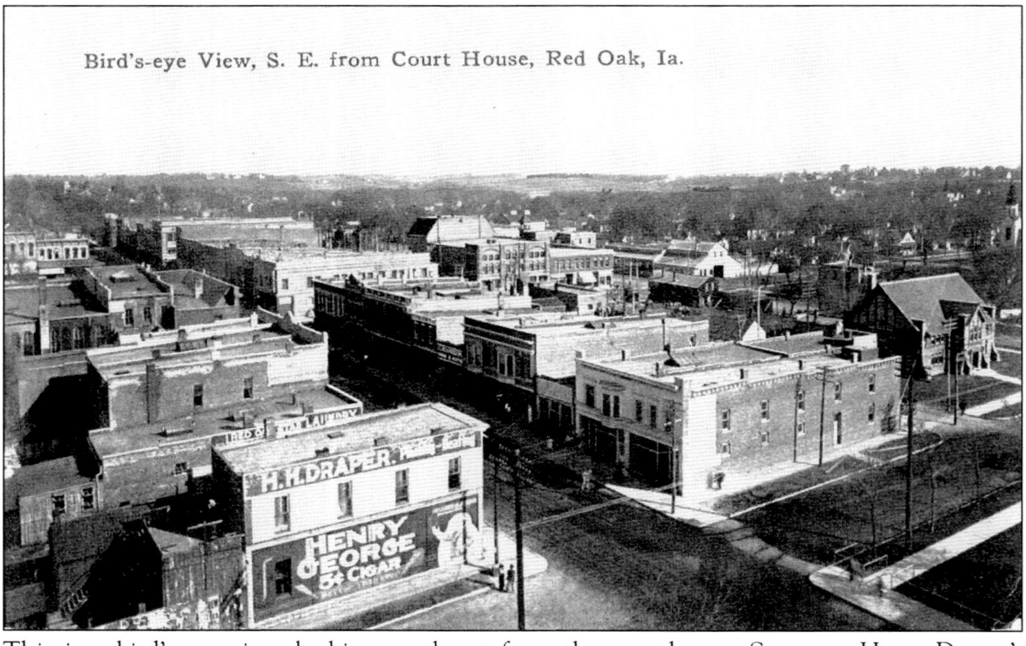

This is a bird's-eye view, looking southeast from the courthouse. Seen are Harry Draper's Plumbing and Heating Company, with an advertisement for Henry George Cigars on the side of the building; then the Red Oak Star Laundry, with the Stevens brothers as proprietors; and the public library on the far right.

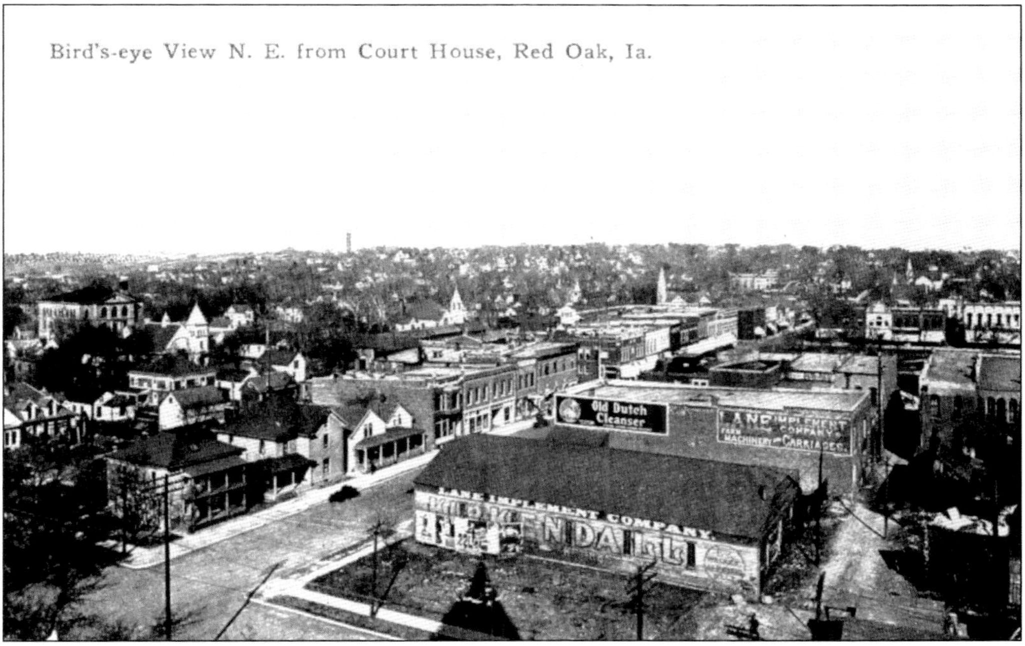

This northeast view from the courthouse shows, on the horizon, the roof of the Chautauqua Pavilion by the water tower, the high school on the far left near the horizon, and the Lane Implement Company, which backs up to Draper's. Notice that the buildings on the square still have the alleyways mid-block.

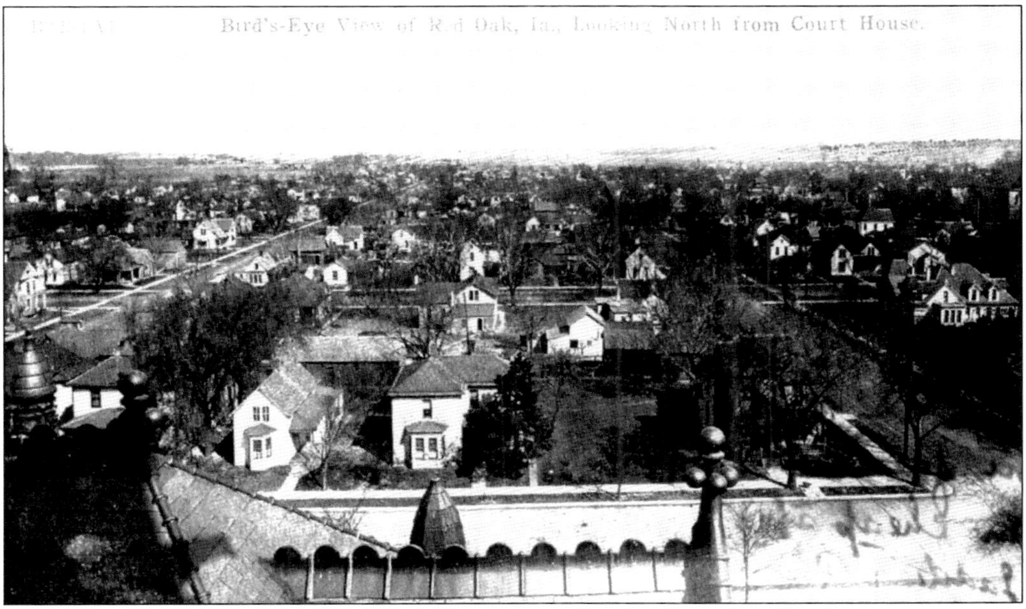

This is a bird's-eye view taken from the courthouse looking north into a residential neighborhood. Many of these houses are still standing.

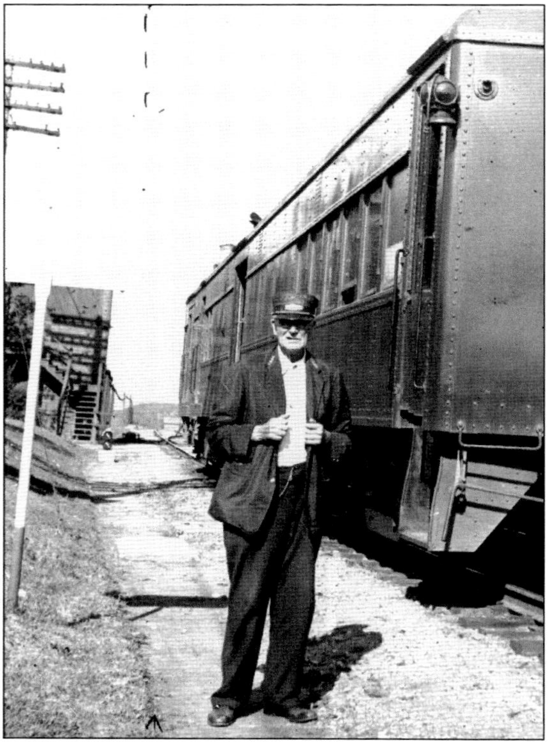

Charles Shank, a longtime railroad employee, is pictured here.

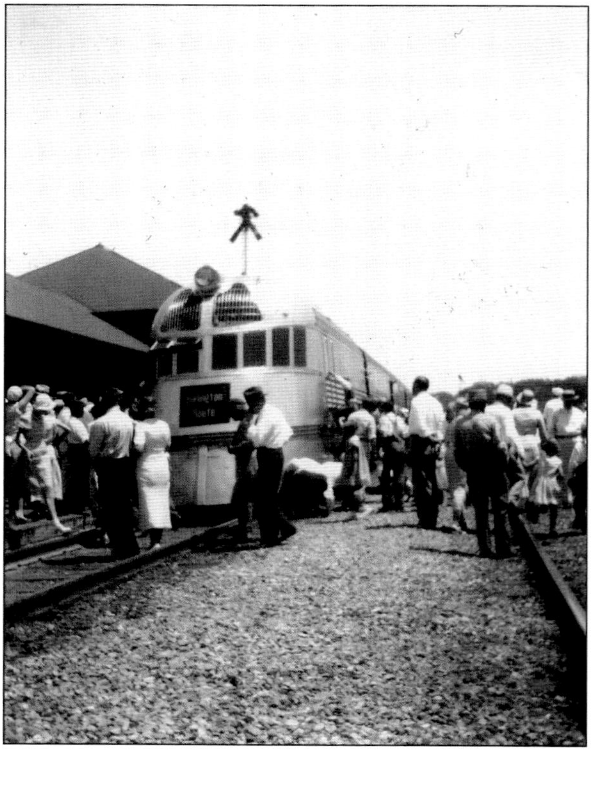

The new Burlington Zephyr created quite a stir when it came through Red Oak.

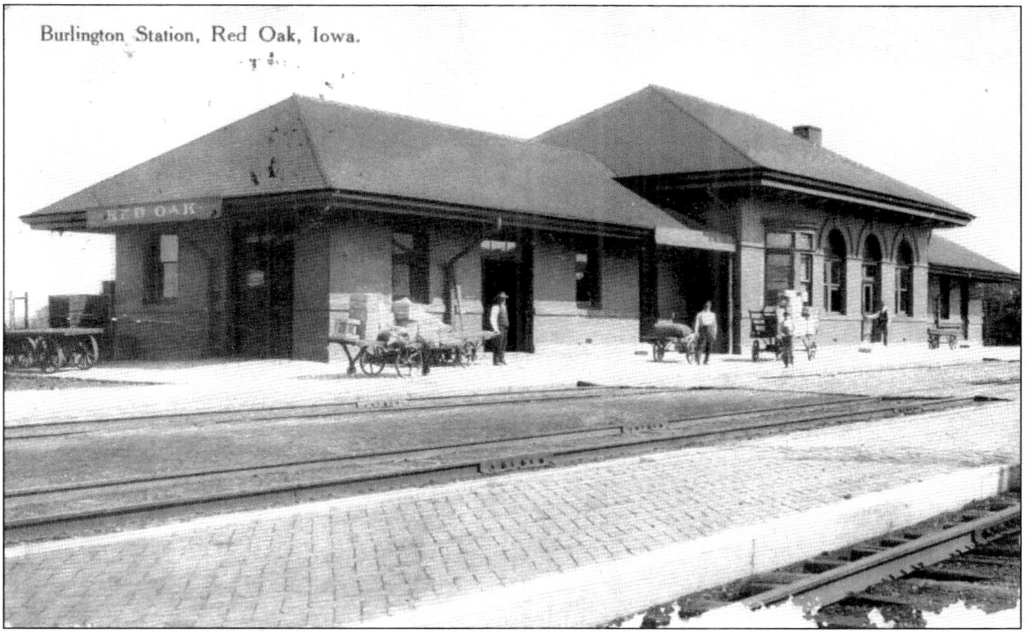

This postal card pictures the Burlington Passenger Depot.

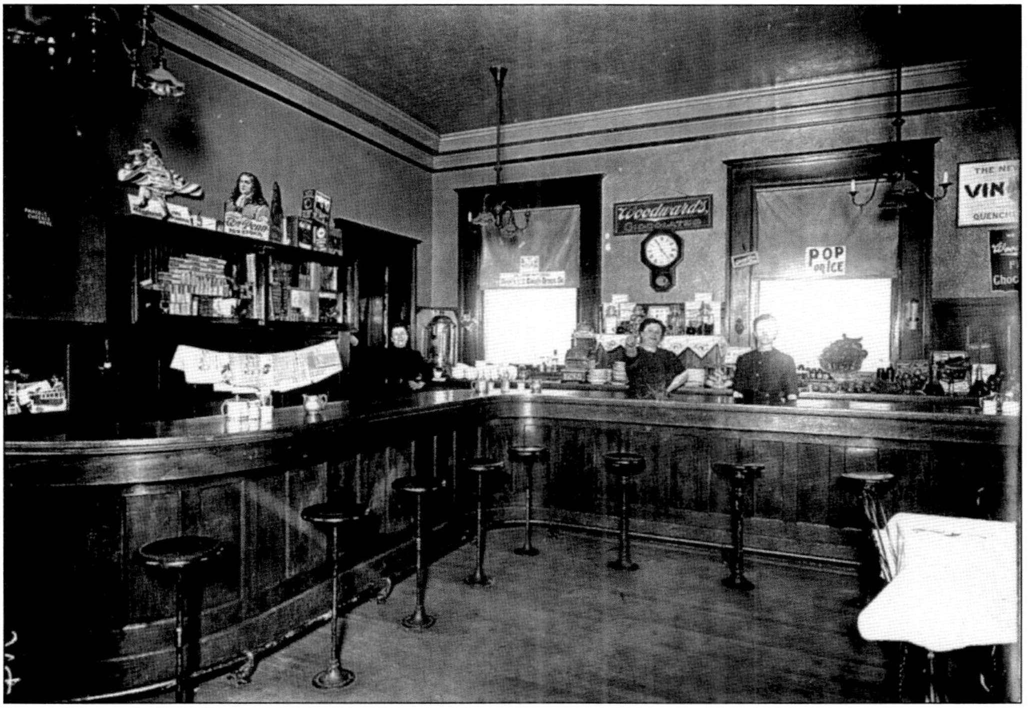

This is the interior of a depot lunchroom in the 1920s. Lillian Carmichael is at the far right with two unidentified women. When the No. 4 train arrived at noon, the passengers got off and ate lunch during the 20-minute stop.

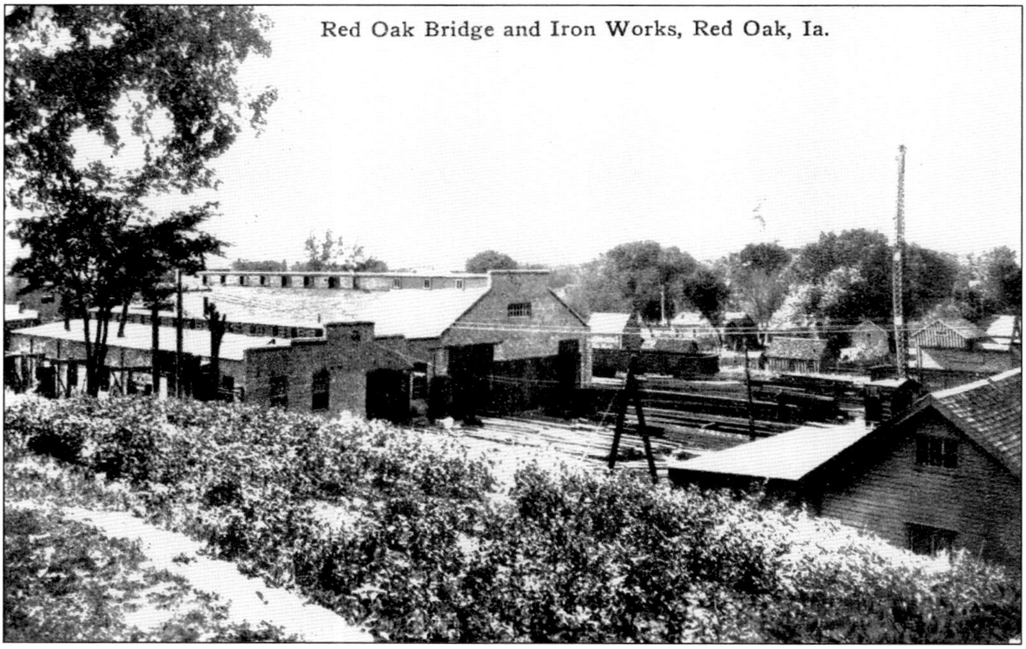

This postal card pictures the Red Oak Bridge and Iron Works. This company built many of the bridges across many rivers in the state—the Coolbaugh bridge included. This company was founded by Charles H. Wilson who first came to Red Oak as a bridge builder. As he was building infrastructures around the area, the idea came to him to make a reinforced concrete pipe. From this idea a patent and a corporation were born.

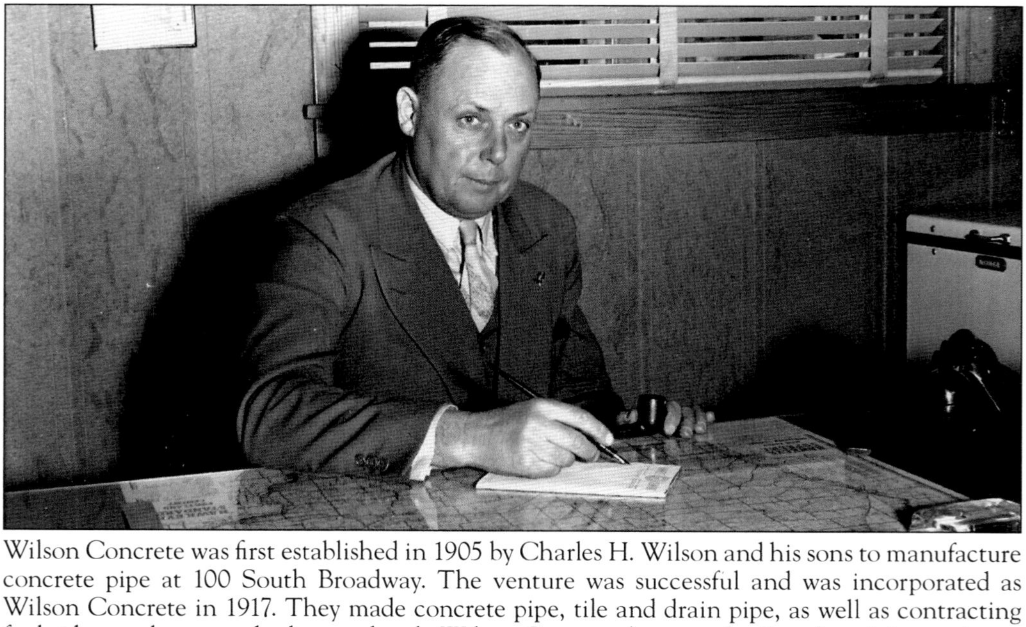

Wilson Concrete was first established in 1905 by Charles H. Wilson and his sons to manufacture concrete pipe at 100 South Broadway. The venture was successful and was incorporated as Wilson Concrete in 1917. They made concrete pipe, tile and drain pipe, as well as contracting for bridges, culverts, and other roadwork. Wilson Concrete has paved miles of roads in southwest Iowa. It became one of Iowa's largest manufacturers of concrete tile and pipe. C. Frank Wilson, pictured here in his office about 1940, ran the business after his father's death in 1920.

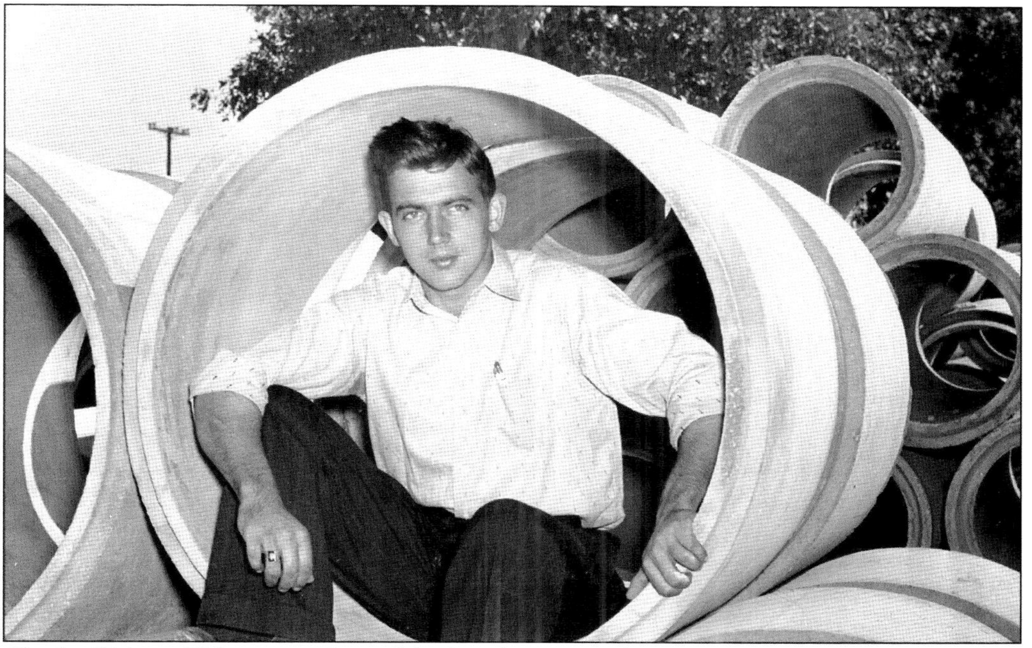

Charles Webster Wilson, grandson of the founder, sits inside one of the culvert pipes made at the Wilson Concrete factory in 1940. After graduating from Iowa State College with an engineering degree he came to work for his father. By 1953, he had become president.

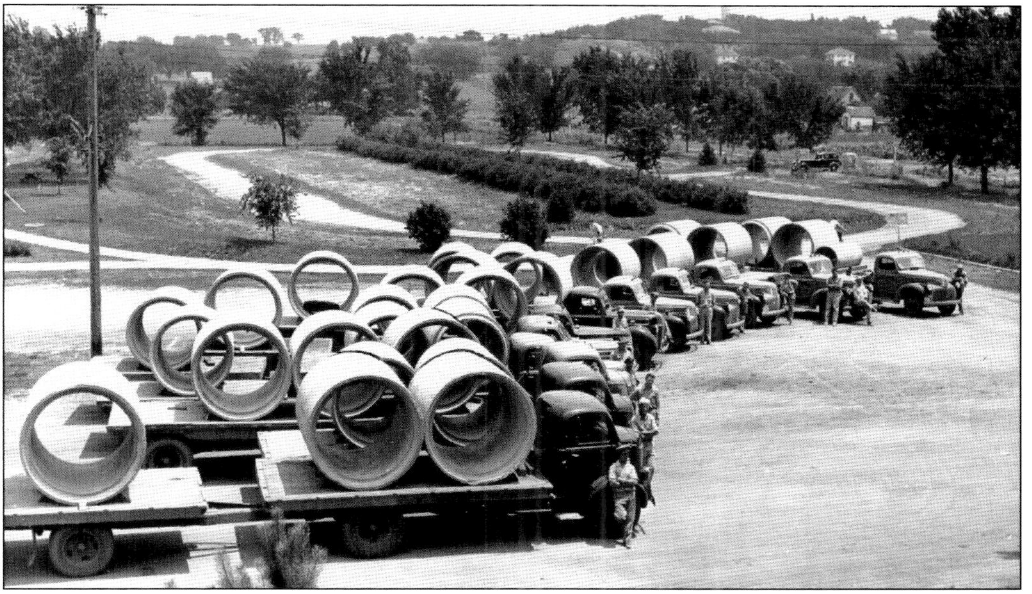

The concrete was shipped out by truck and rail, but as it became cost prohibitive, branch offices were opened in Nebraska, Missouri, Kansas, and Illinois. Wilson Concrete has been utilized in many important building projects around the Midwest. In 1965, it was used in building Busch Stadium in St. Louis. Some other building projects include the North West Bell offices in Omaha, Blue Cross and Blue Shield building in Omaha, the Durham Scout Center, the expansion of Rosenblatt ballpark, and casino's in Council Bluffs.

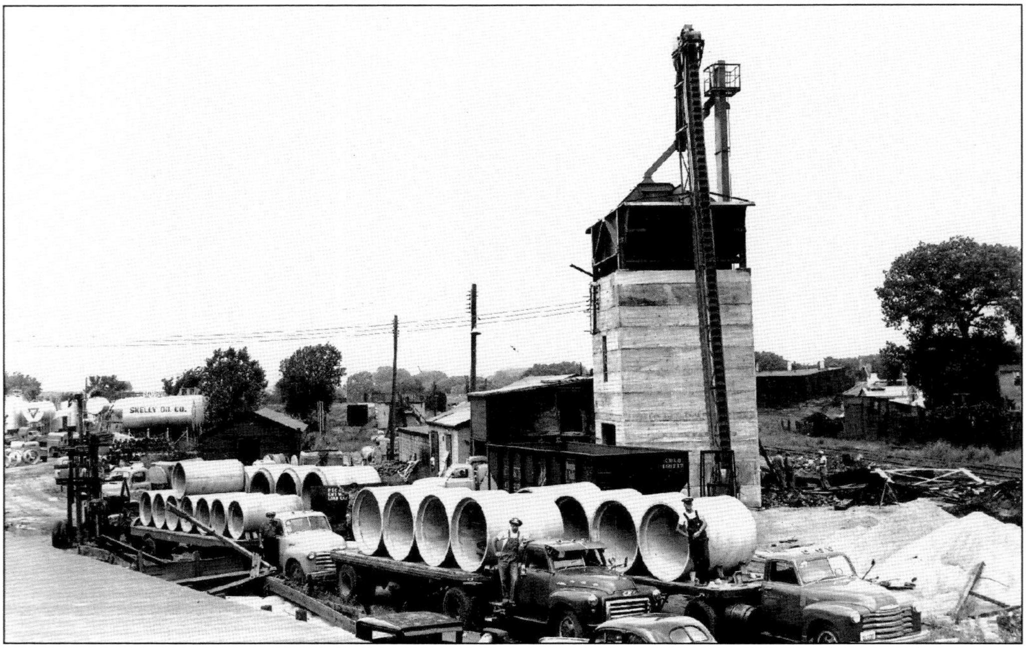

These trucks are ready to head out from the plant. They drive past the sand conveyer where the sand is mixed with cement to get the right mix for the pipes. Cement has been around since Roman times. The manufacture of portland cement began in England about 1825. In the United States, the manufacture of portland cement did not begin until about 1872, but little progress was made until the grinding machinery was capable of reducing the hard lime rock to the right consistency. Once this was achieved, cement was an affordable building material and has been utilized in building all over the world.

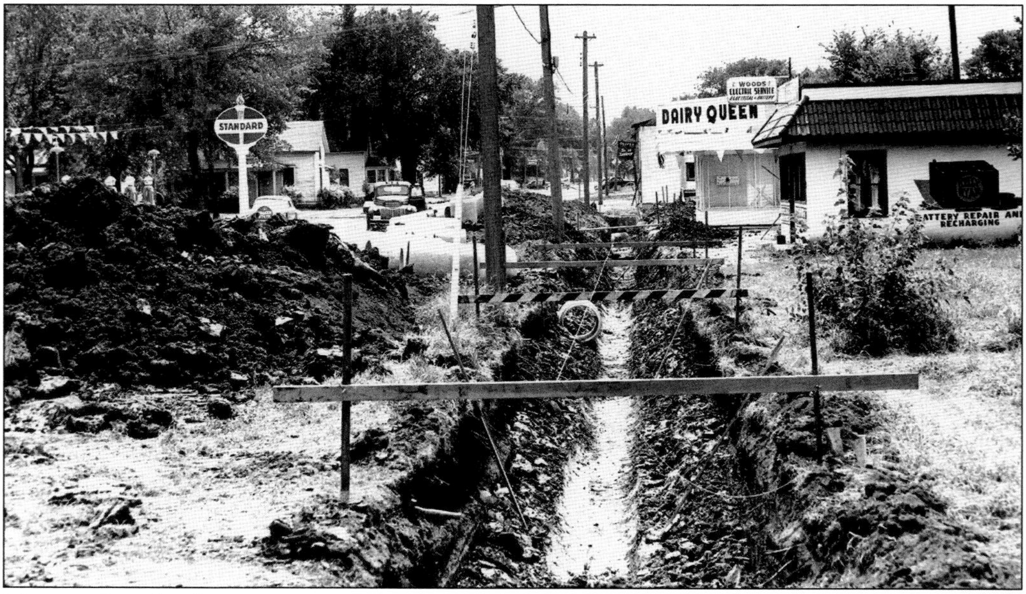

Many miles of culvert concrete pipe were laid throughout Red Oak as the infrastructure was improved. Of course, Wilson Concrete's culverts were used.

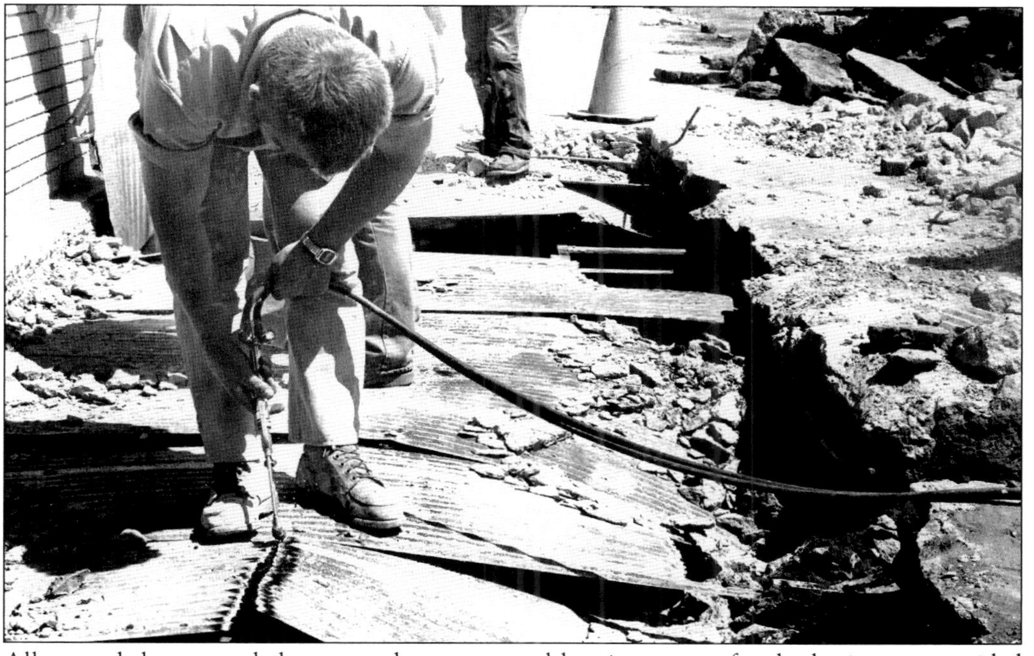

All around the square below ground was a central heating system for the businesses provided by the steam from the power plant. Around the 1950s, it was taken apart and filled in. A worker breaks apart the sidewalk and removes the corrugated metal sheeting over the underground system.

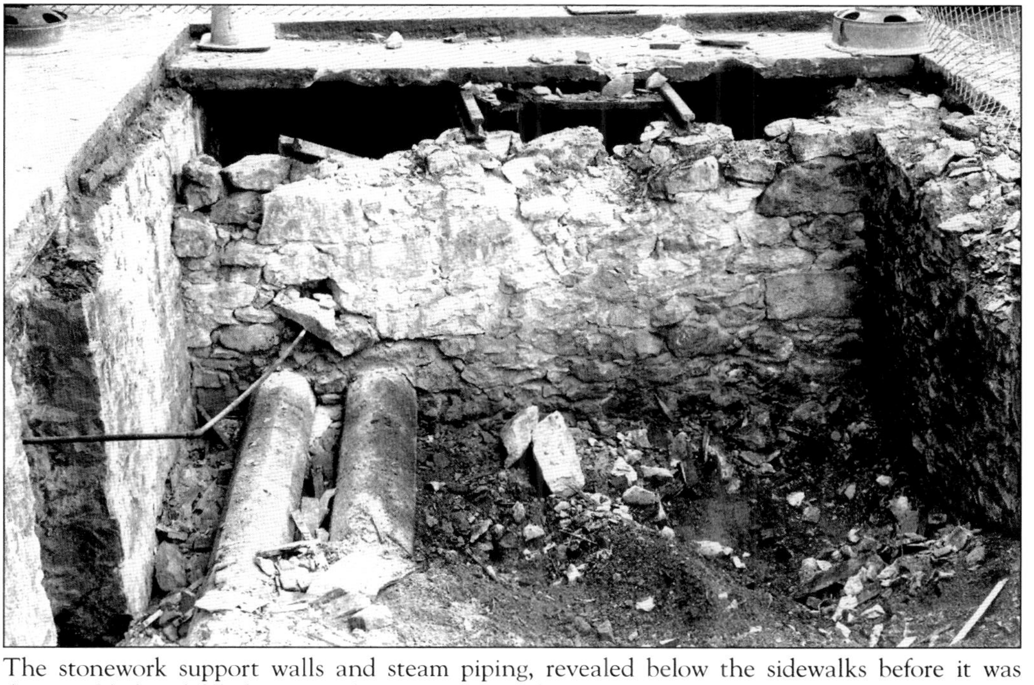

The stonework support walls and steam piping, revealed below the sidewalks before it was disassembled and filled in, reveals an amazing infrastructure that was very far-sighted when it was created.

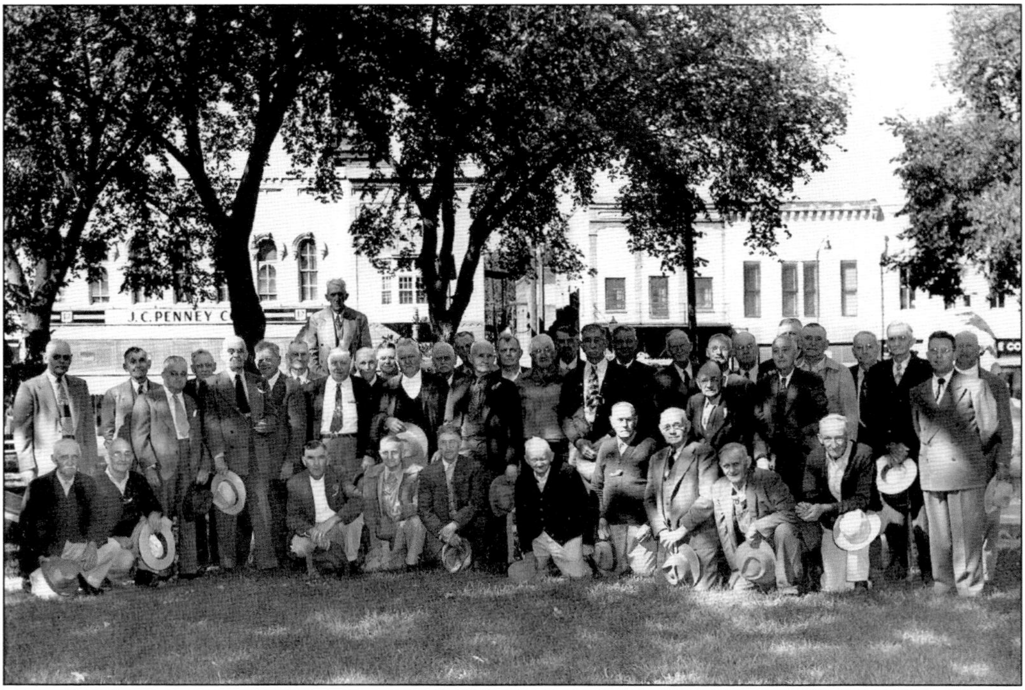

Red Oak had the unique honor of hosting the Checkers and Dominos Tournament in 1949. Entrants pose together in the square under the shade of the trees on a summer afternoon before these men began to play until there was a winner.

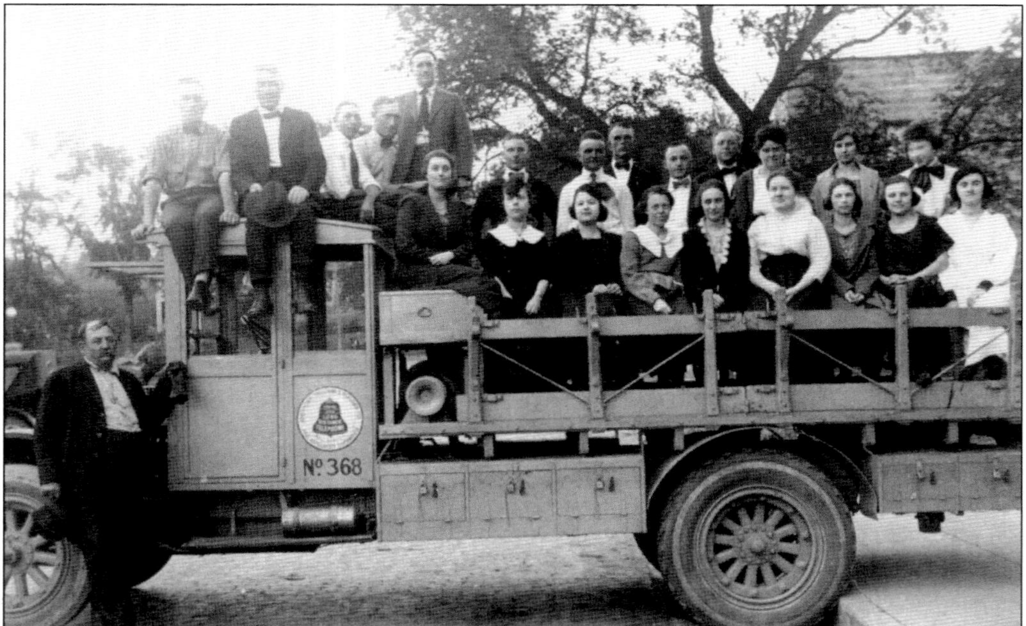

About 1930, the workers for Iowa Bell Telephone pile on one of their utility trucks for a company outing.

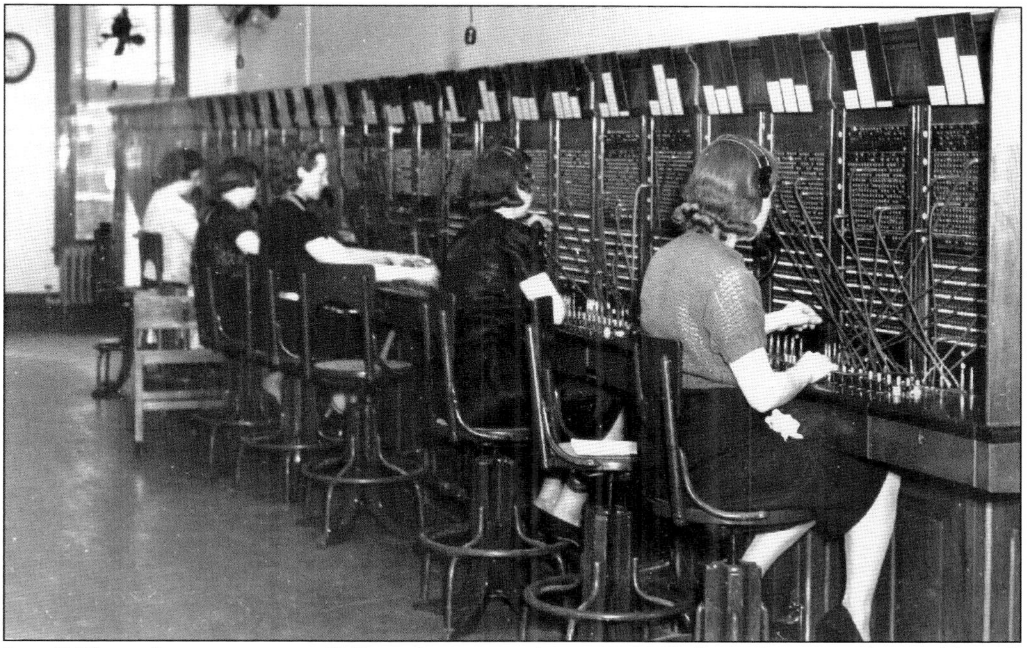

It is 9:50 in the morning in 1939 and a team of operators work at the manual switchboard. They answer, "Operator, number please." Phone service in Red Oak has grown; there are more switchboard units, and more operators to assist callers. In December 1973, as part of an $83,000 improvement program, Northwest Bell Telephone made direct dialing of long distance available to its customers.

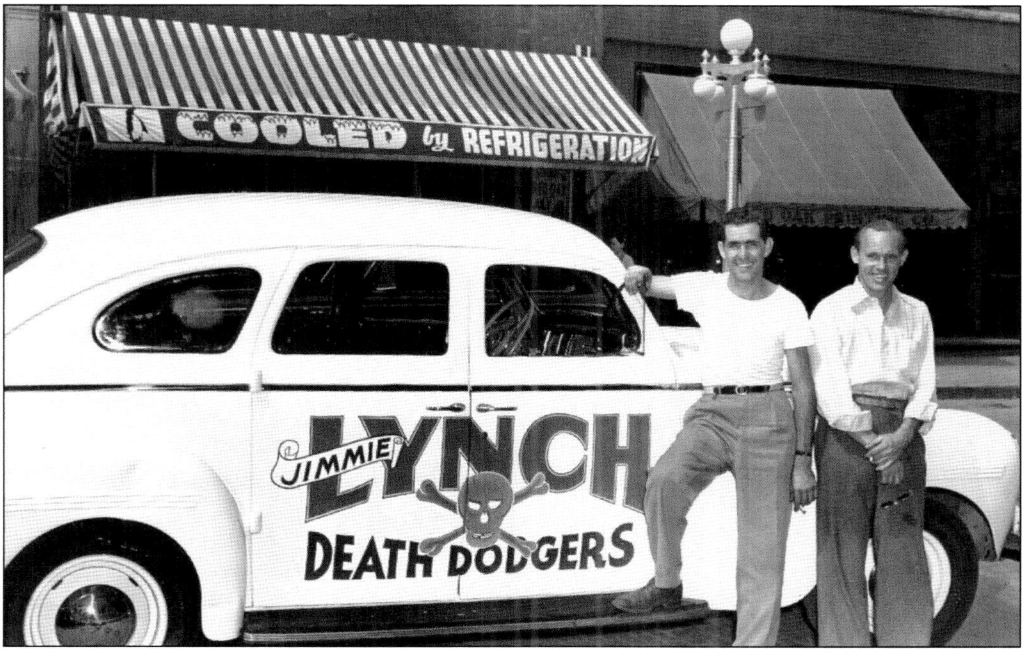

Jimmie Lynch's Death Dodgers pose by the car on the 400 block of Coolbaugh Street; Red Oak Printing and the Red Oak Café are in the background.

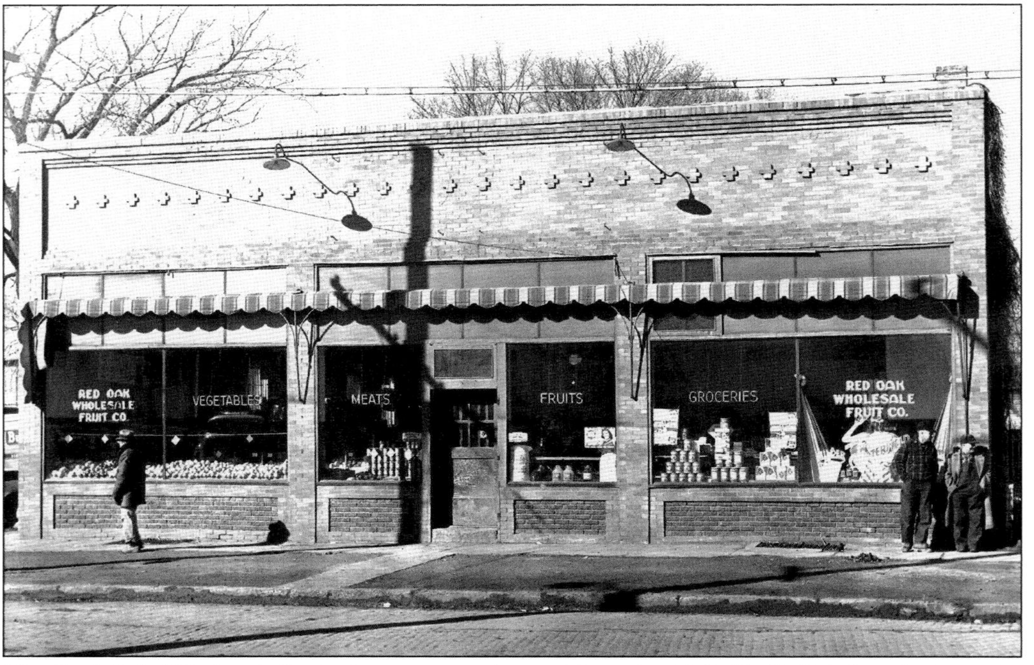

The Red Oak Wholesale Fruit Company is pictured here. In 1929, R. K. Belt bought into the Red Oak Wholesale Fruit Company. It was one of 15 grocers in town, some of which had stores on the square.

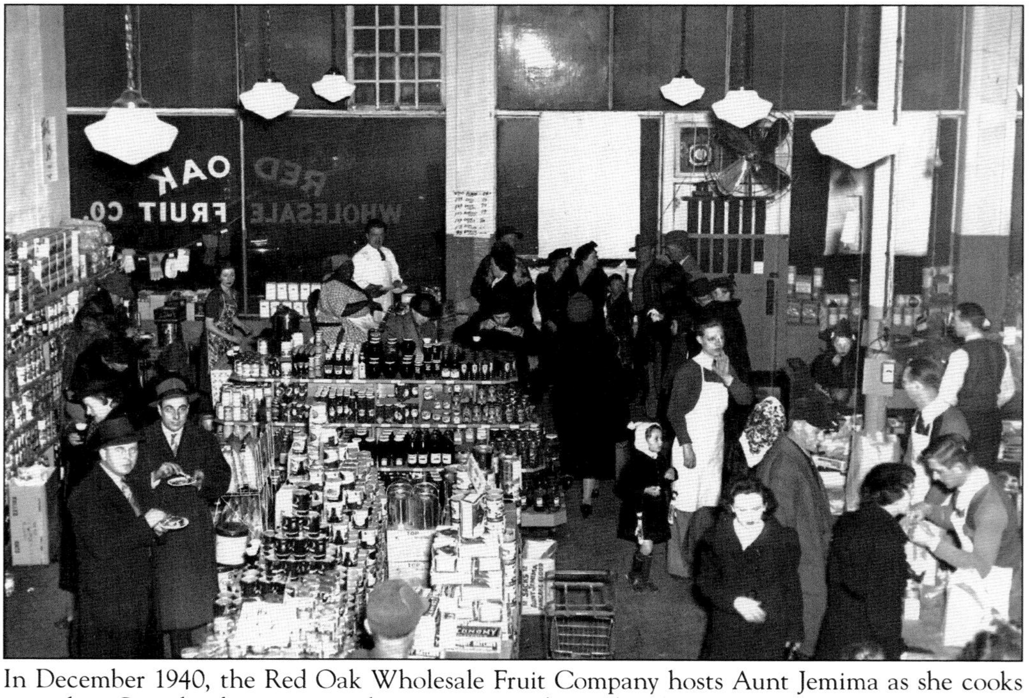

In December 1940, the Red Oak Wholesale Fruit Company hosts Aunt Jemima as she cooks pancakes. Crowds of curious people venture into the Red Oak Wholesale Fruit Company for a special promotional treat. She is by the window flipping flapjacks.

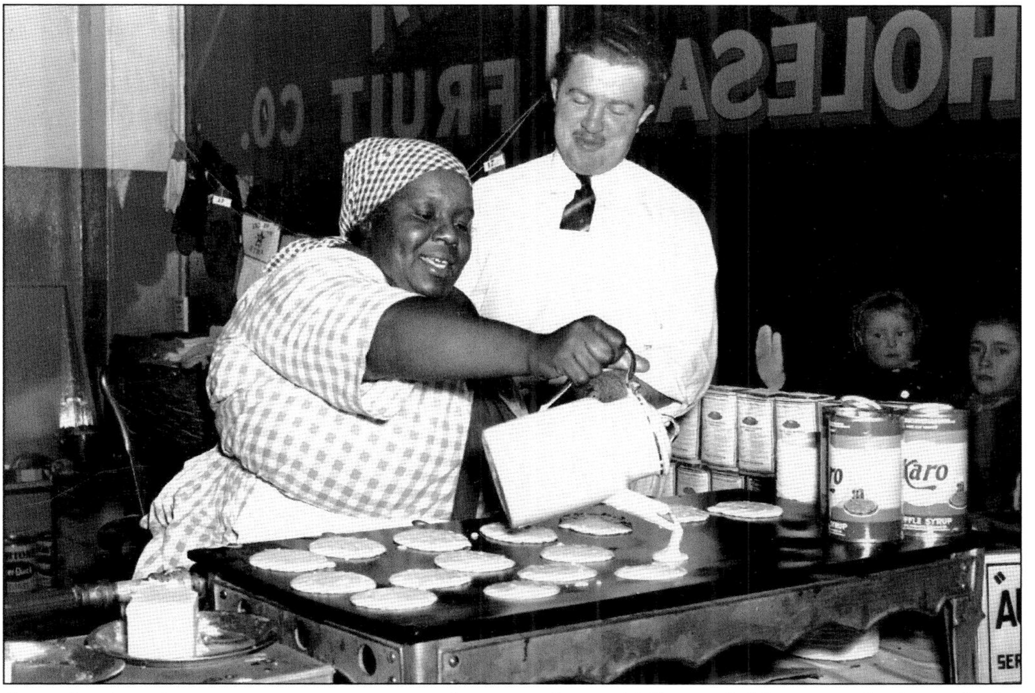

Aunt Jemima in person pours out pancakes on a hot griddle as children watch through the window. Karo syrup and a huge chunk of butter, a hot grill, and her famous pancakes are just great on a chilly December morning.

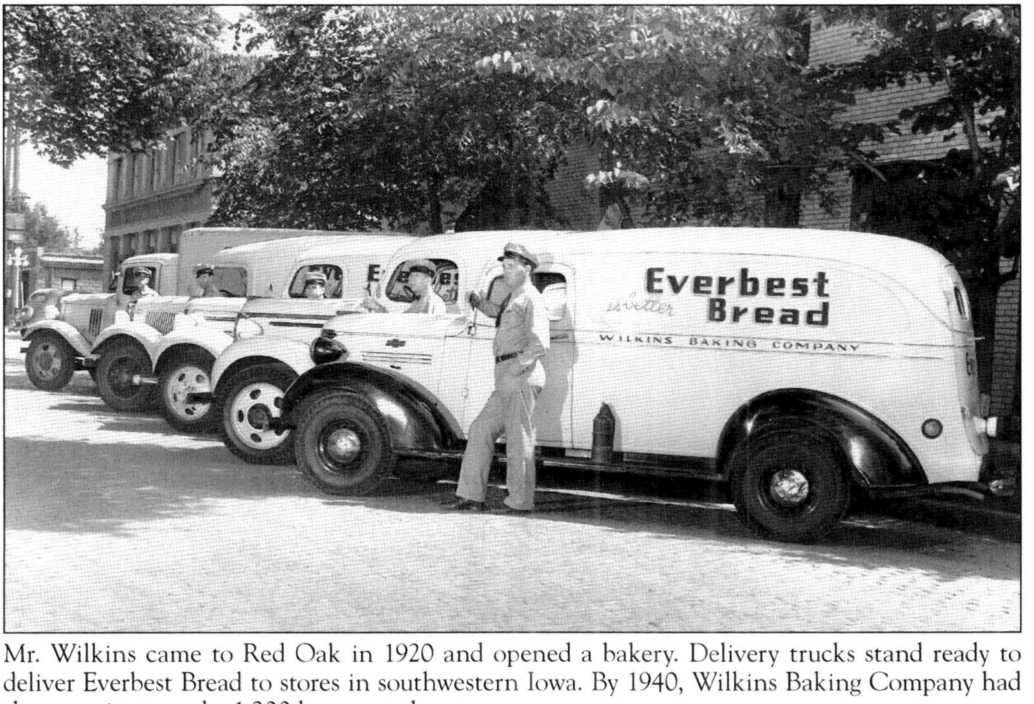

Mr. Wilkins came to Red Oak in 1920 and opened a bakery. Delivery trucks stand ready to deliver Everbest Bread to stores in southwestern Iowa. By 1940, Wilkins Baking Company had the capacity to make 1,200 loaves per hour.

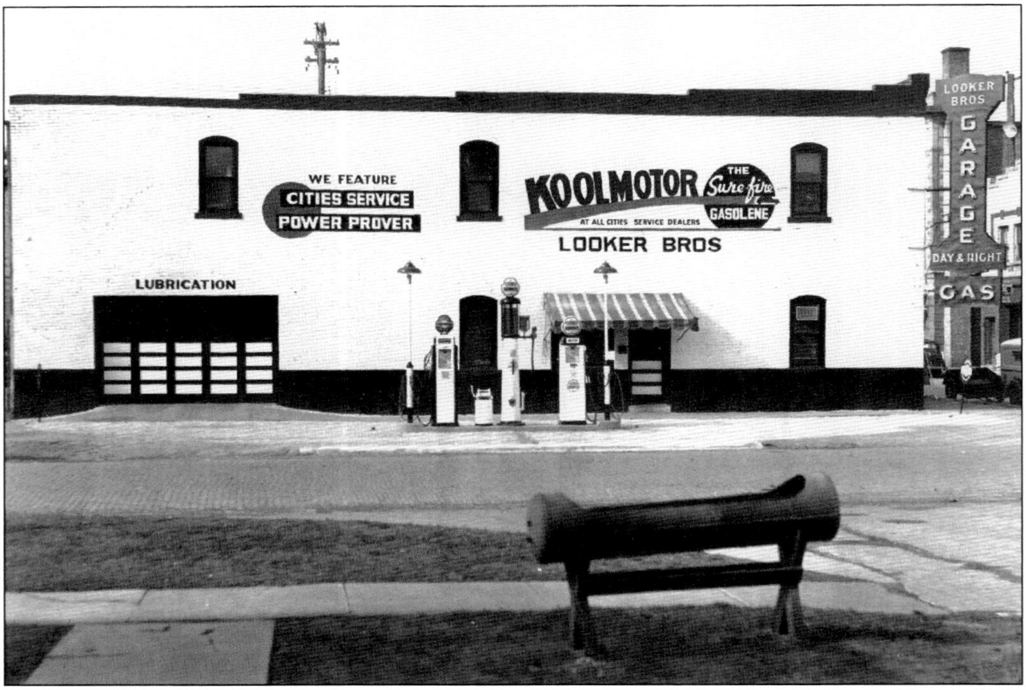

In 1939, the Looker brothers remodeled and updated their garage service located at 401 Fourth Street.

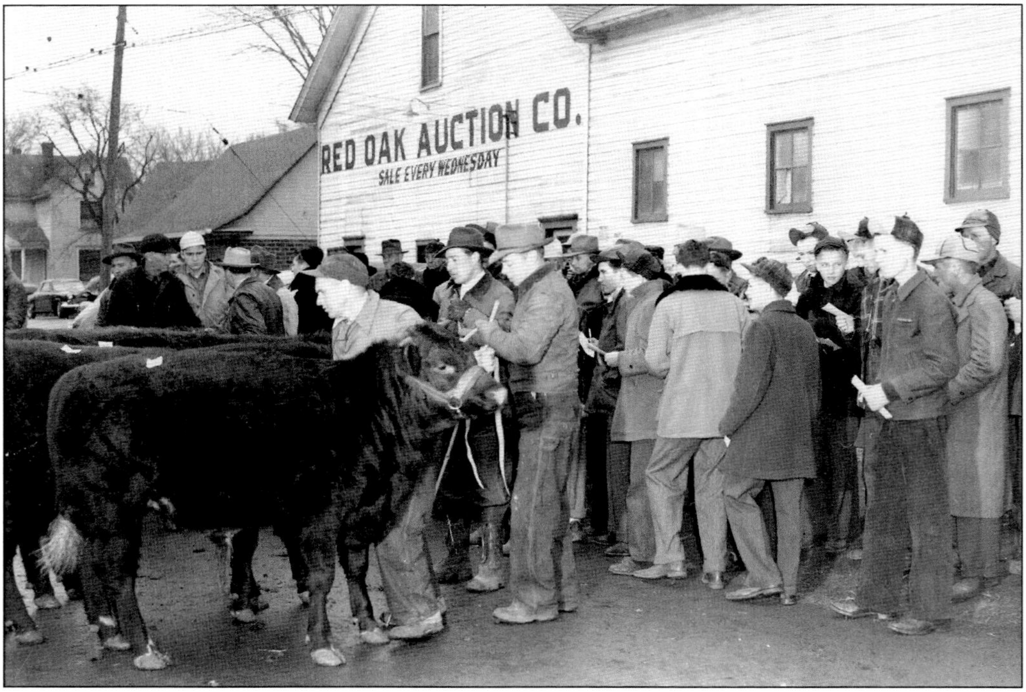

Red Oak Auction Company had an auction every Wednesday. Men line up to check out the beef being offered this day in the 1950s.

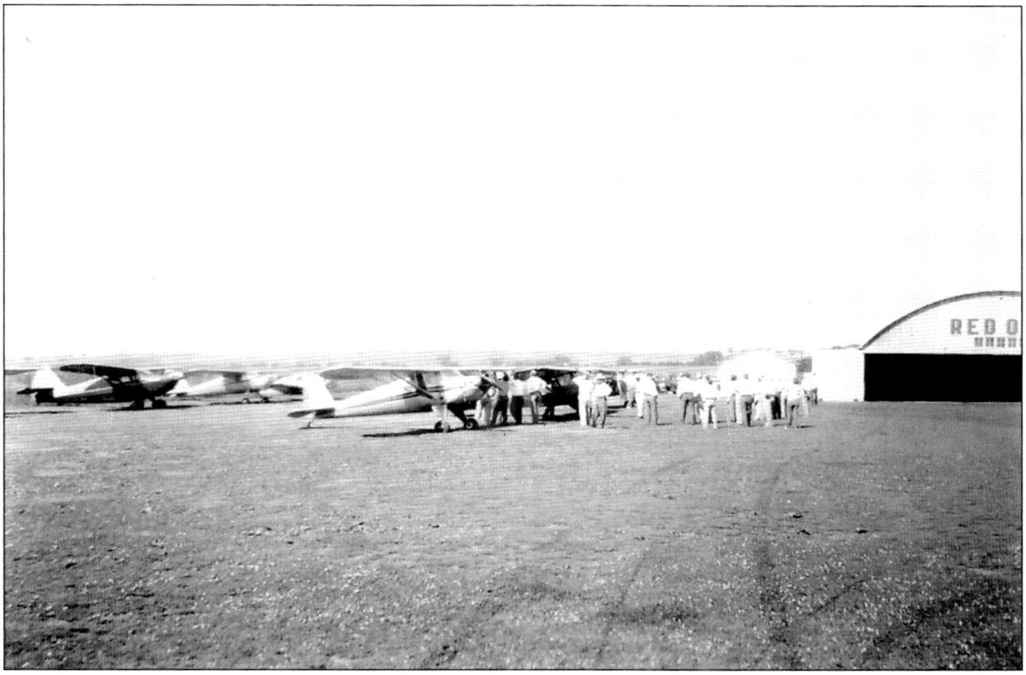

Red Oak continued to strive for excellence. In the 1950s, the city purchased 160 acres along old Highway 34 and built an airport.

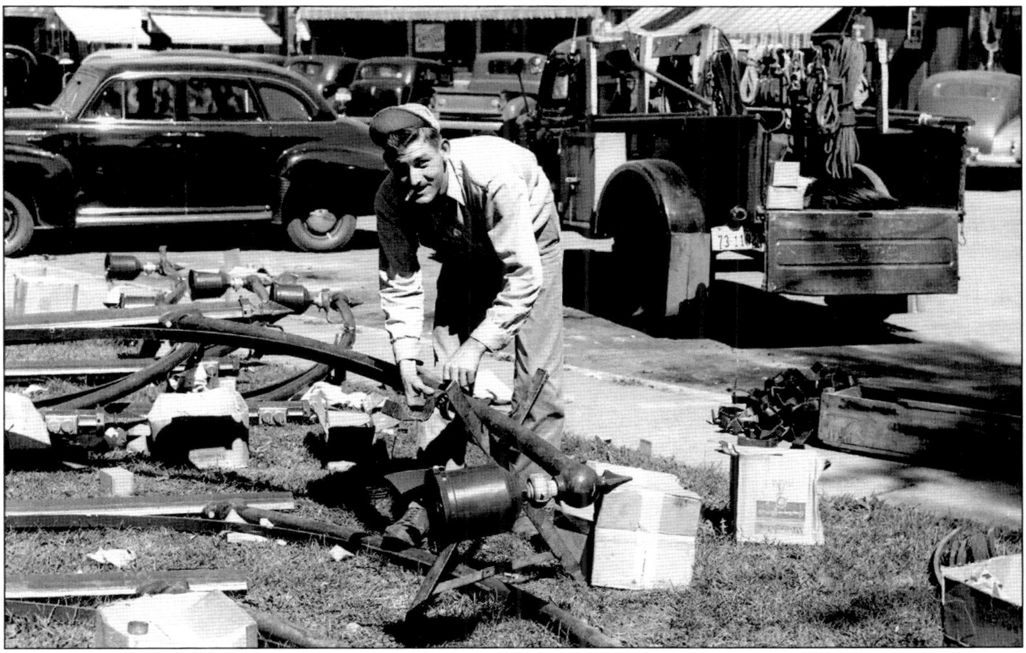

In June 1948, a new lighting system began to be installed in the business district on Coolbaugh Street between First and Second Streets. Fifty-one poles and luminaries were installed and Iowa Power and Light held the contract. A city worker is assembling some of the poles in this photograph.

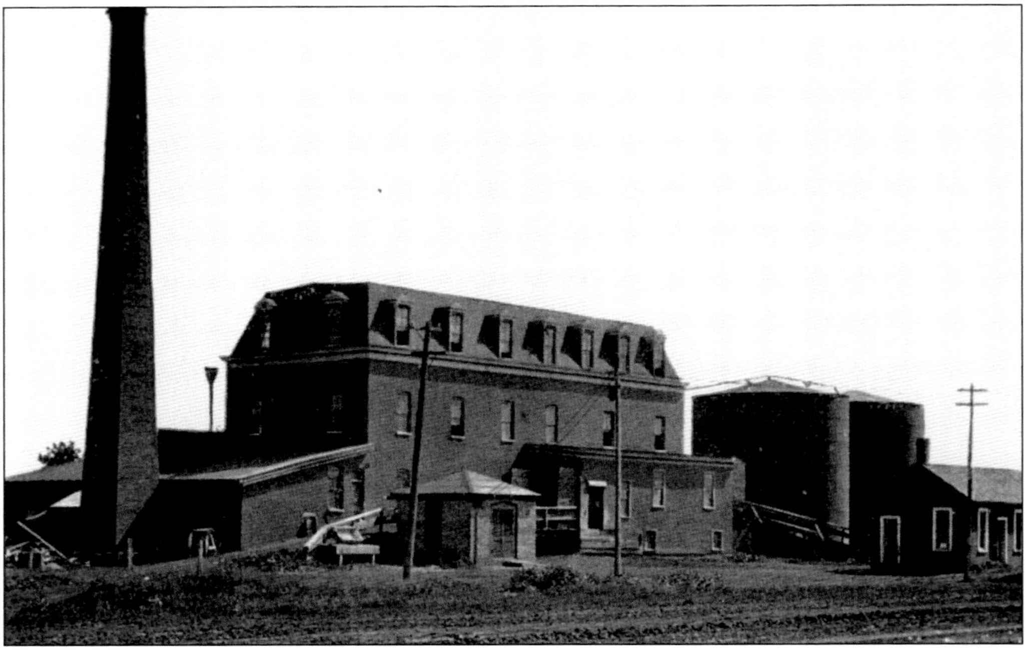

In 1889, Replogle and Company was founded. The mill burned to the ground on June 15, 1892, but by November of that same year it was back in business. Replogle was an integral part of Red Oak and Montgomery County for many years. The mill grew over the years and produced fine-quality flours.

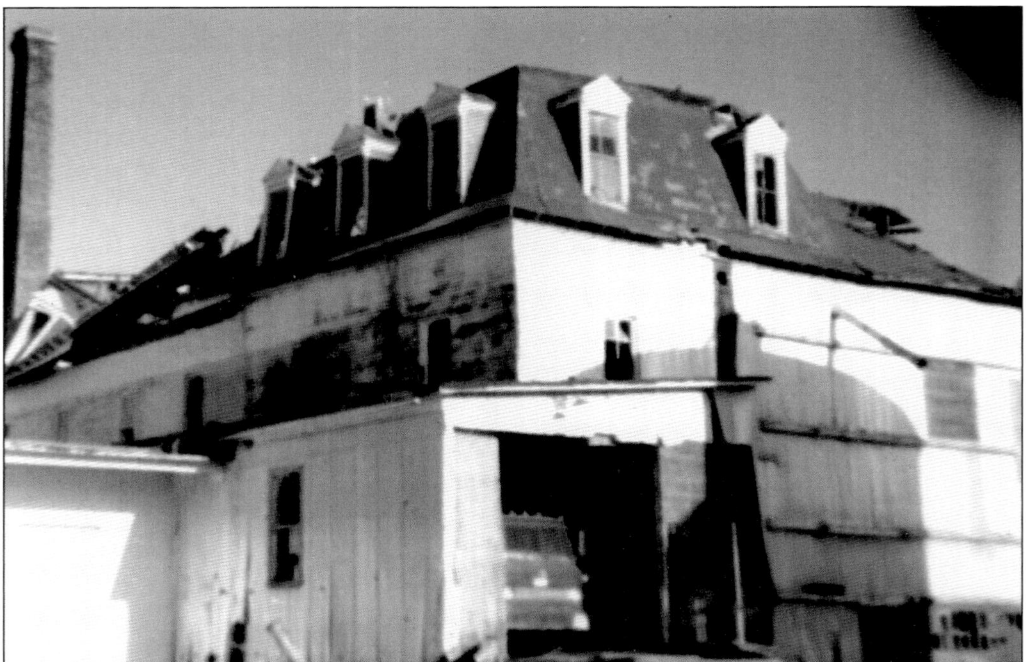

The Replogle mills survived many years of floods and storms. In the 1960s, the buildings were razed.

Four

The War Years

From the time Iowa was only a territory to the present day, the men and women of Red Oak have served proudly. Although Montgomery County was sparsely settled with a population of only 1,256 souls in 1860, it met the enlistment quota for volunteers. Mary Jane Wiley Zuber was a new bride when her husband, Joseph, enlisted. Word came to her that he was ill in a Southern camp. In boy's clothing, she stole away to find him. She enlisted, was called Frankie, and served as a stable boy for eight months until discovered.

According to U.S. Army records on May 17, 1879, Company K, the 5th Infantry Regiment of the Iowa National Guard was organized. In 1892, Company K was reorganized as the 3rd Infantry. By October 18, 1893, Company K was redesignated as Company M, 3rd Infantry Regiment of the Iowa National Guard with three officers and 26 enlisted men. When they applied, they were so well organized they enlisted the men immediately.

On May 30, 1898, Company M, 51st Infantry, was mustered into service for the Spanish-American War. Darwin Merritt was one of two officers killed on the ill-fated battleship *Maine*.

For World War I their full strength of 250 men served in many major campaigns, were a part of the Rainbow Division, remained through the armistice, and served in the occupation.

World War II again saw Company M serving the nation. March 6, 1943, was a black day in that over 100 telegrams arrived in Red Oak. While fighting in North Africa, Company M was overrun by Germans and was taken prisoner at Fiad Pass. One hundred men were missing in action, and officially 27 men were taken prisoner. In 1946, the *Saturday Evening Post* declared that proportionally, the casualties in Red Oak were the highest mortality rate compared to any other community in America.

The D-Day invasion in 1944 found Floyd Keeton, a 24-year-old army infantryman of the 85th division, on Omaha Beach. During breaks in the fighting, and with no one to talk to, he turned to God. He wrote "Footprints in the Sand" that day; he holds one of three copyrights to the poem.

Company M continued to serve the country proudly through the years in Korea, Vietnam, the Gulf War, and service in the Middle East.

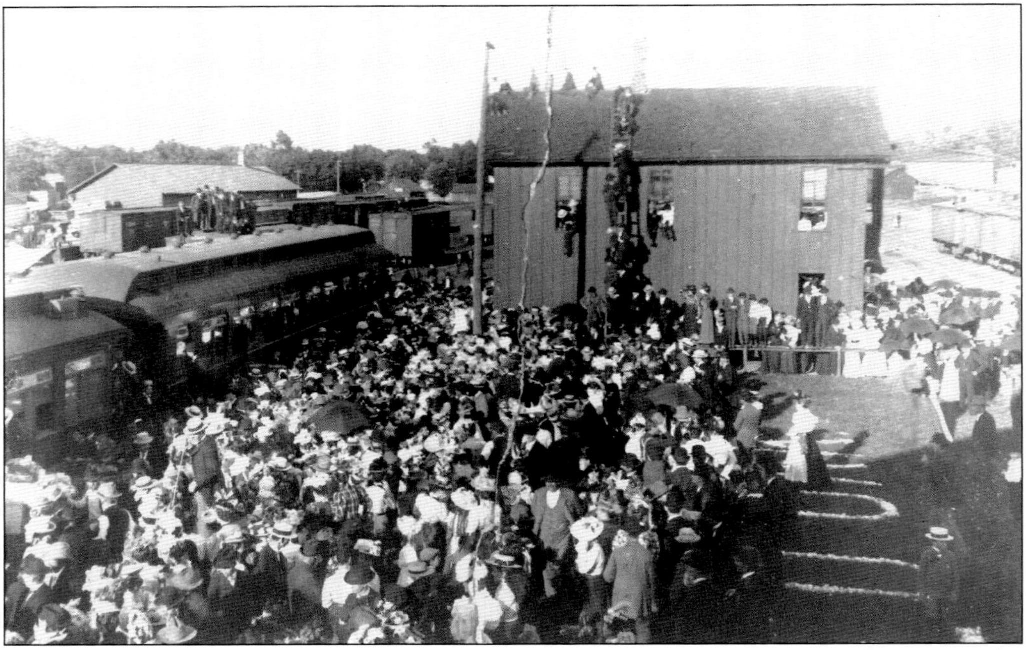

The Spanish-American War had broken out and Red Oak men answered the call to serve. The people of Red Oak turn out at the old passenger depot in 1898 when Company M went through from Des Moines to the Philippines. The depot was located one block west on Highway 48 on the old main line.

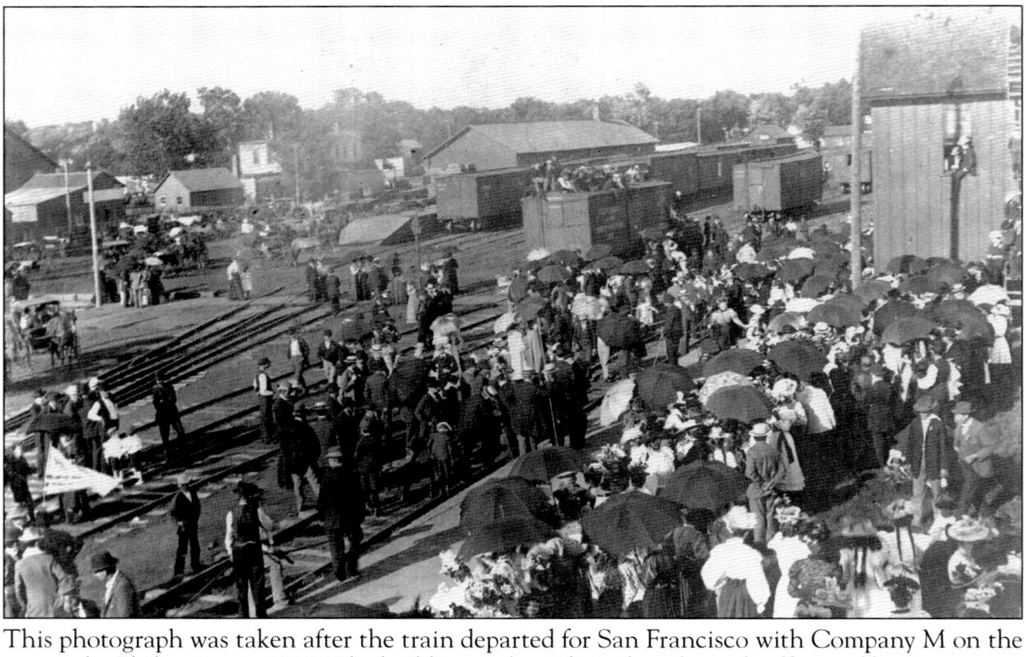

This photograph was taken after the train departed for San Francisco with Company M on the way to the Philippines in 1898. The building at the right is the telegraph office and baggage room. The building in the center is the freight depot, beyond that is Draper's Store. The passenger depot and Depot Hotel are just out of the photograph.

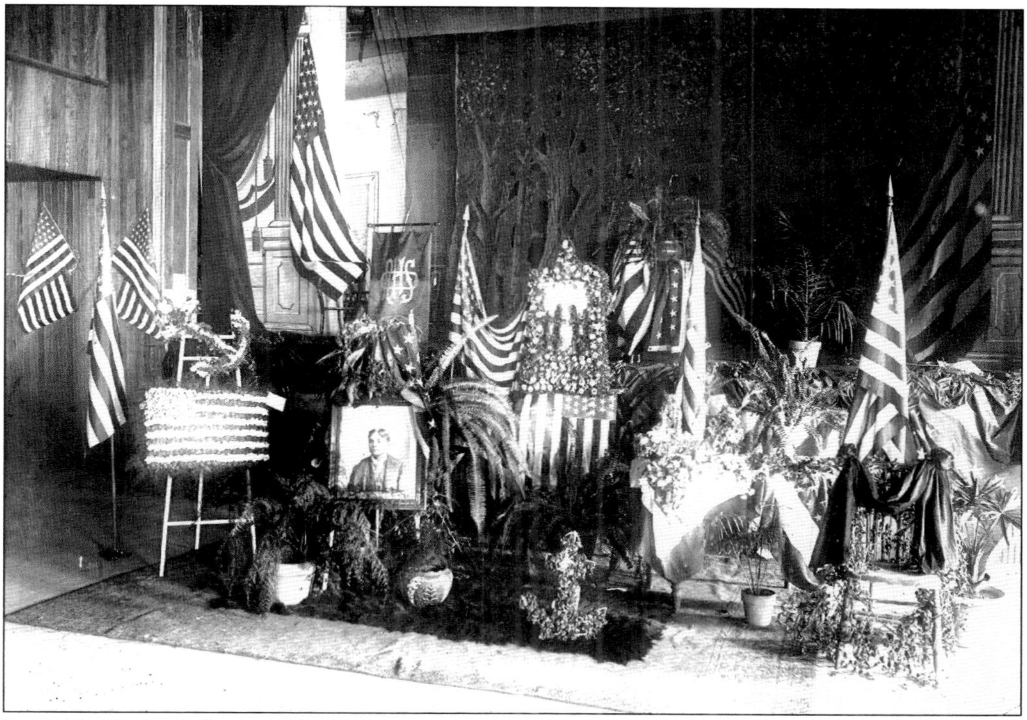

In 1899, Vern Hysham died in camp in San Francisco, he was 16 years old. His photograph stands among the floral arrangements at his funeral.

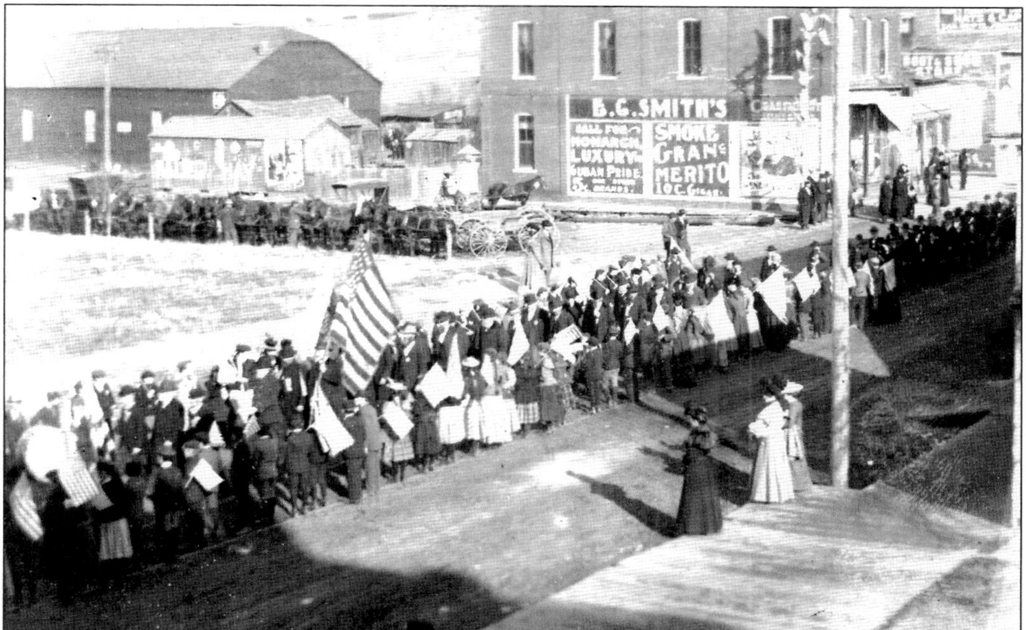

The people of Red Oak line the streets to welcome their men back home after the Spanish-American War.

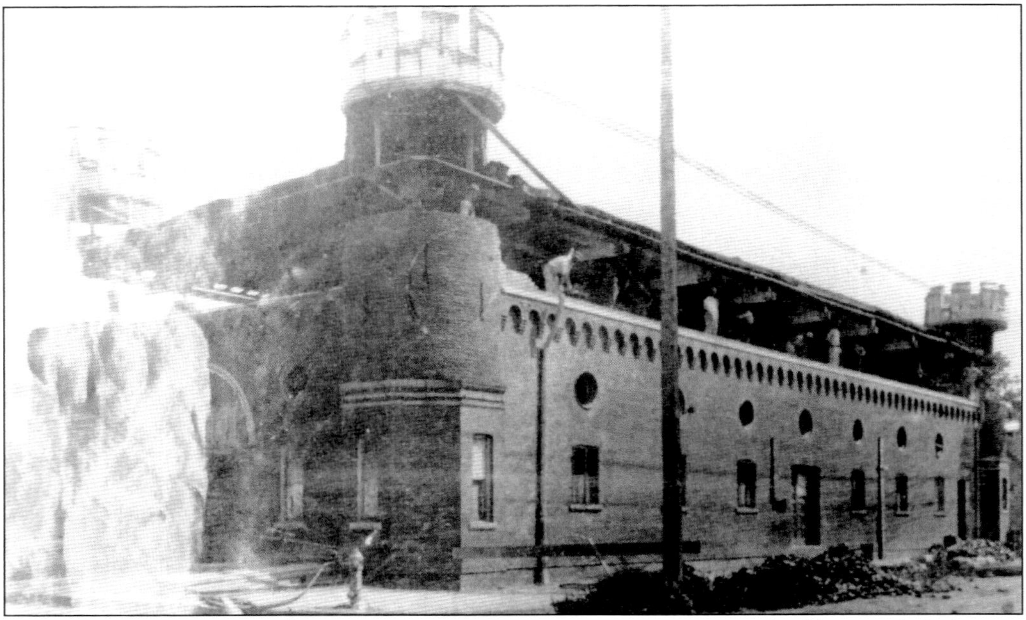

Built in 1896 at a cost of $6,000, the original armory was a one-story building with balconies inside on the east and west ends of the hall. It was used as a theater, civic meetinghouse, and was headquarters for the Iowa National Guard, Company M. In 1905, Pratt and Pratt, a Red Oak contractor, raised the roof on the armory building at Fifth and Coolbaugh Streets. L. D. Pratt is shown standing by the building cornice at the extreme right. Charles Pratt, L. D.'s father, is standing in the middle wearing the white shirt. They used screw jacks and blocks to raise the entire roof and then added the second story.

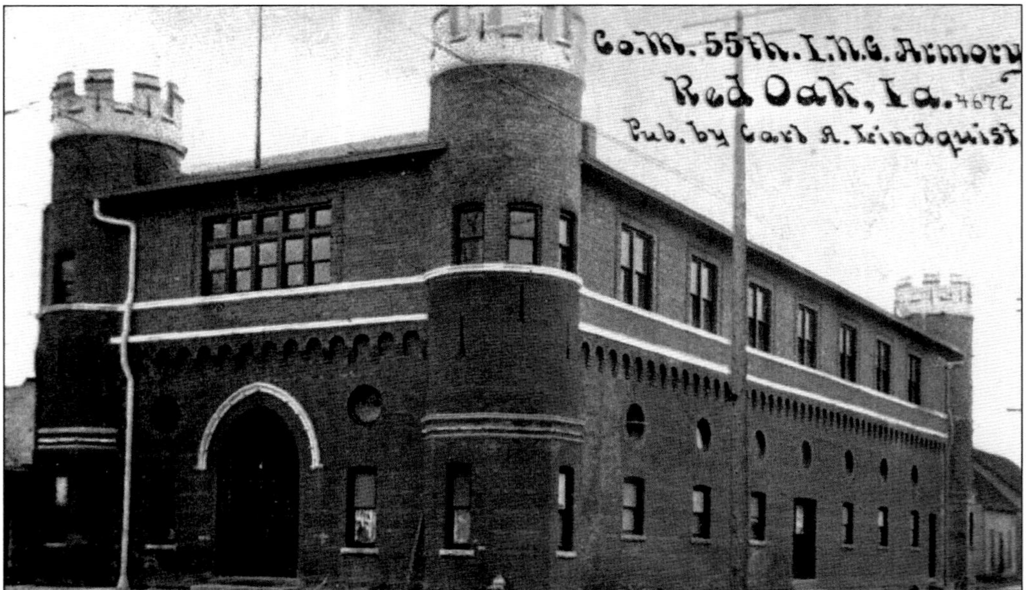

After the roof was raised and the second story completed, the photograph for this postal card was taken. This is the Company M 55th Iowa National Guard Armory, Red Oak.

Fisher Company is seen here decked out in honor of Company M. Mr. Fisher had come in the late 1800s and was a wholesale grocer established in 1870.

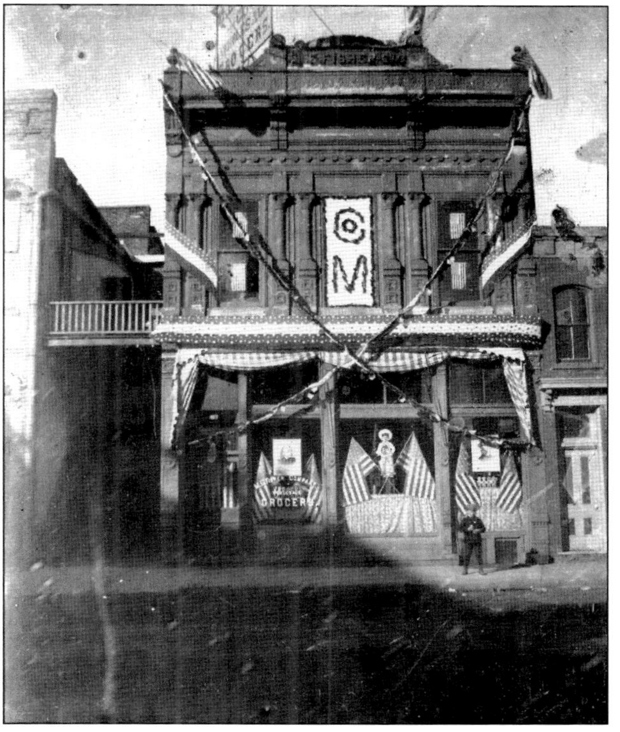

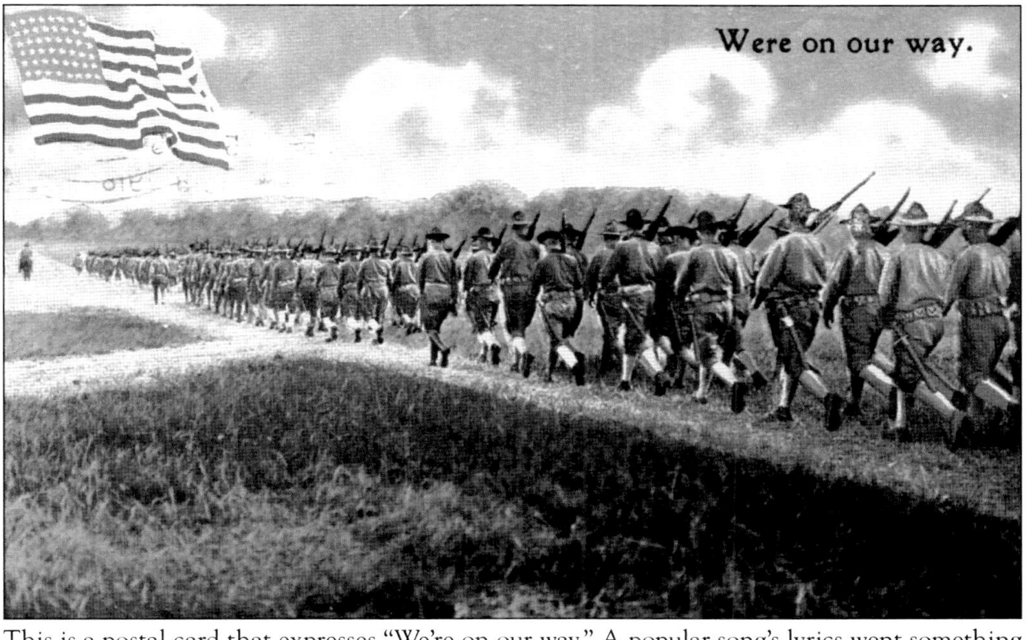

This is a postal card that expresses "We're on our way." A popular song's lyrics went something like this: "Over there, over there, send the word send the word to prepare! That the Yanks are coming; the Yanks are coming the drums rum-tumming everywhere. So prepare, say a prayer, send the word, send the word over there, that the Yanks are coming, the Yanks are coming, and we won't be back 'til it's over, over there."

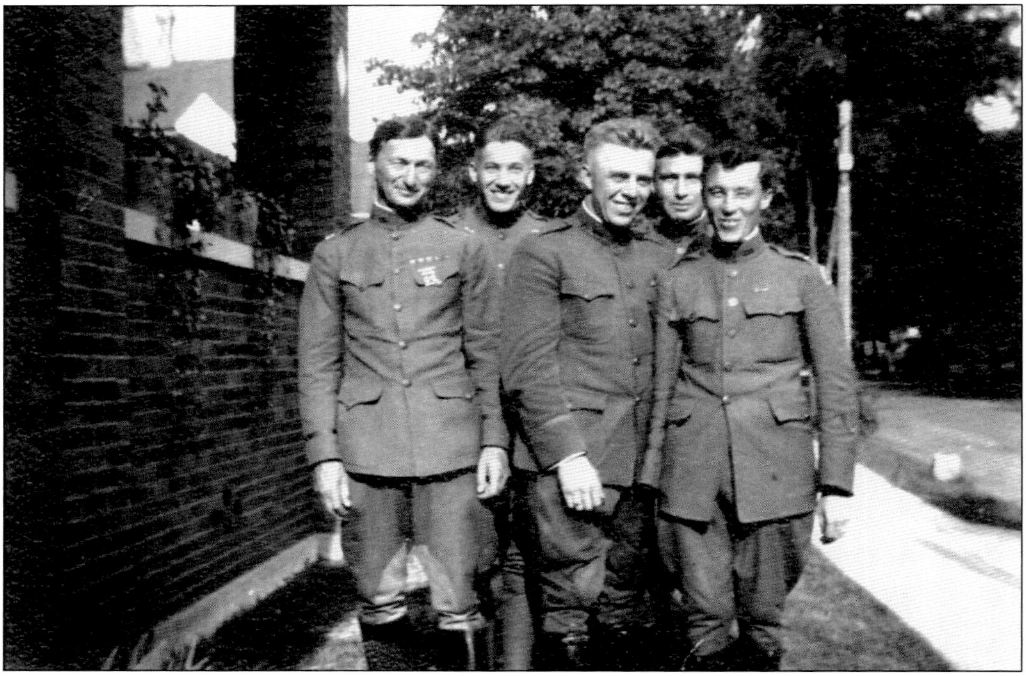

Charles Binns at the left and his friends in World War I uniform are ready to serve their country. They served in the cavalry.

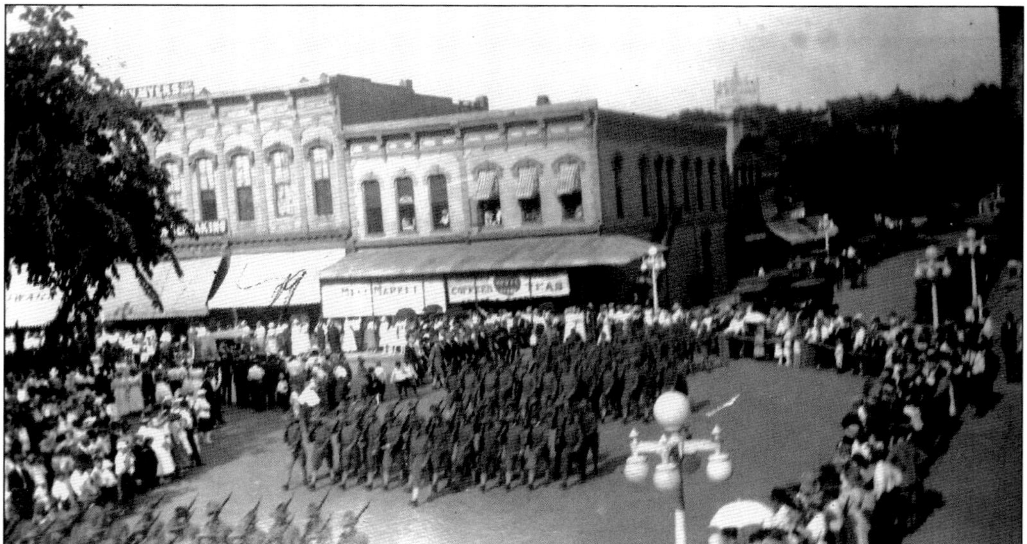

Troops on parade at the corner of Coolbaugh and Fourth Streets, ready to go off to the fighting in Europe, are pictured here.

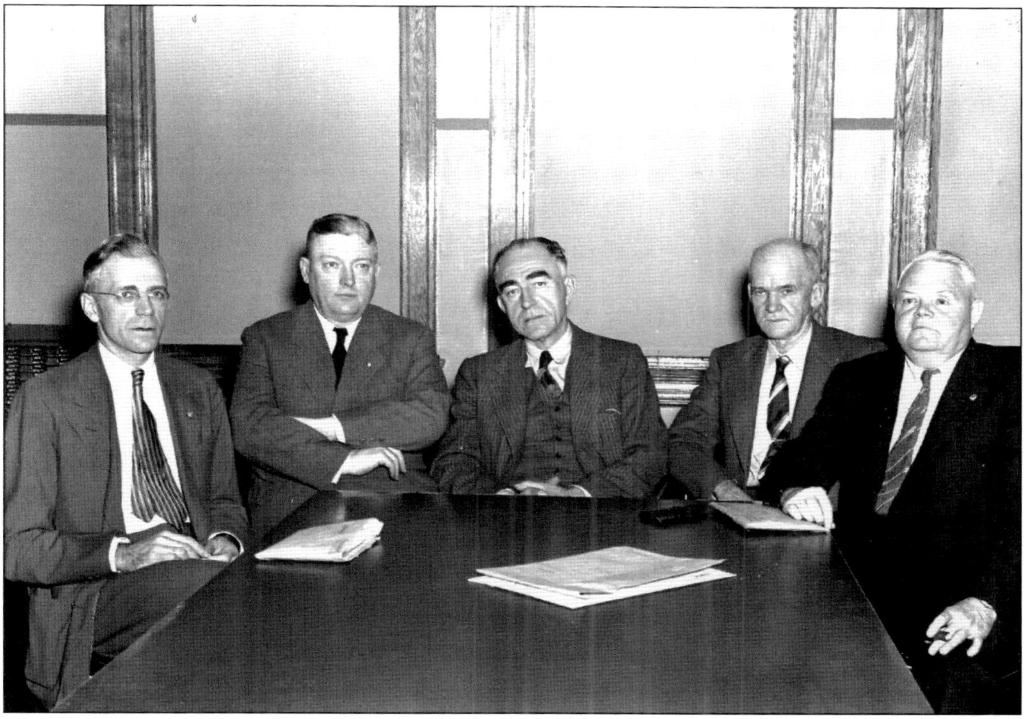

During World War II, the gentlemen of the draft board are seen in this picture.

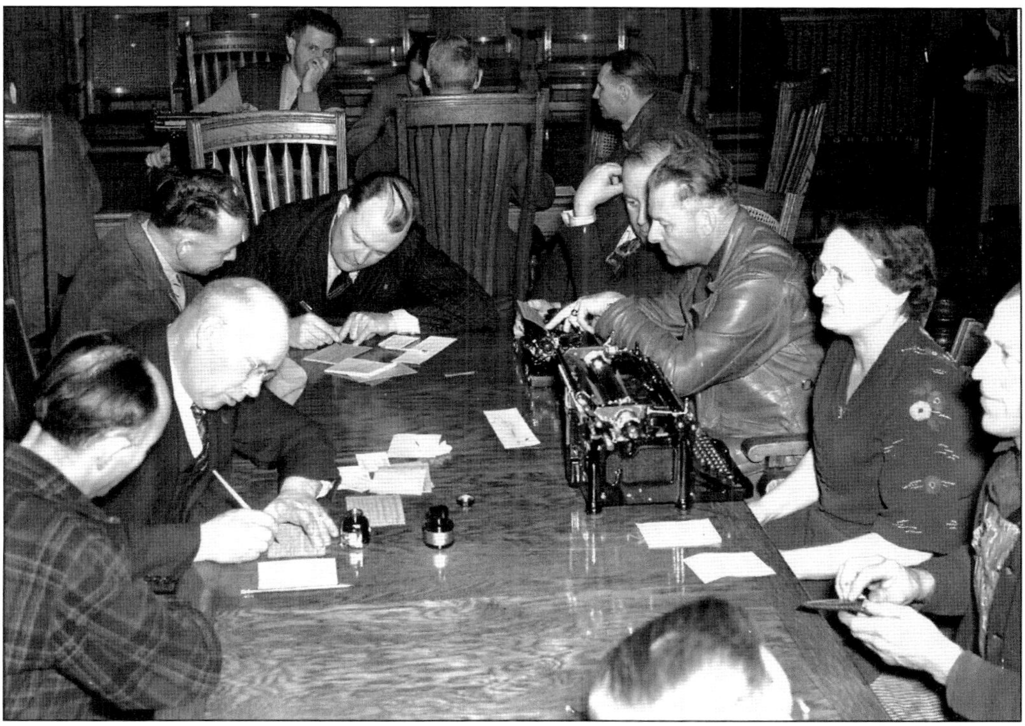

Men registered for the draft in the Montgomery County Court House.

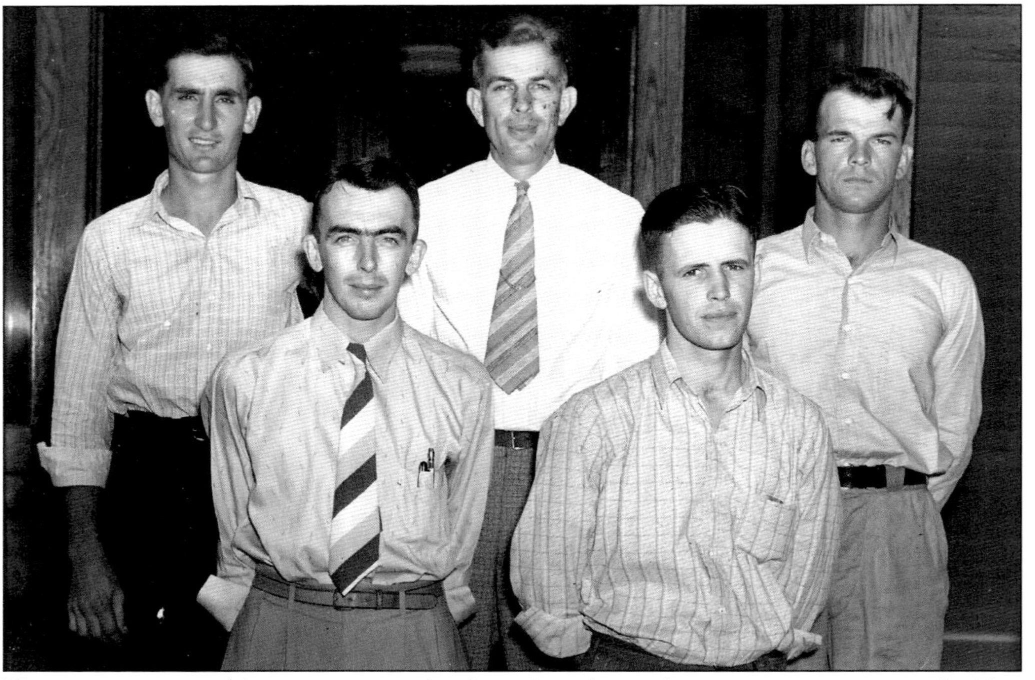

There was a quota of five men expected to be inducted into the service every six months. Five brave men stand ready to serve in August 1941.

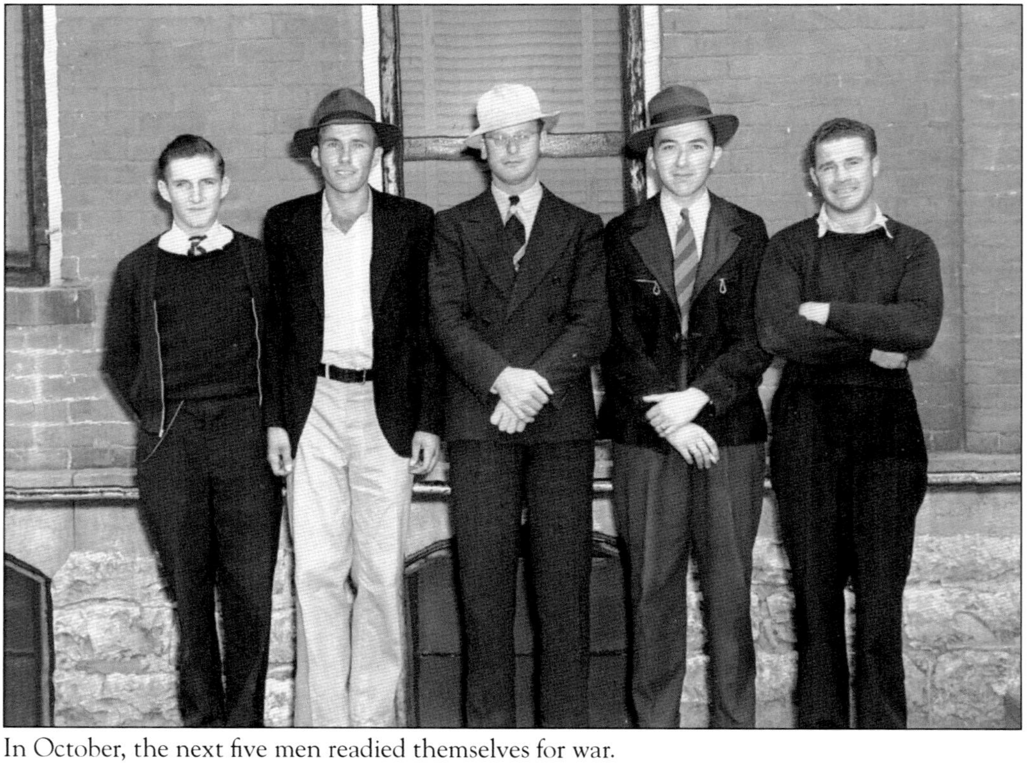

In October, the next five men readied themselves for war.

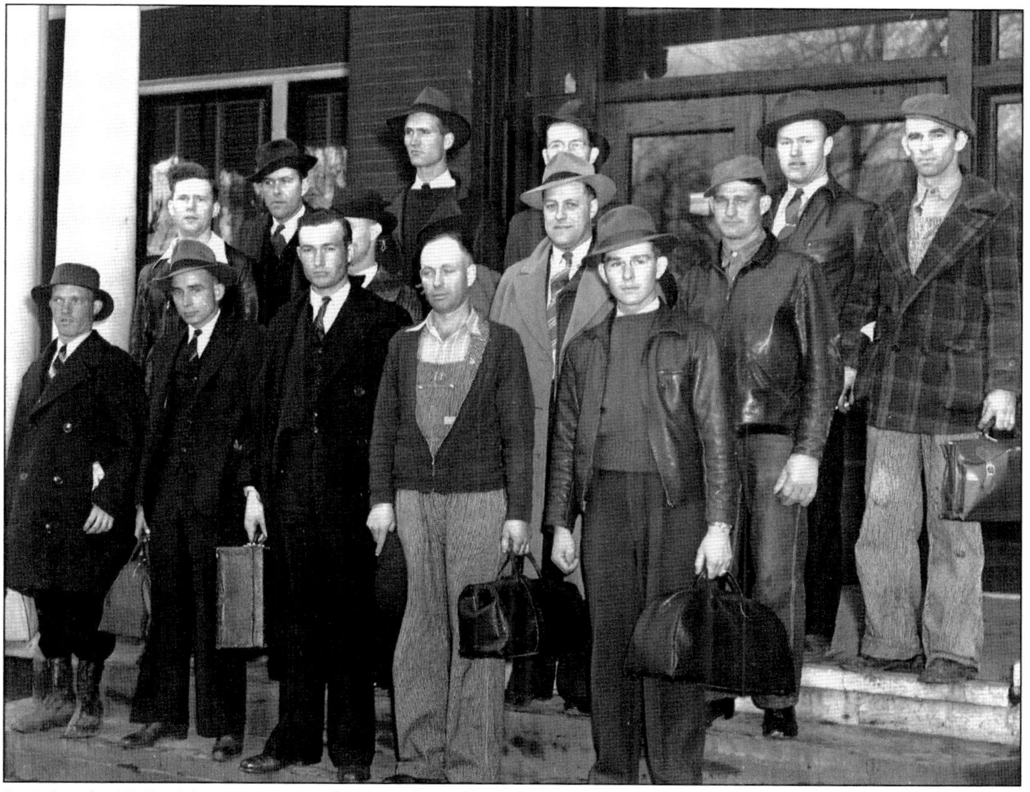

In March 1942, 14 men are packed and ready.

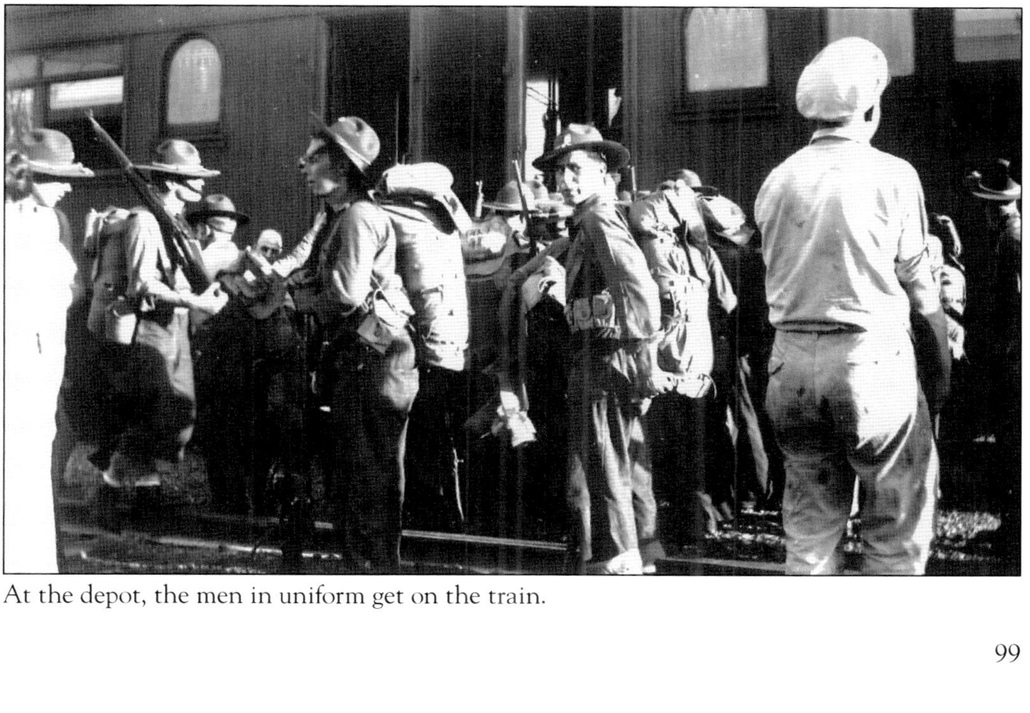

At the depot, the men in uniform get on the train.

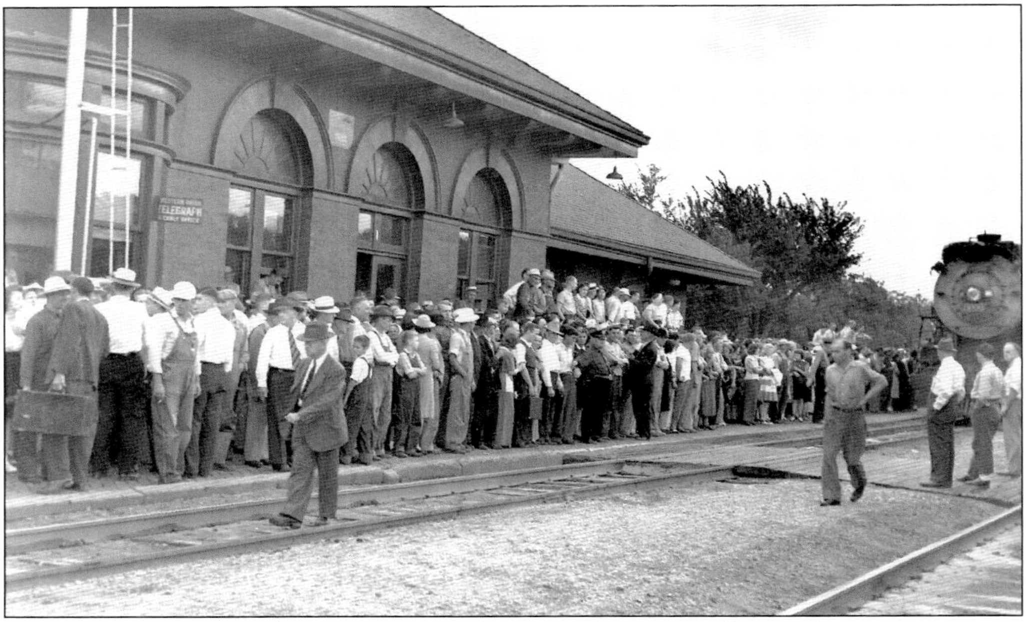

On a cloudy warm Monday in early September 1942, the train pulls into the station with the 24 inductees from Montgomery County. They are on board the train coming through Red Oak before they head off for eight weeks of basic training and then off to the war.

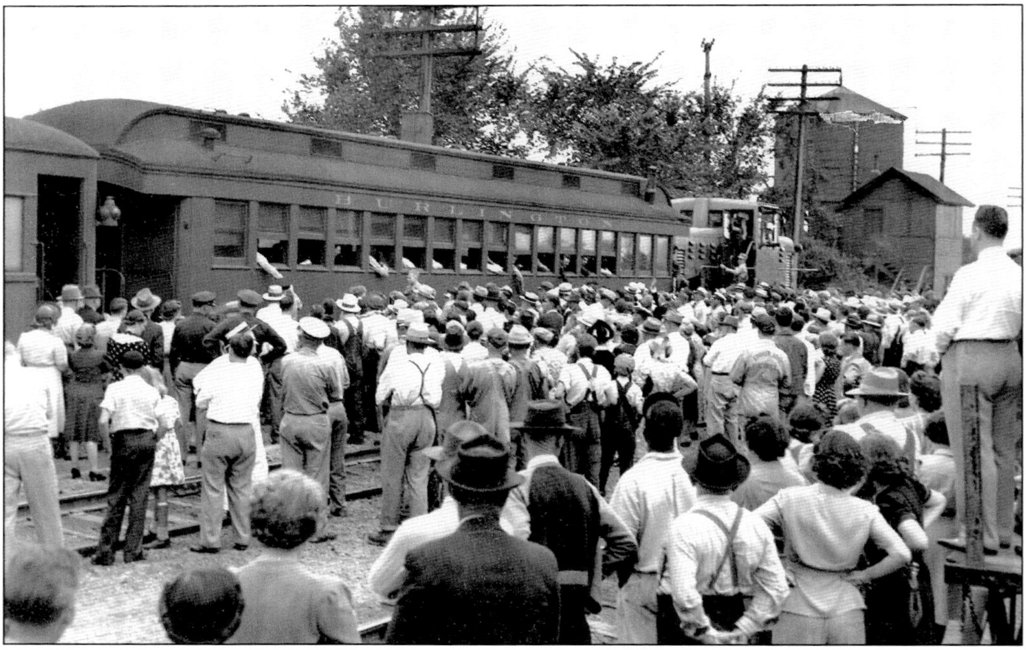

Teddy Buffon, Jack Liddick, Charles Winn, Paul Dumler, Syke Woods, Alfred Anderson, Glendon Woods, Earl Samples, Alva Herren, John Frank, Frank Helm, Loring Laire, Carl Nelson, Morris Steffen, Elmer Anderson, Howard Bradley, Floyd Whitney, Fred Fritz, Jack Vannausdle, Clifford Trively, Bob Smith, Carl Swanson, Marion Bergren, and Charles Good were each provided with $89 worth of military clothing before departing for basic training.

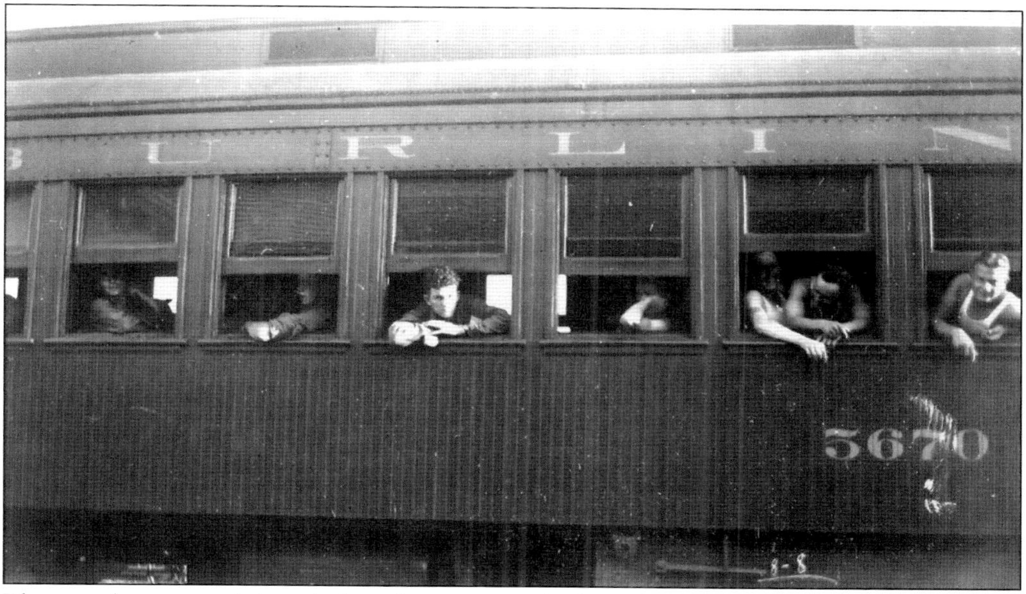

The men hang out of the windows for one more look, some teasing, some anxious, and each feeling a touch of uncertainty for the unknown that was ahead of them, but each willing to give his all for the nation they loved and believed in.

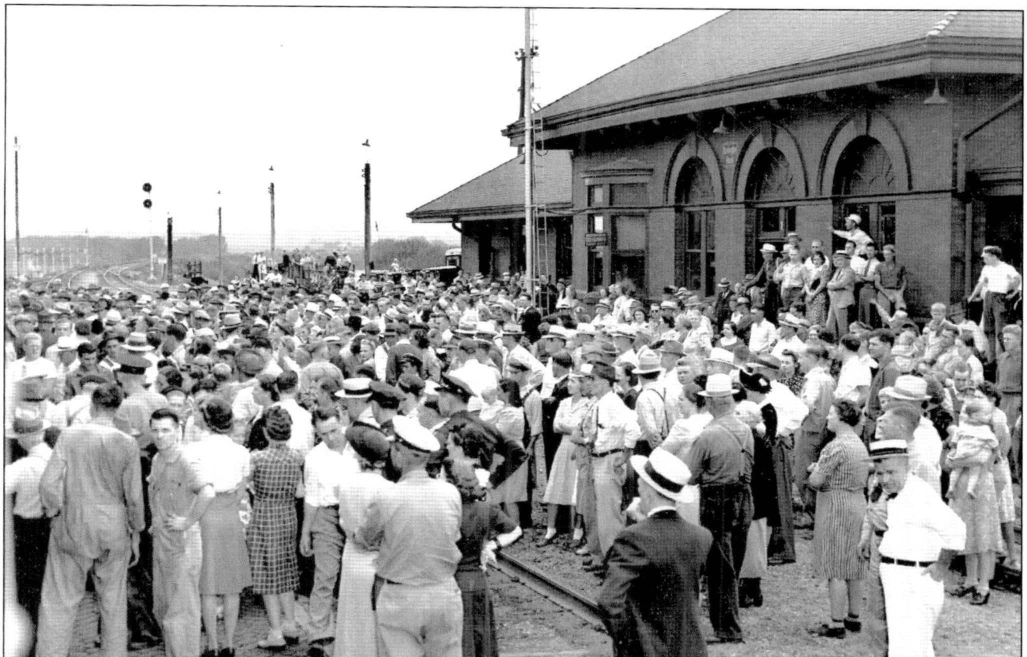

The train has pulled out of the station, and the people mill about before heading home. Those who stay at home will pray for their loved ones. They will continue with their lives, always with listening to the radio for news, and reading the papers to keep themselves informed, every hour hoping that their loved ones will come home to them safe and unharmed.

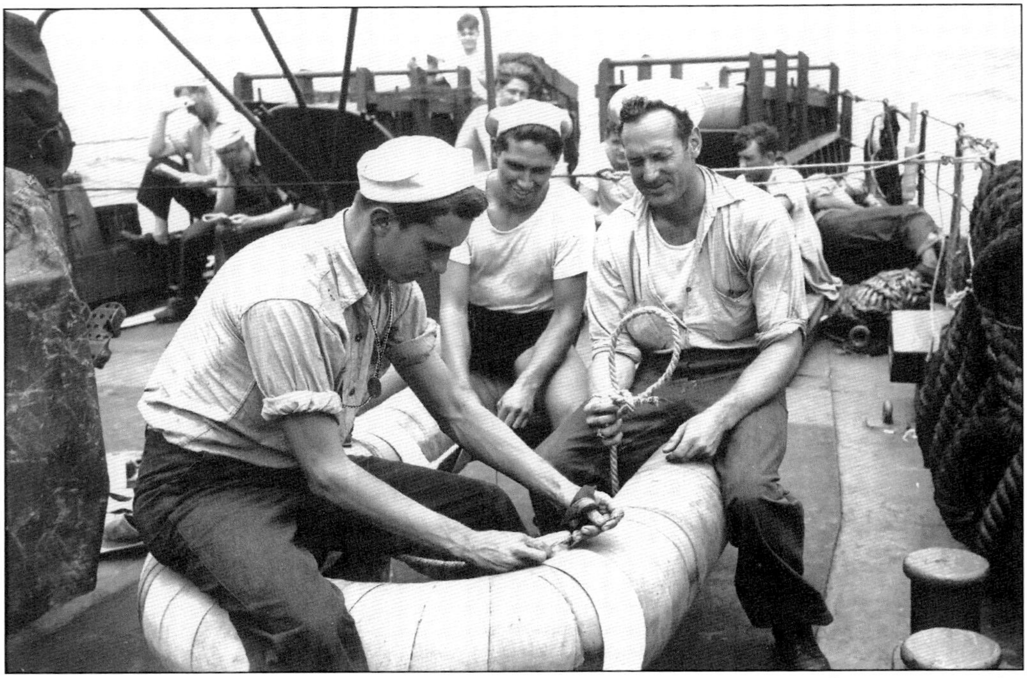

On the deck of the Coast Guard–manned troop transport carrying reinforcements to the battlefront in France, three guardsmen repair a life raft. From left to right they are Warren Horne, seaman first class of 207 Hammond Street, Red Oak; Roy Hicks, seaman second class of Lookout, West Virginia; and Winfield Peters, coxswain of 2746 Hampden Street, Chicago, Illinois.

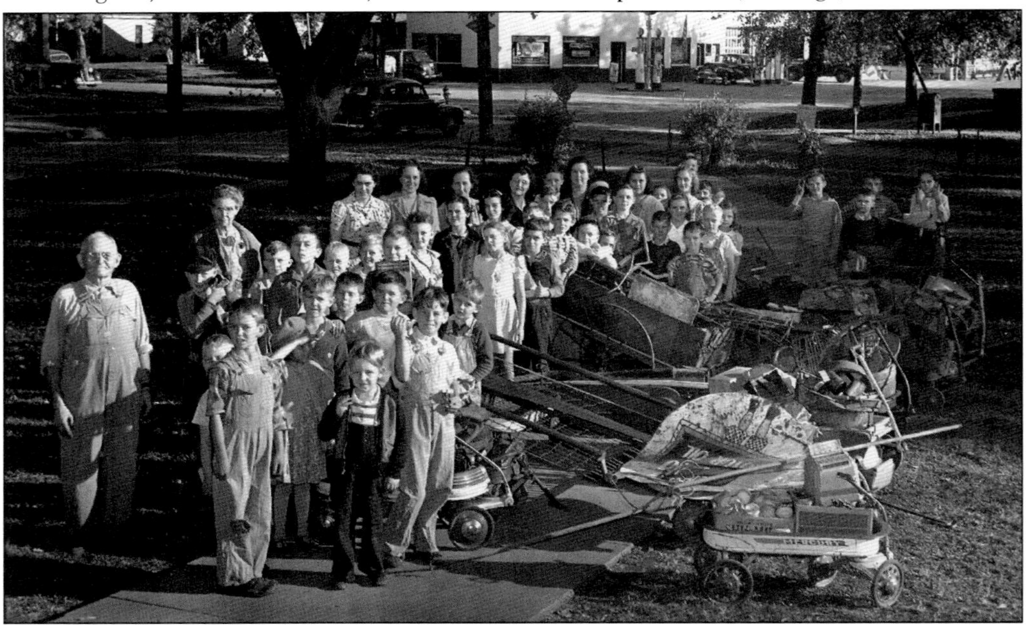

While the men were serving overseas, everyone at home did what they could to help the war effort. The children gathered scrap metal. Even the old cannon on the courthouse lawn was sent along with all the other scrap metal.

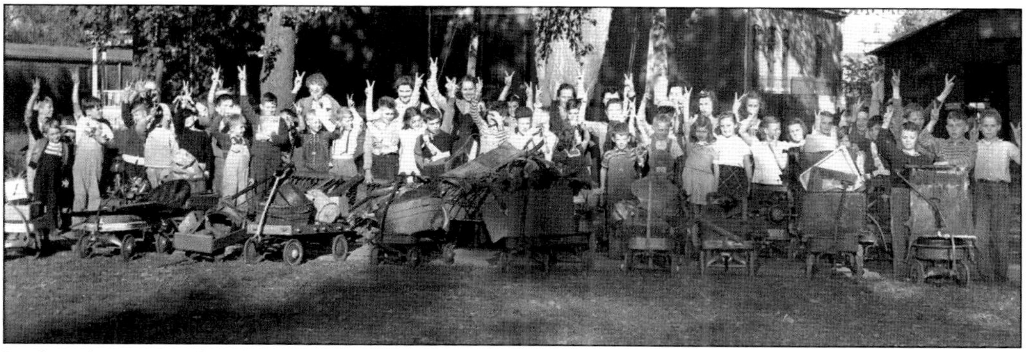

In October 1942, the children of the Washington School proudly display the haul of scrap metal they collected. They hold up their fingers in the *V* for victory.

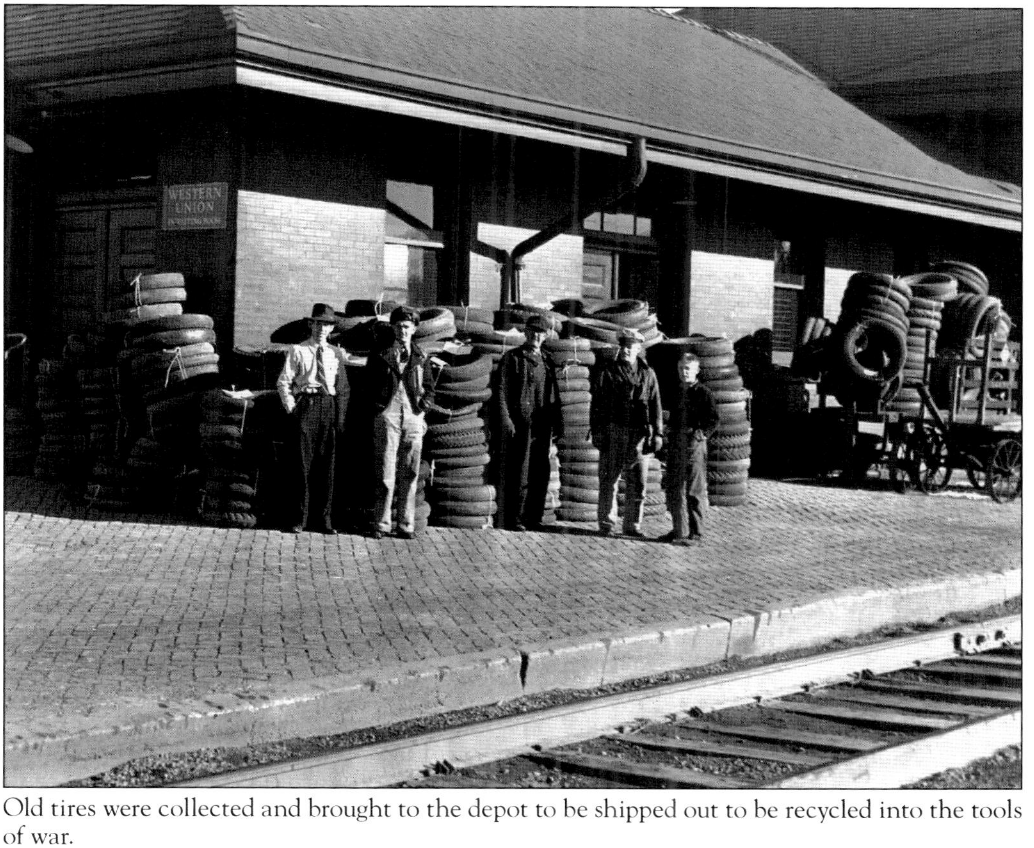

Old tires were collected and brought to the depot to be shipped out to be recycled into the tools of war.

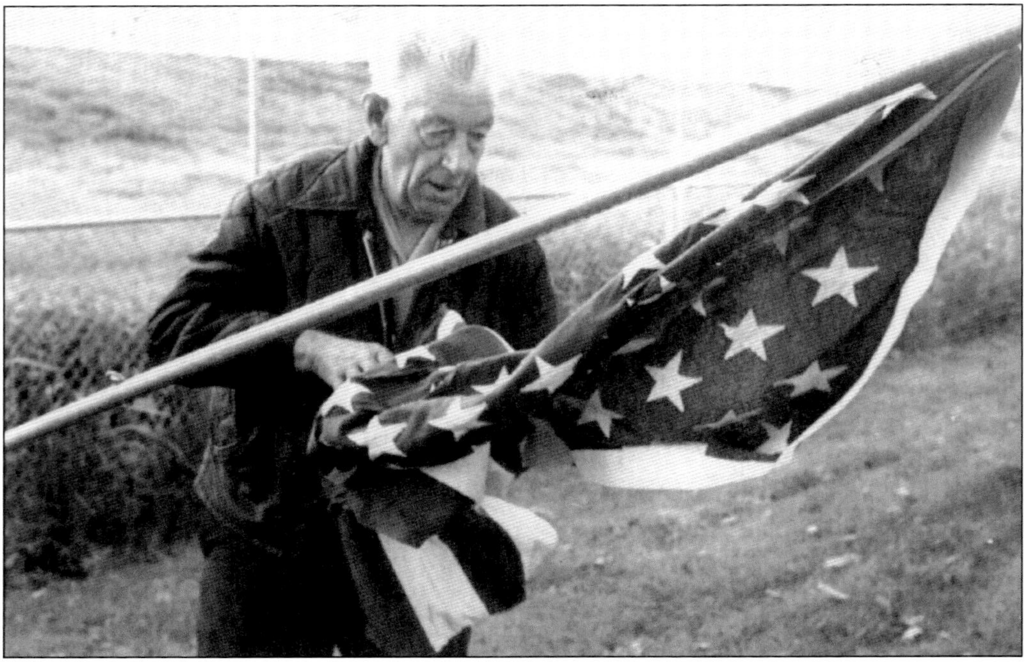

Memorial Day is when all who have sacrificed so much for this great nation are remembered. The men and women of Montgomery County have bravely served in all wars since the Civil War.

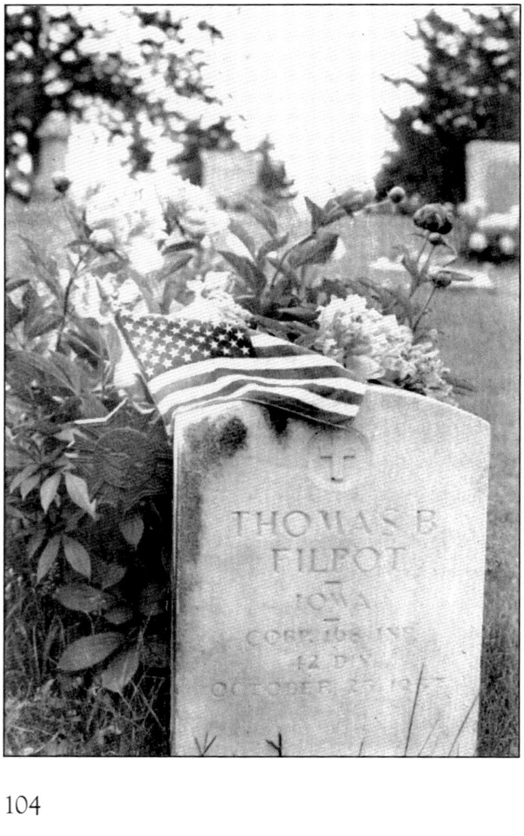

On Memorial Day the graves of those lost in the wars are decorated. Wreaths, flowers, and flags are placed with care at loved ones' graves.

Five

Politics, Parades, Revelry, and Disaster

By law, Iowa has the unique distinction of being first in the nation for the presidential race and is unique in the method of the caucus. Iowans are fortunate enough to have the candidates come to them, to look in their eyes, shake their hands, and tell them why they want to be the next president. Gen. Ulysses S. Grant came on November 5, 1879, and between 4,000 and 5,000 people turned out to greet him. Their train arrived at the depot around noon, Julia Grant was called for, and she waved her handkerchief to a cheering crowd. On October 13, 1898, 3,000 people came to greet Pres. William McKinley, along with several members of his cabinet. Over the years, William Jennings Bryan, Franklin Roosevelt, Richard Nixon, and George Bush have come to Red Oak, and people will continue to come, as long as there is a caucus to win and voters to meet.

Down through the generations, parades reflected current events, captured the mood of the nation, and the personality of the town. Circuses, soldiers, town leaders, politicians, and children have all paraded around the heart of the city, the town square, each one proud to be a part of what was happening. When Red Oak was 50 years old, the pioneers gathered and remembered the early days. Then when the city had its first 100 years to celebrate, they looked back with great pride having parades and celebrations that acknowledged those who went before them. There were still some who recalled their parents' and grandparents' stories of how it was. Red Oak has celebrated 150 years, and looks forward to celebrating the next milestone of 200 years.

Red Oak has had its share of disasters through the years. Fires, floods, and tornados could not deter the people of Red Oak. The coldest summer day on record was August 12, 1856, when temperatures dropped to 26 degrees and all the crops froze. In 1936, the temperatures topped out at 117 degrees in a run of 15 straight days with temperatures over 100 degrees. The harvest of 1936 was rated the worst on record.

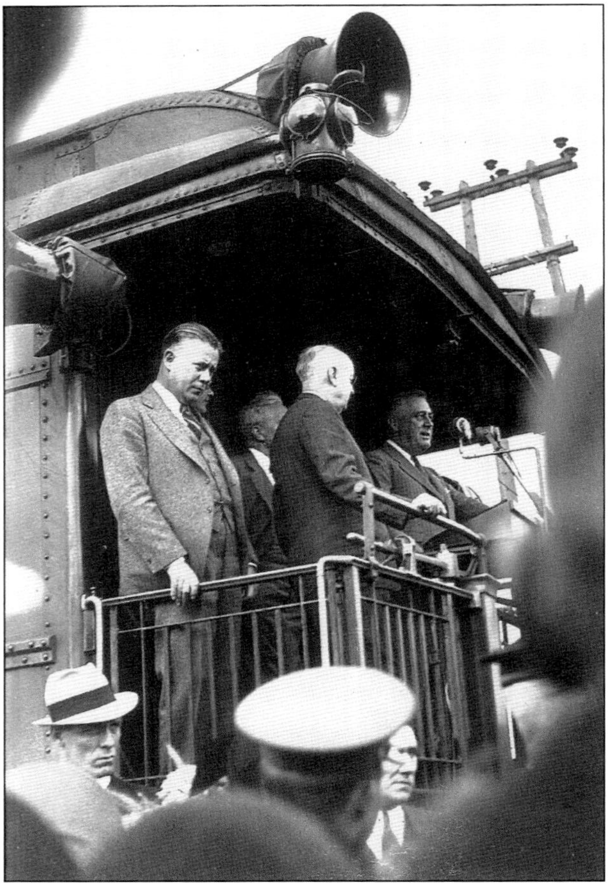

In 1936, Franklin Delano Roosevelt and his wife Eleanor Roosevelt came to Red Oak on a whistle-stop tour. Franklin Delano Roosevelt is making a speech.

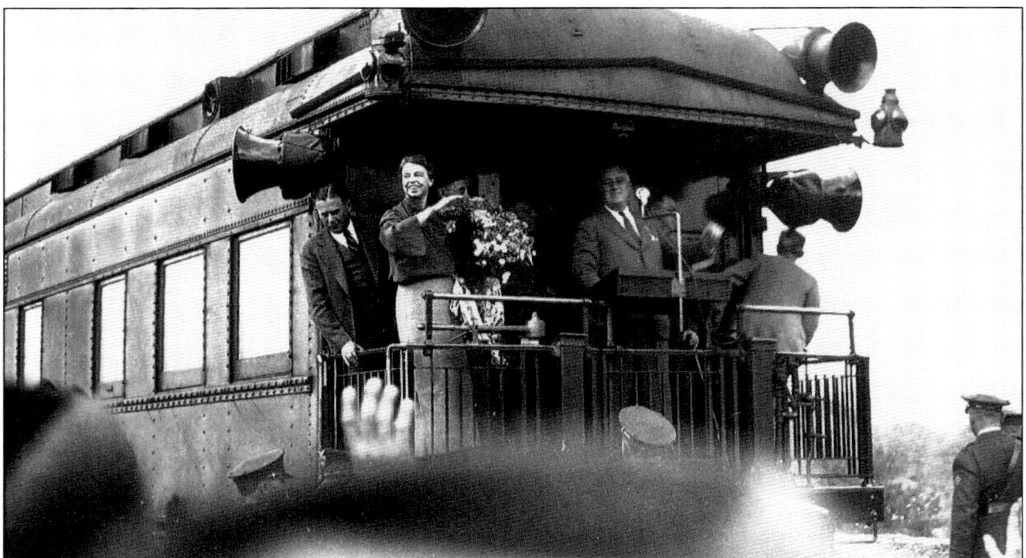

Eleanor has been given a great bouquet of flowers.

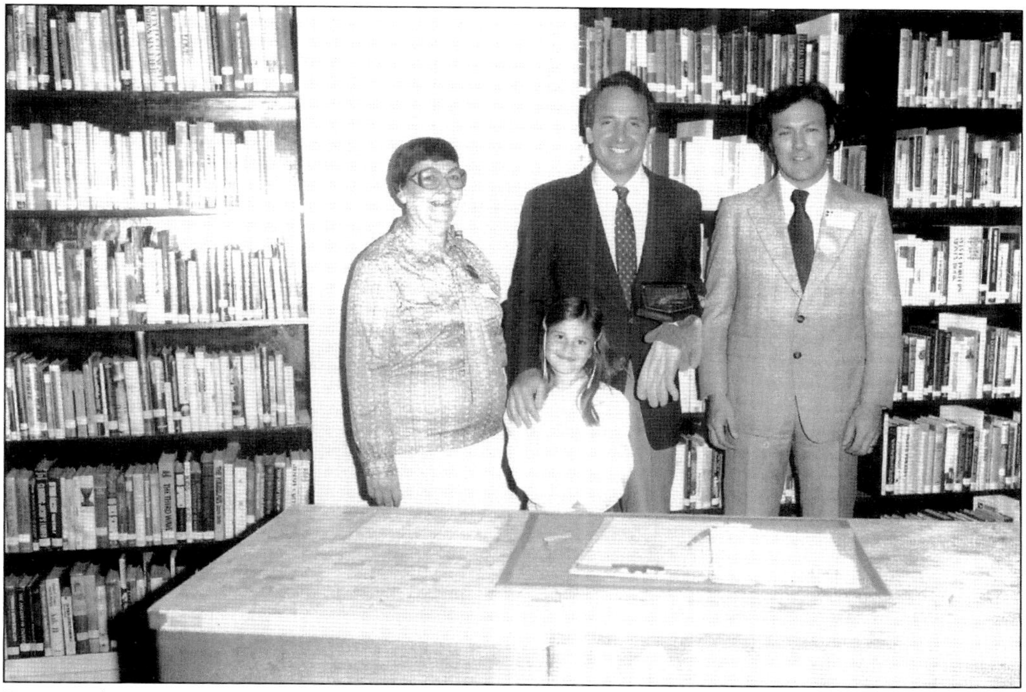

Tom Harkin is pictured here in 1973, campaigning for the Iowa 5th Congressional District. He won and served from 1974 to 1984, before he ran for the Senate in 1984. Harkin is the first Iowa Democrat to serve four Senate terms.

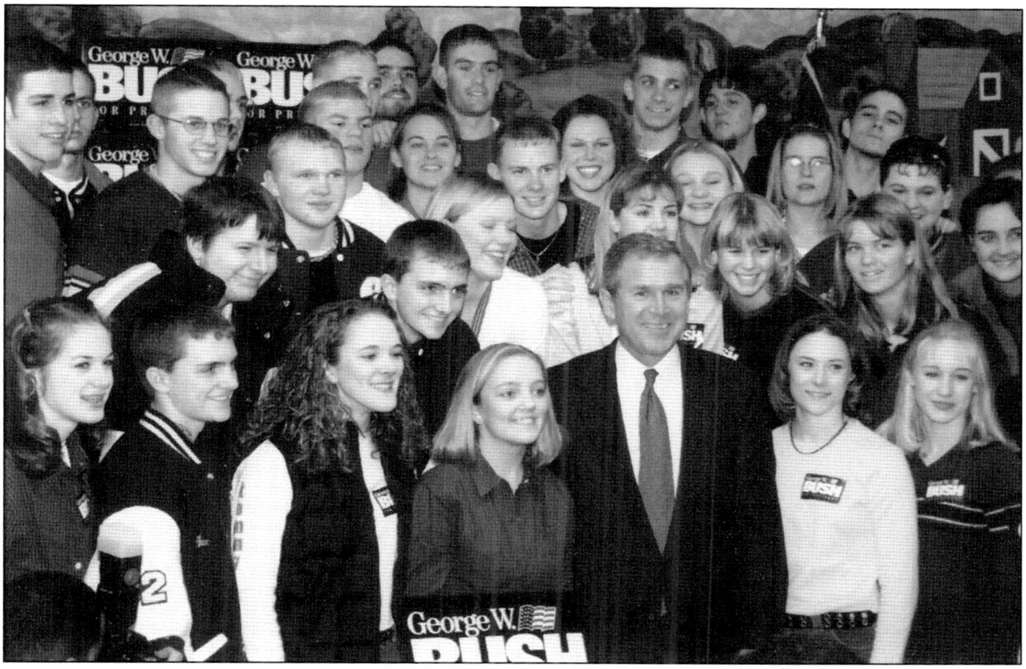

George W. Bush, while caucusing for president in 1999, stopped in the area to be with the young Republicans of Red Oak. He served as president from 2000 to 2008.

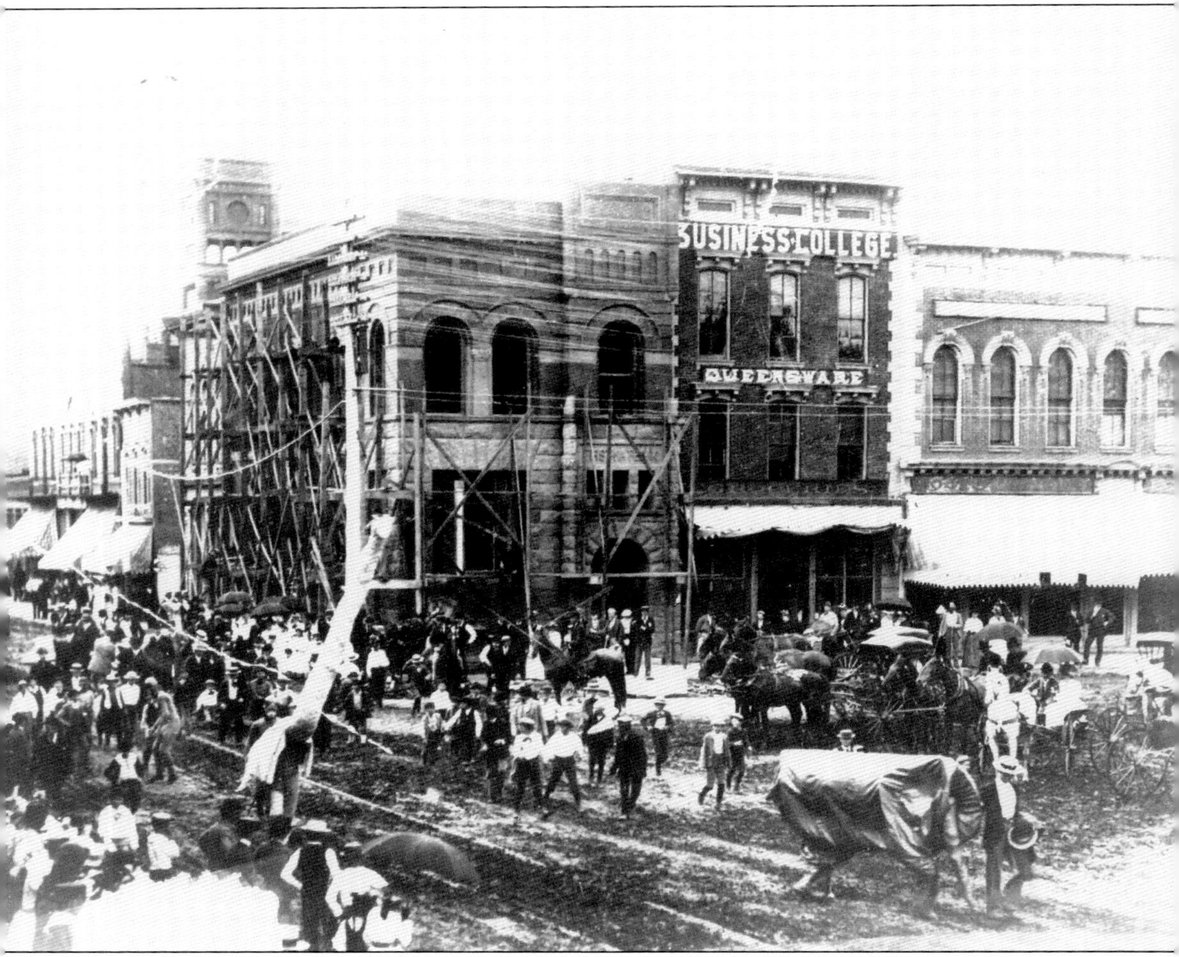

As a parade ambles along Coolbaugh Street around 1894, the First National Bank is covered in scaffolding for its remodeling but is nearing completion, and there is no clock yet in the clock tower of the courthouse. Trolley tracks can be seen in the dusty street, a business college and Queensware are advertised on the facade of the store next to the bank and Hughes and Olson Grocery. A fabric giraffe and elephant draw the attention of the crowds on the southwest corner of the square.

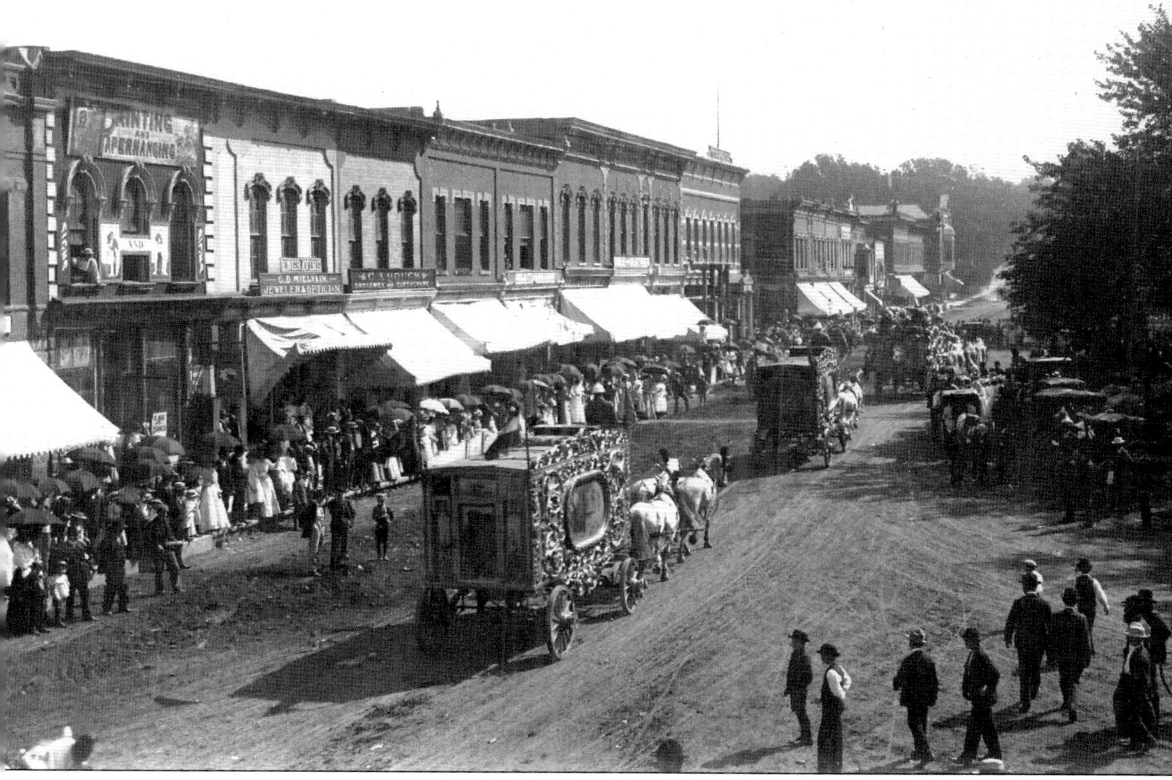

In 1899, this is a circus parade on Reed Street through the square. When Barnum and Bailey's circus came to town, the elephants assisted in moving the Civil War emolument up the hill and into place in the graveyard.

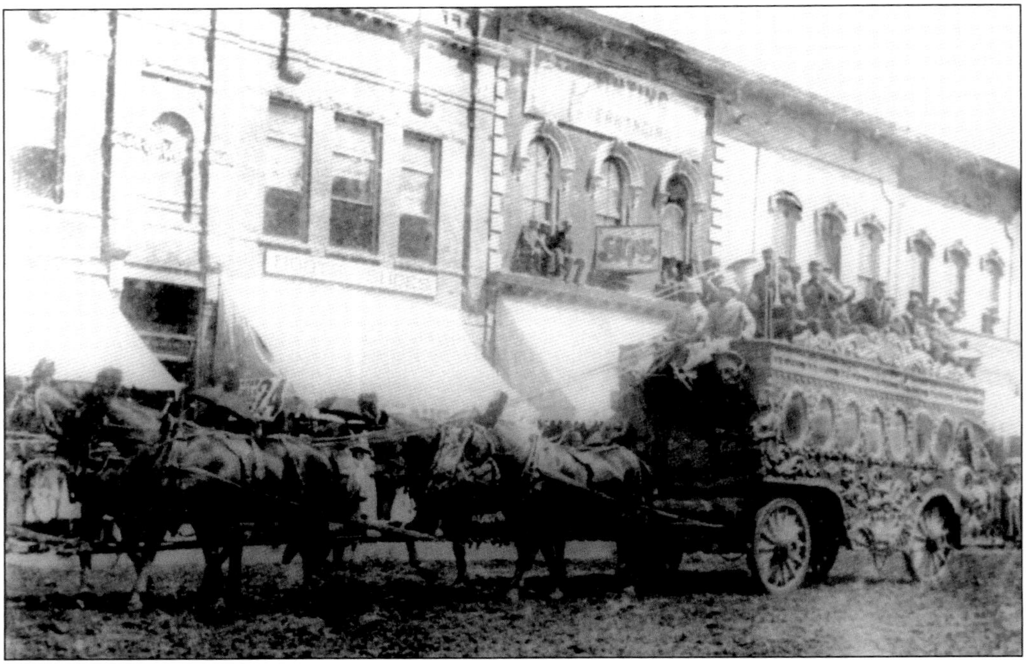

On Friday, August 28, 1900, the Forepaugh-Sells Show came to Red Oak and paraded through the square to announce their arrival. This circus bandwagon was originally built for Howes Great London Circus in 1871. During the 1880s, it was used in the Barnum and London Circus, later Barnum and Bailey. In 1898, it was pulled by a 16-horse checkerboard team, meaning four horses abreast with two whites and two blacks in alternate pairs. In 1897, this wagon ended 39 years of service.

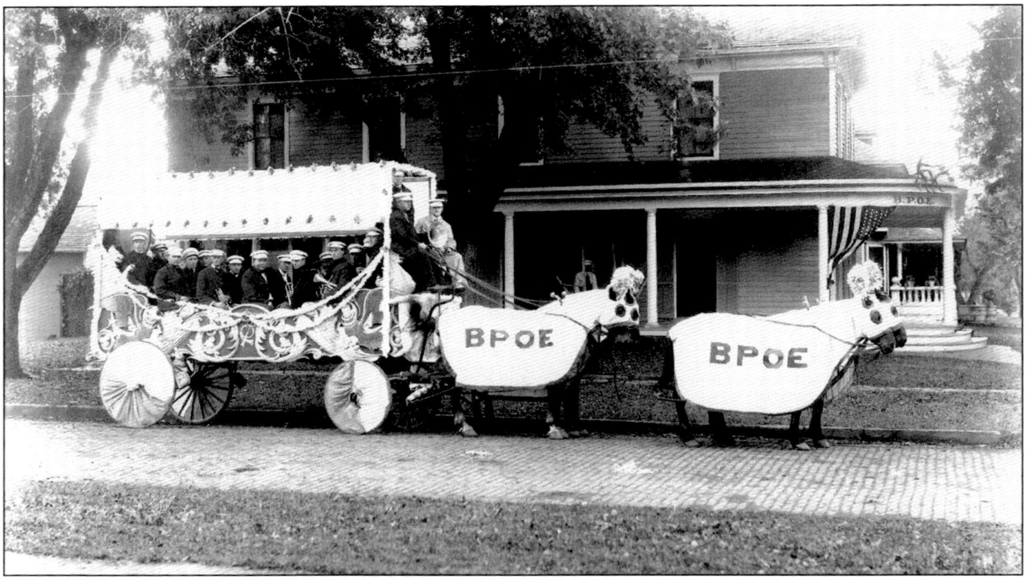

The Benevolent and Protective Order of Elks band on the horse-drawn wagon is ready for the parade in front of their lodge. Note the antlers above the door on their hall before the new one was built across from the courthouse.

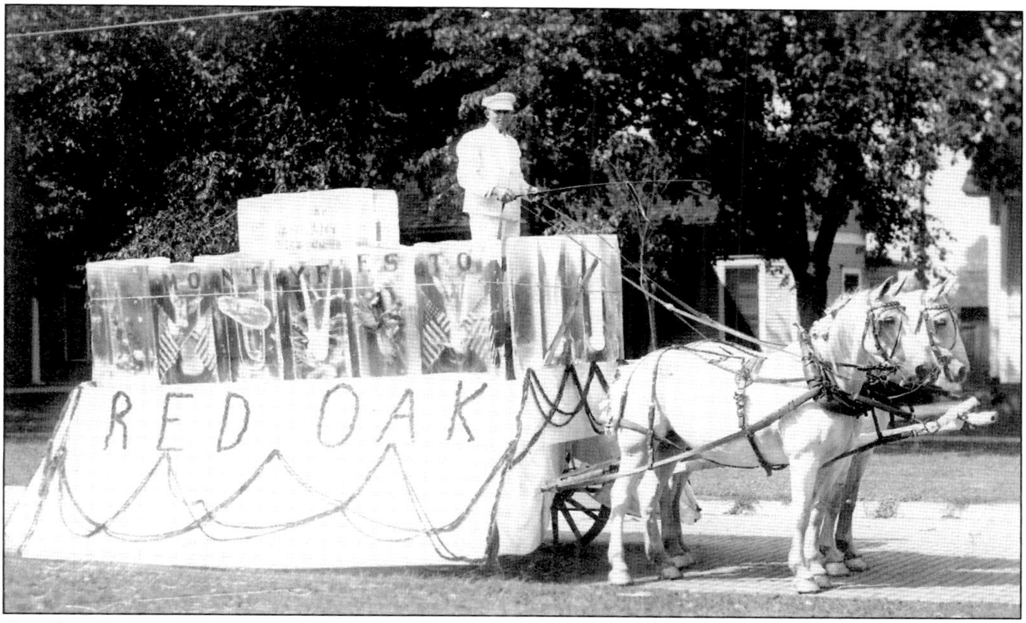

On the Sanitary Ice Company's float in the Monty Festo parade, flags frozen in blocks of ice show how pure the ice was. Edward C. Knight founded the company and F. J. Nims went into the venture with him. In 1915, they built a new plant with a capacity to produce 10 to 12 tons of ice a day with storage for 100 tons.

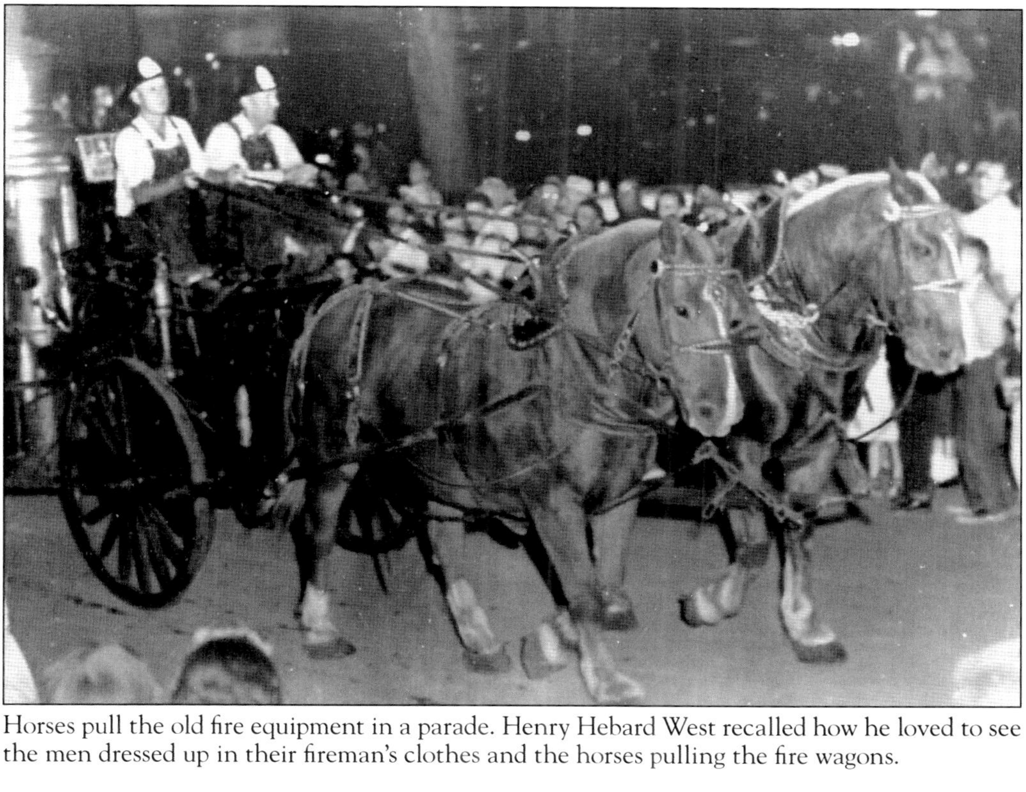

Horses pull the old fire equipment in a parade. Henry Hebard West recalled how he loved to see the men dressed up in their fireman's clothes and the horses pulling the fire wagons.

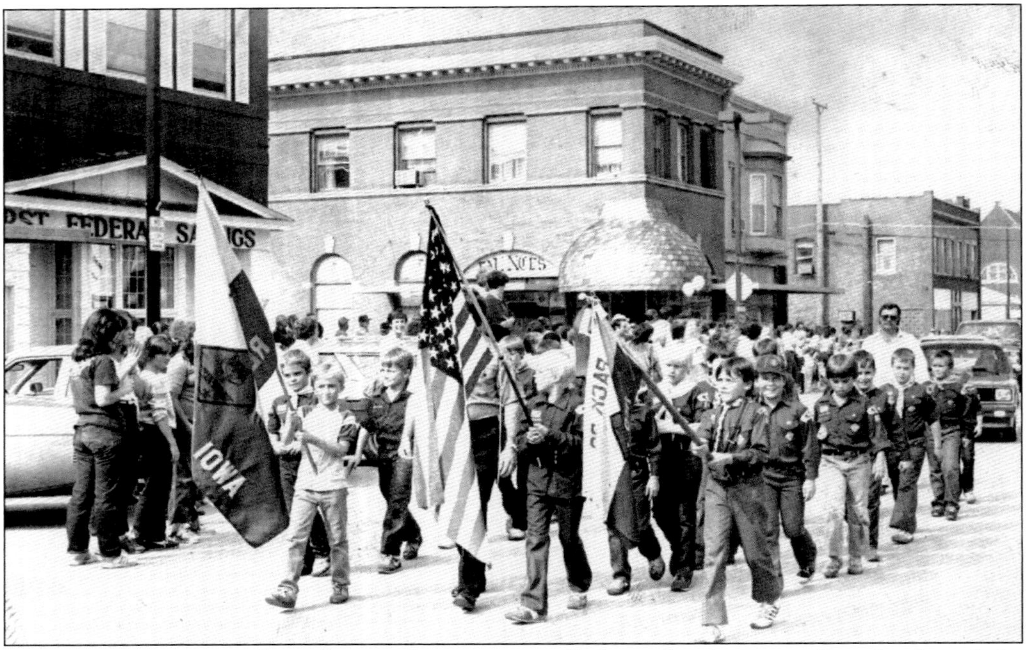

Kids love to be in parades. These Cub Scouts proudly bear the American flag, the flag of the State of Iowa, and their pack flag. Red Oak had the first Boy Scout troop in the state of Iowa.

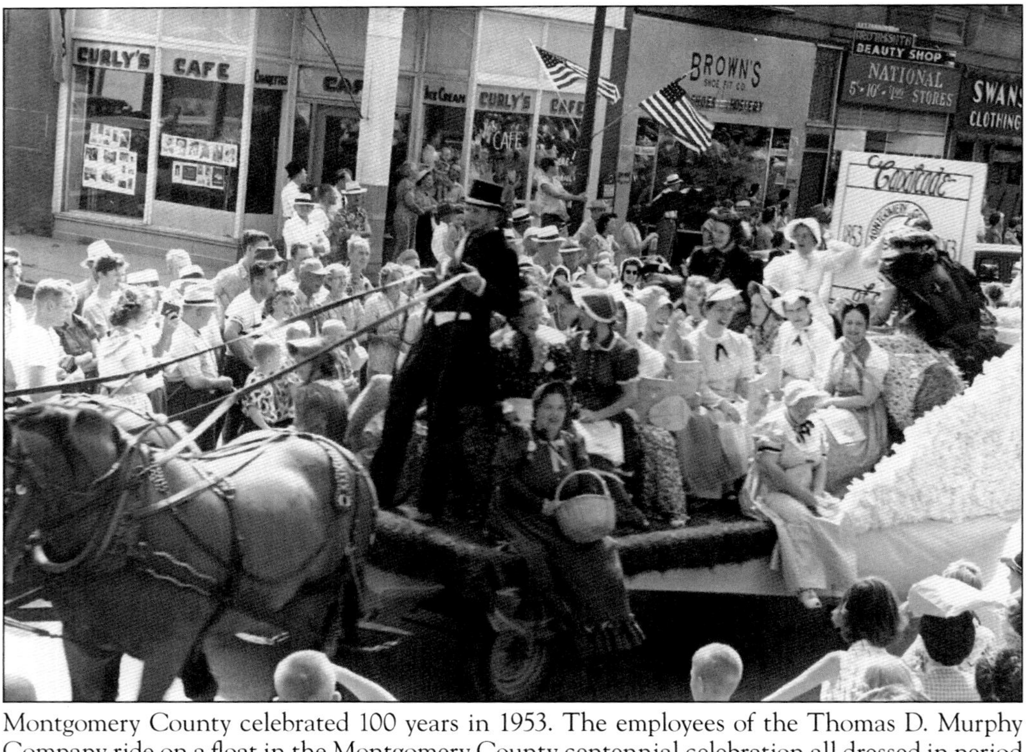

Montgomery County celebrated 100 years in 1953. The employees of the Thomas D. Murphy Company ride on a float in the Montgomery County centennial celebration all dressed in period clothing for the occasion. Many of the men of the county grew beards especially for the event.

This is a program from the Monty Festo. Horace Deemer was the district court judge from 1886 to 1890 and was appointed by Gov. Frank D. Jackson to the Iowa Supreme Court and served for 28 years. Deemer wanted people to remember their history and spent three years researching before he and others mounted the Montgomery Festival in College Park. Mr. Sampson abbreviated it to Monty Festo.

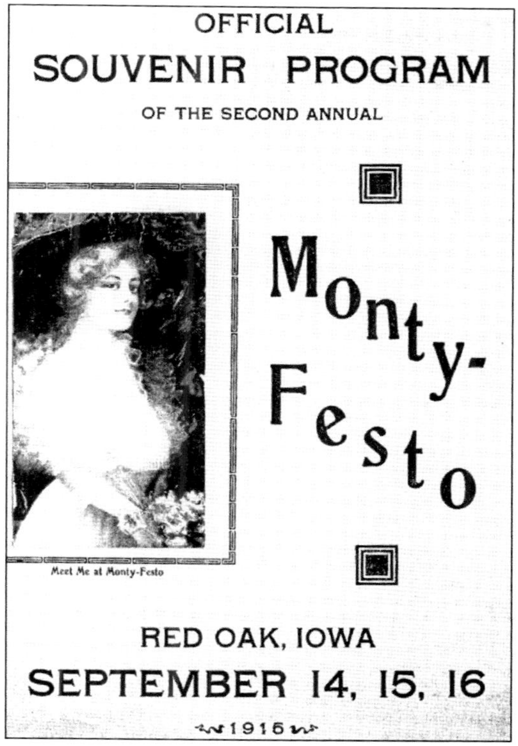

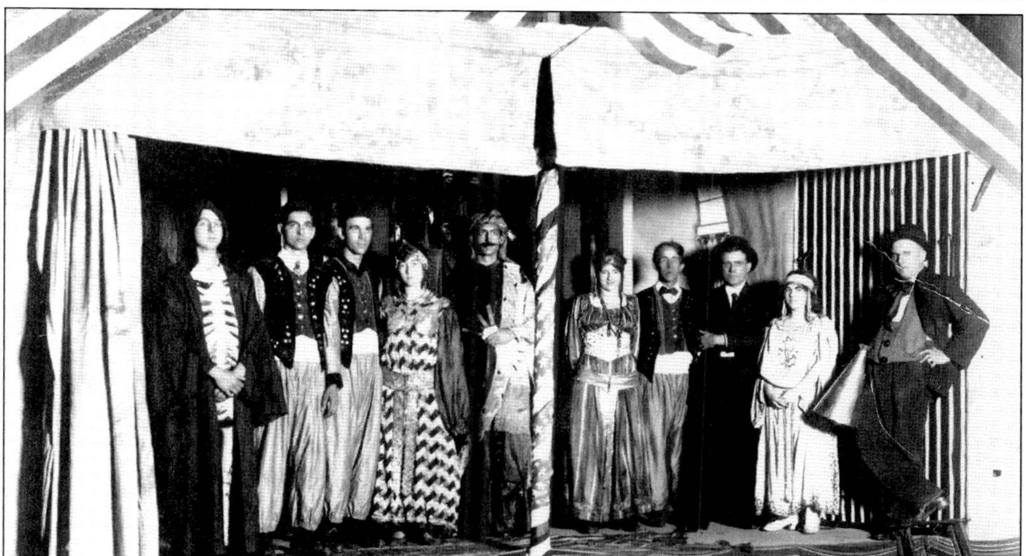

There was an Indian Night, Pioneer Night, and Jollification with fireworks. Company M put on a battle scene from real life, there were band concerts, automobile races, farm exhibits, drills, athletic events, and lectures by Iowa State College and University representatives. Auto Polo was the only event with a fee. The Monte Festo Indian Night cast includes, from left to right, Ed Smith, Art Hickert, unidentified, Laura Gossrick, Jim England, Geraldine Coag Leory, Ralph Hiatt, Ed Kerrihard, unidentified, and Ed Hatcher.

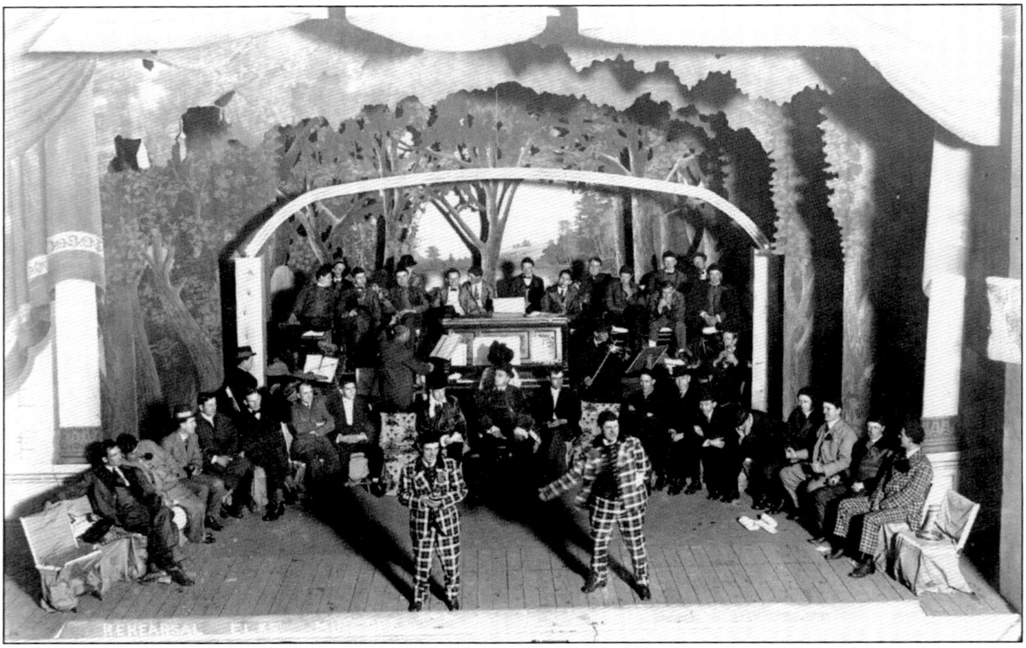

The November 26, 1914, Elks Club rehearsal for their minstrel show at the Beardsley Theatre is seen here.

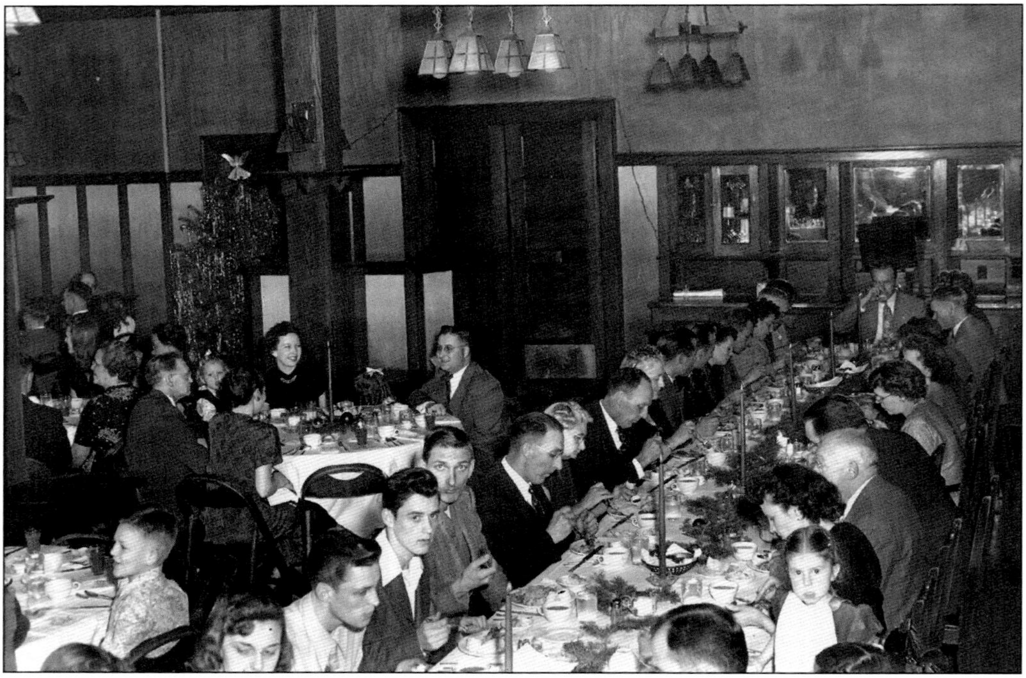

The Ko-Z-Air Company, which was located at 401 Coolbaugh Street, employees enjoy their annual Christmas party at the Hotel Johnson in 1945. Thomas Kerrihard was a pioneer who had a sawmill, foundry, and was involved in many ventures over the years. The Ko-Z-Air Company made furnaces.

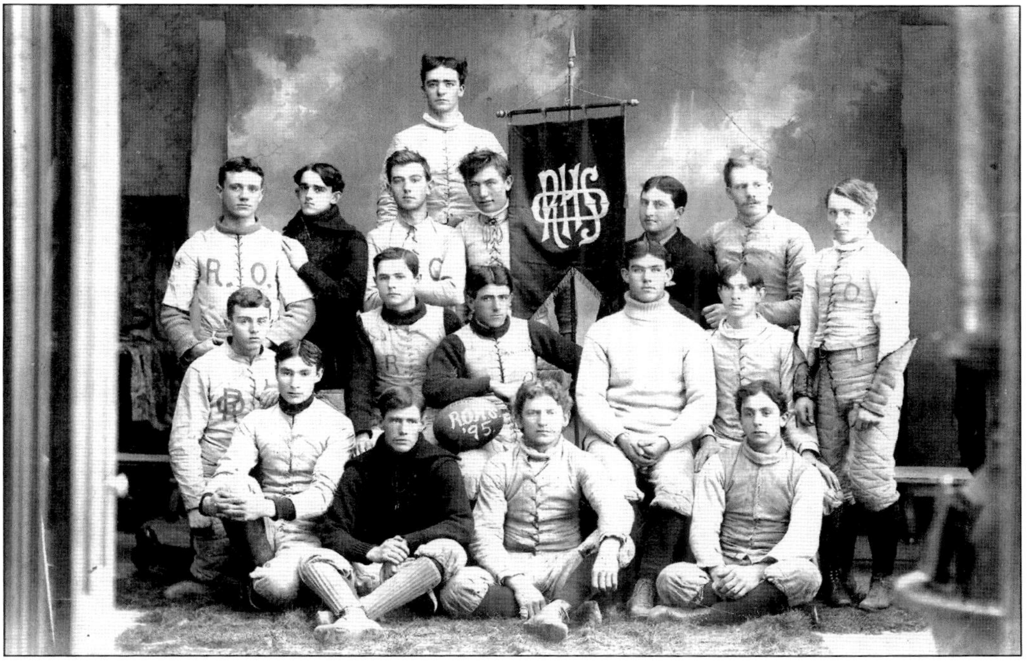

The Red Oak 1895 football team is pictured here. At first, Red Oak did not have a very good football team. Their first game, againt Corning, was so bad they did not even score a point (80-0). The Presbyterian minister had been to Yale and offered to help coach the team. They improved dramatically.

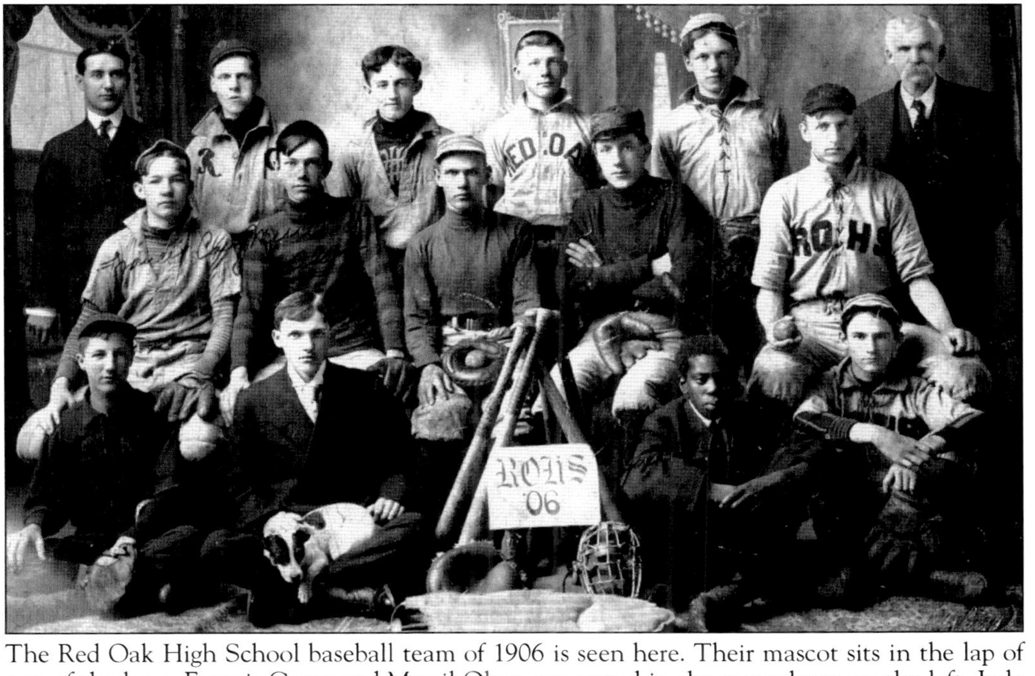

The Red Oak High School baseball team of 1906 is seen here. Their mascot sits in the lap of one of the boys. Francis Carey and Merril Olsen are seated in the second row on the left. Jude Alexander is the black boy seated in the front row.

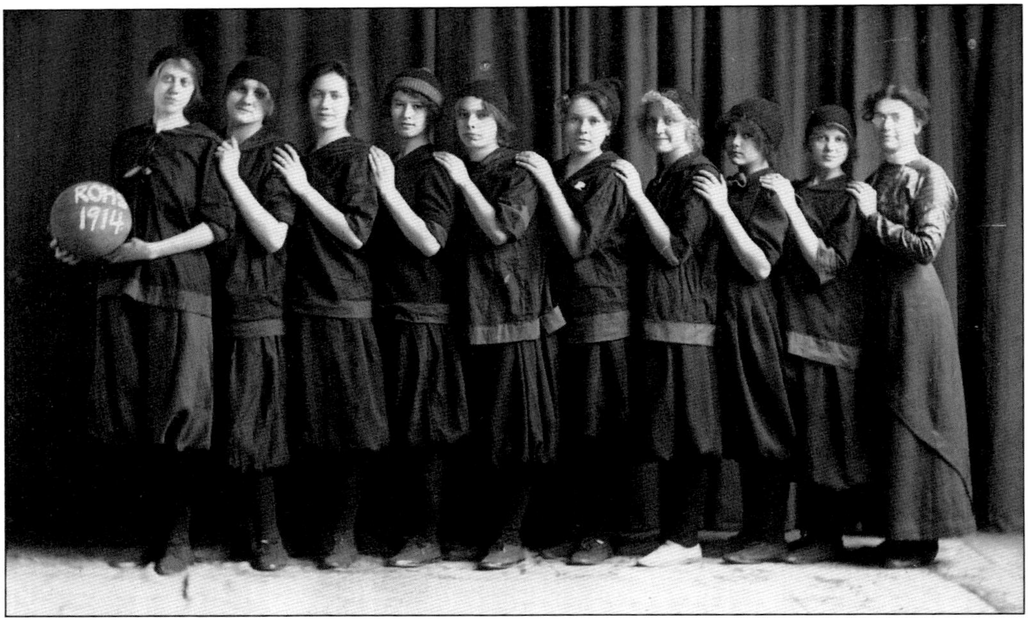

The Red Oak High School women's basketball team in 1914 includes, from left to right, Dora Johnson, Ruth Bass, Margaret Leper, Vera Braden, Lena Rubey, Velma Wallace, Josephine Jenkins, Goldie Mitchell, Grace Peters, and coach Thompson.

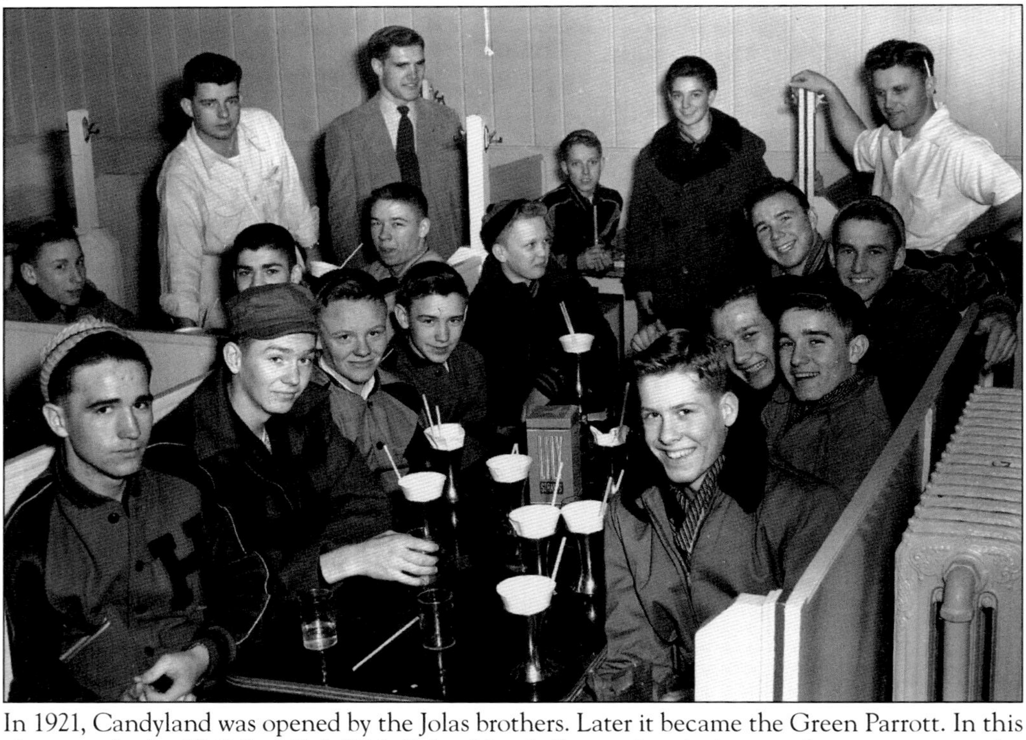

In 1921, Candyland was opened by the Jolas brothers. Later it became the Green Parrott. In this photograph, the 1948 Red Oak High School football team is enjoying an afternoon treat at the Green Parrott.

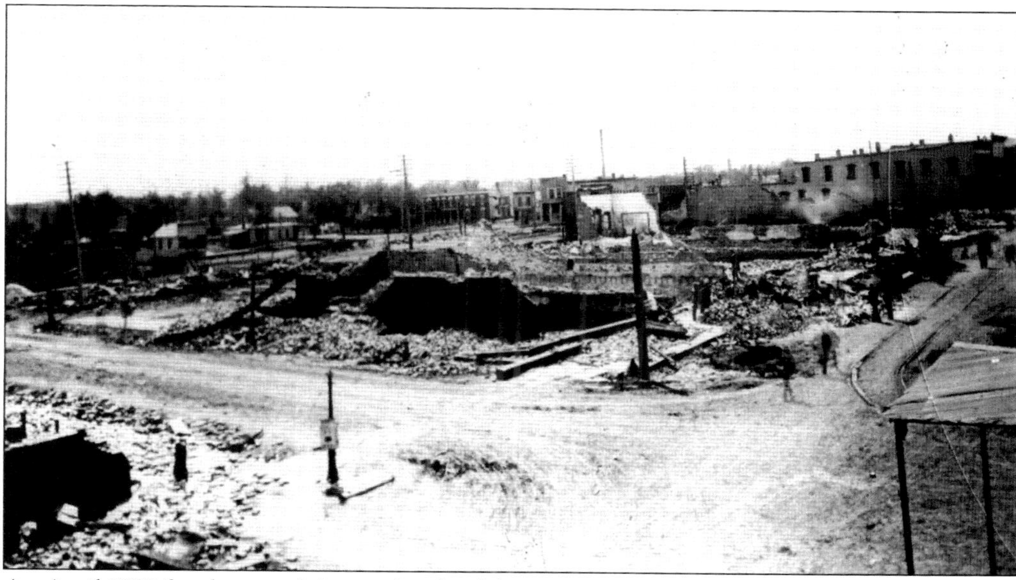

An April 1902 fire destroyed the south side of the square. Frank Askey was the first photographer on the scene to record the devastation. This photograph was taken looking west from Fourth Street along Coolbaugh Street. The fire started in the bank building at the lower left, jumped the street, and spread west and north. The fire even destroyed some of the trees in the square. The smokestack in the distance is believed to be the old brick foundry.

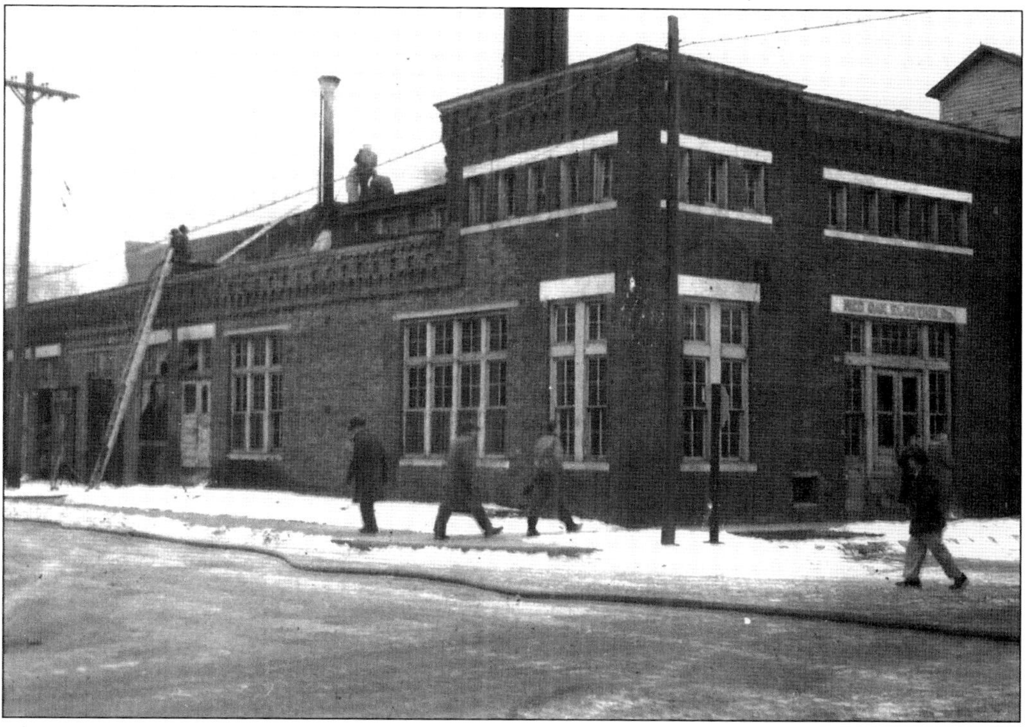

The Red Oak Electric Company, at Second Street and Washington Avenue, was destroyed by fire in the 1940s.

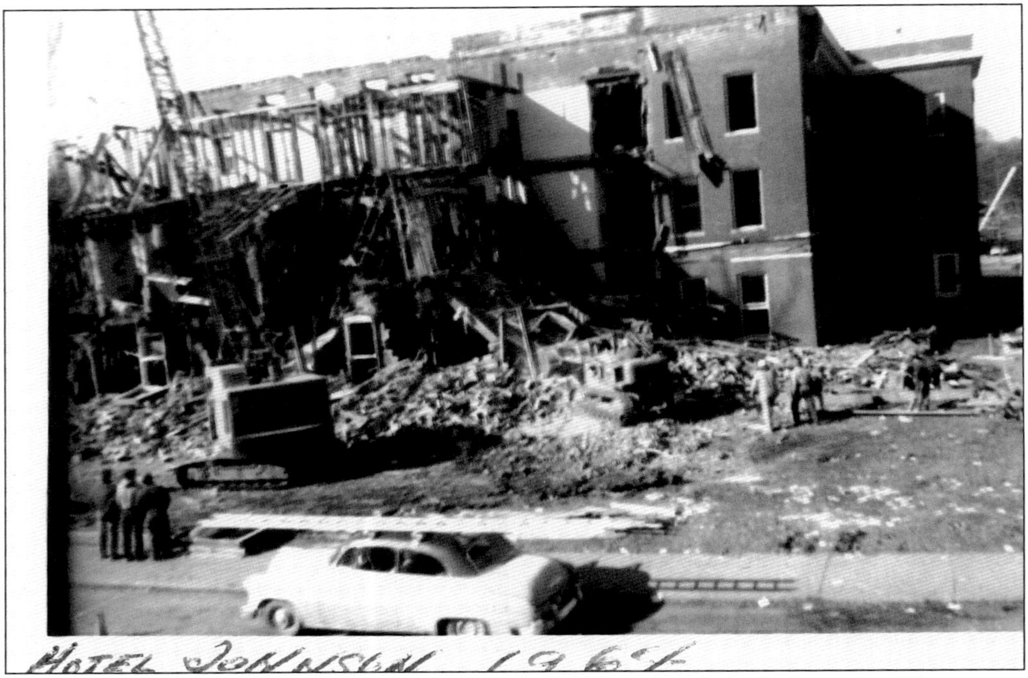

In 1964, the end of an era came as the Johnson Hotel was demolished after a fire. The newest wing is being torn down first.

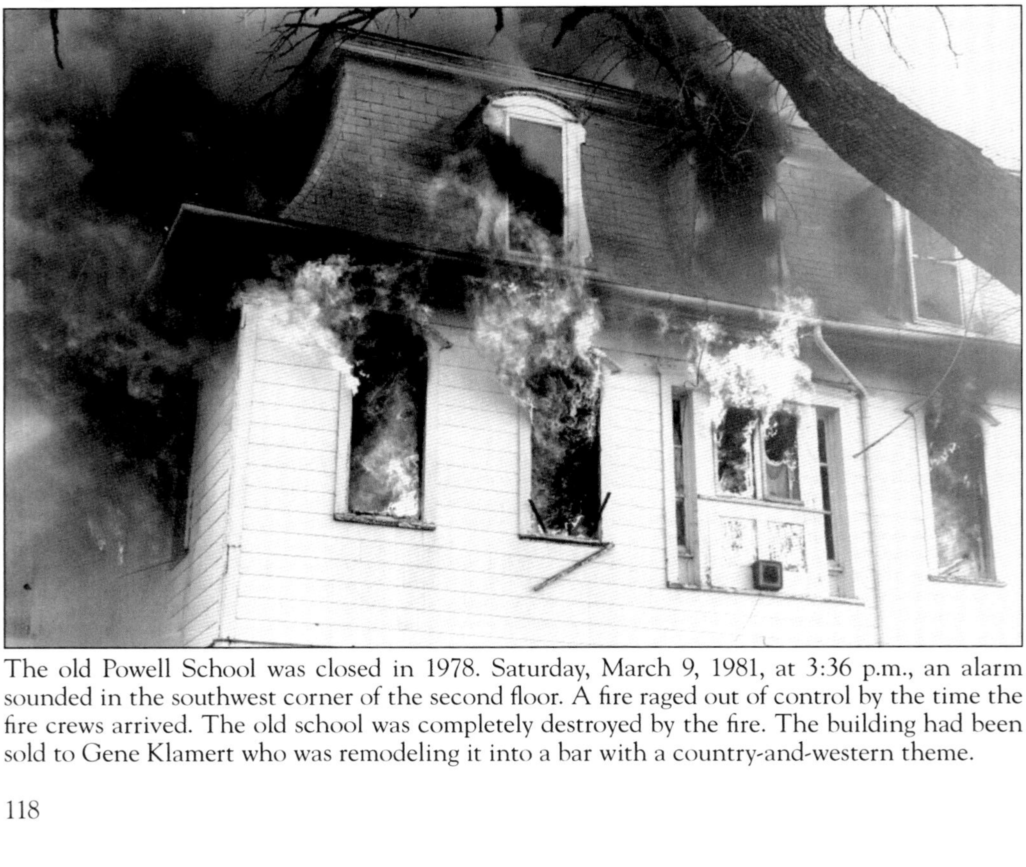

The old Powell School was closed in 1978. Saturday, March 9, 1981, at 3:36 p.m., an alarm sounded in the southwest corner of the second floor. A fire raged out of control by the time the fire crews arrived. The old school was completely destroyed by the fire. The building had been sold to Gene Klamert who was remodeling it into a bar with a country-and-western theme.

On April 17–19, 1941, rain, hail, and cyclone damage tore through Red Oak and Montgomery County. This is a photograph of the twister that destroyed homes and farms in the area.

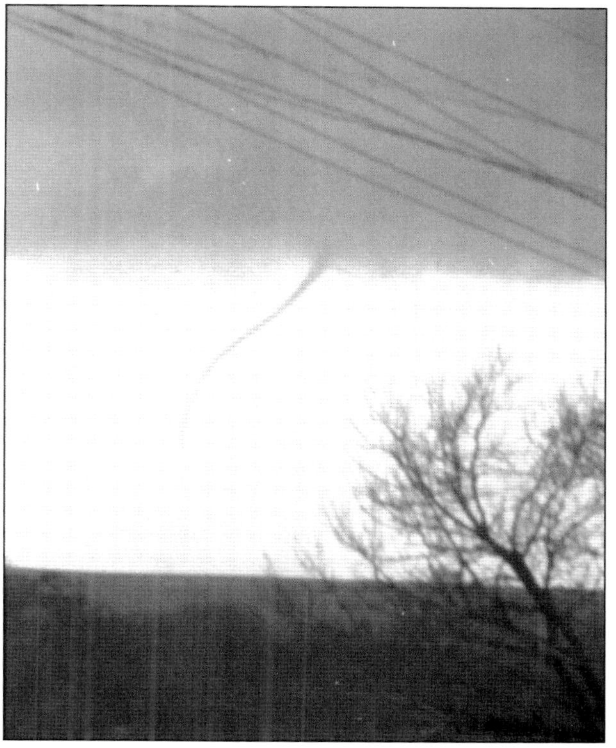

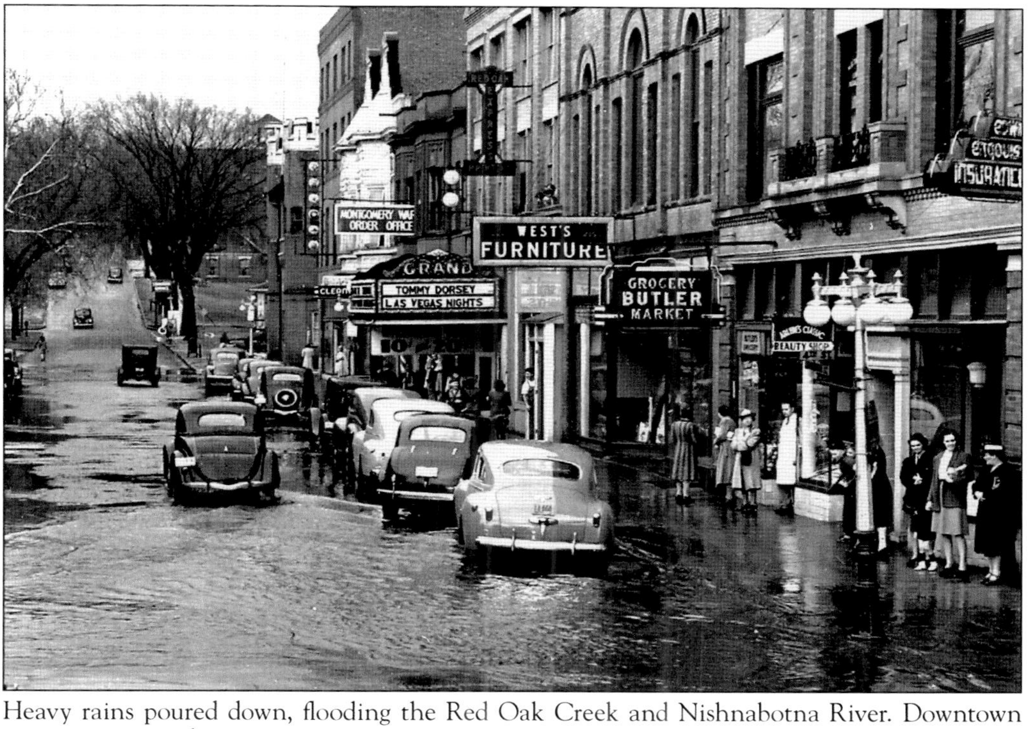

Heavy rains poured down, flooding the Red Oak Creek and Nishnabotna River. Downtown streets were paved in water.

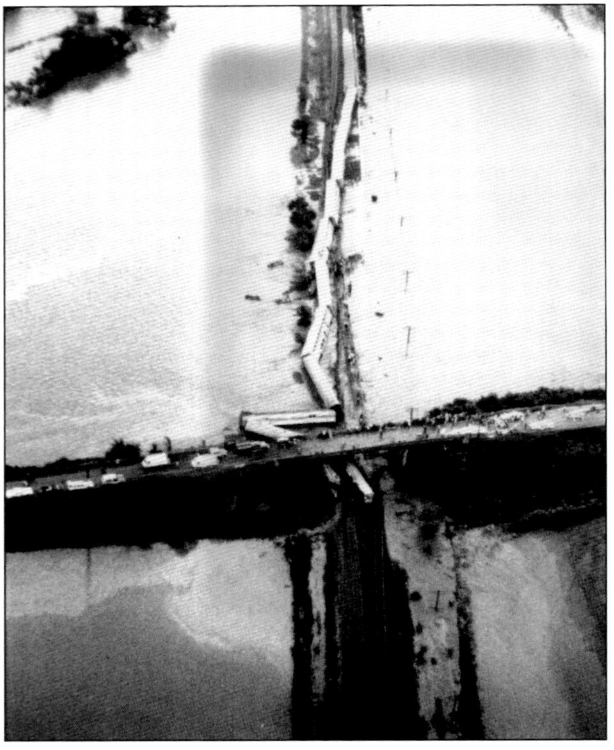

This is an aerial photograph of the damage that the floodwaters created by washing out the railroad track. The train was derailed.

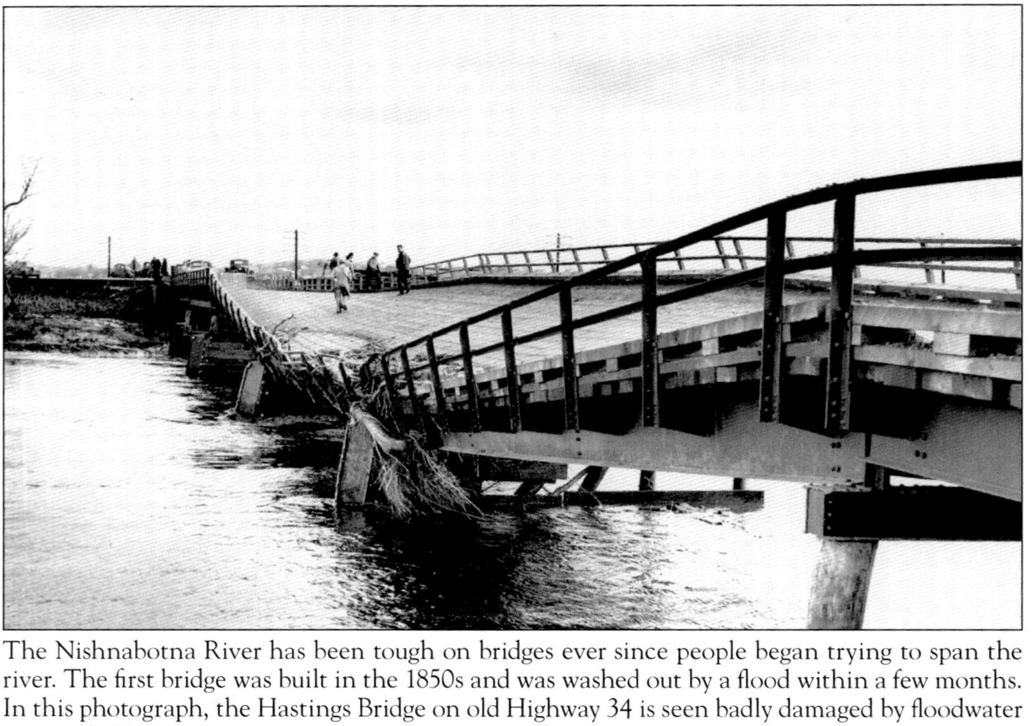

The Nishnabotna River has been tough on bridges ever since people began trying to span the river. The first bridge was built in the 1850s and was washed out by a flood within a few months. In this photograph, the Hastings Bridge on old Highway 34 is seen badly damaged by floodwater in March 1949.

Six

Past, Present, Future

Red Oak did not just happen, it is here because of the dedicated lives of the many men and women who lived through great joys, as well as many disasters, but always came out on top. Each generation has built on what their predecessors had built. They brought their hopes and dreams and offered their best to the city they loved and called their home. They were proud of their city, proud of its history, and proud of their accomplishments.

Red Oak is not a city that will be plowed under by a rapidly changing world. Red Oak has always been a leader in the latest innovations, the telephone, electric power, and plumbing, long before many other cities installed these modern marvels. Red Oak will continue to be a leader in the Montgomery County area and in the state of Iowa, this great nation, and even the world. Red Oak proudly looks at its past, embraces it, and cheerfully looks to the future and the contribution it shall make to the lives of those who are so fortunate to live there.

Red Oak is blessed to have many excellent examples of Victorian homes. Red Oak also had its own radio station; an excellent hospital facility, the Montgomery County Memorial Hospital; a new YMCA; the restored depot museum; a performing arts center, began with a bequest from Johnny Carson and completed thanks to the many gifts of Red Oak's philanthropists; and Betty McKenzie's dream, a new state-of-the-art museum for the Montgomery County Historical Society.

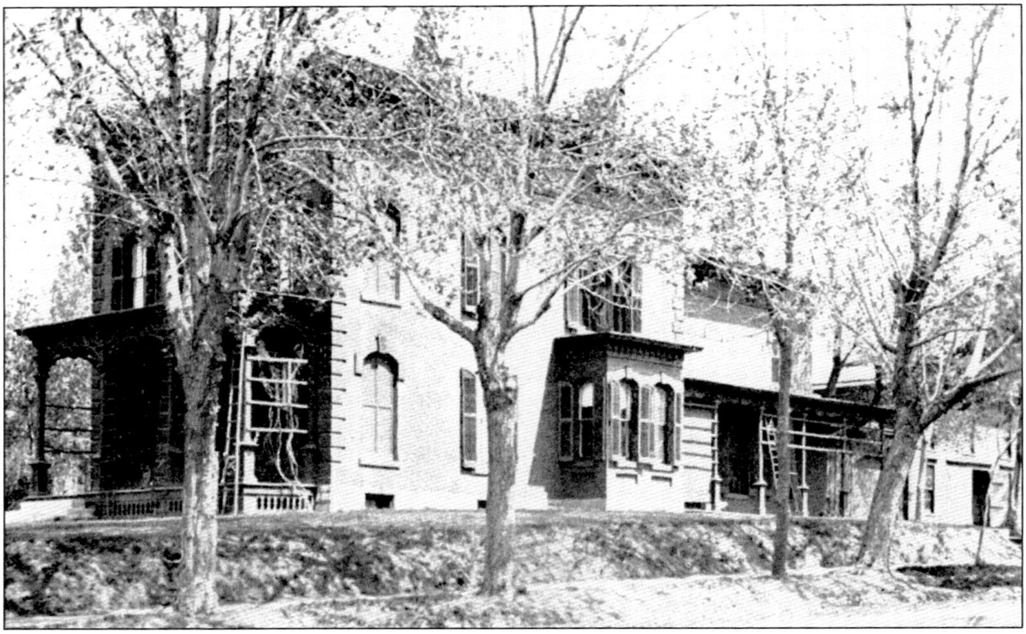

Col. Alfred Hebard is considered to be the father of Red Oak, although he was not the first resident. It was his route for the railroad that made Red Oak a possibility. When the town was in its infancy, he returned and commissioned George West to build a fine brick home on a hill at Eighth Street. The following photographs were taken in 1901.

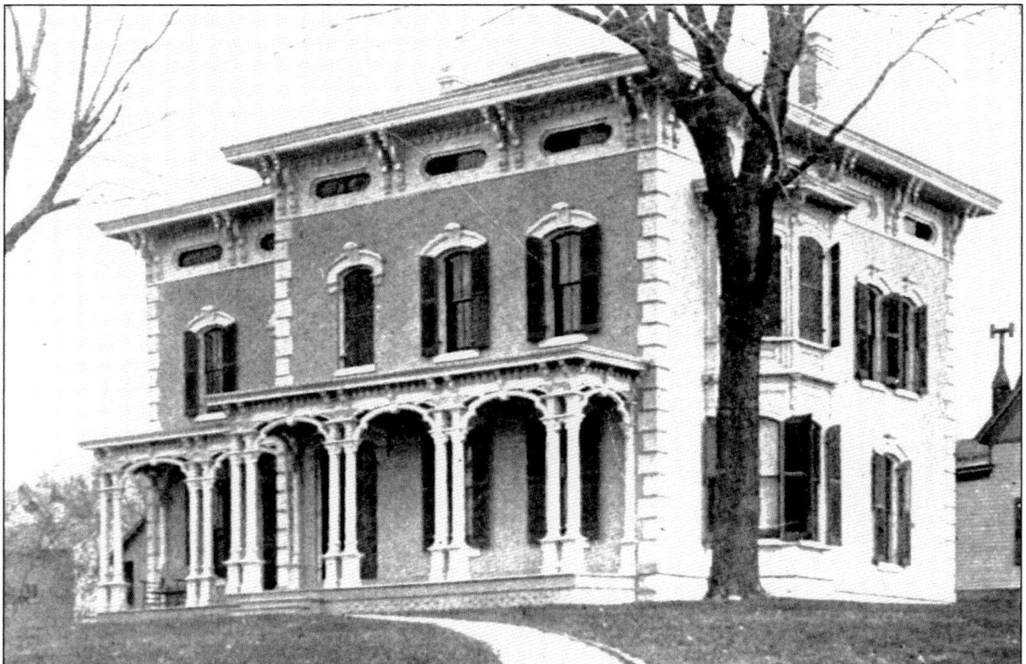

This elegant brick home was that of P. P. Clark, a cashier in the First National Bank of Red Oak. It is located at 601 Reed Street. It is now a multiunit dwelling.

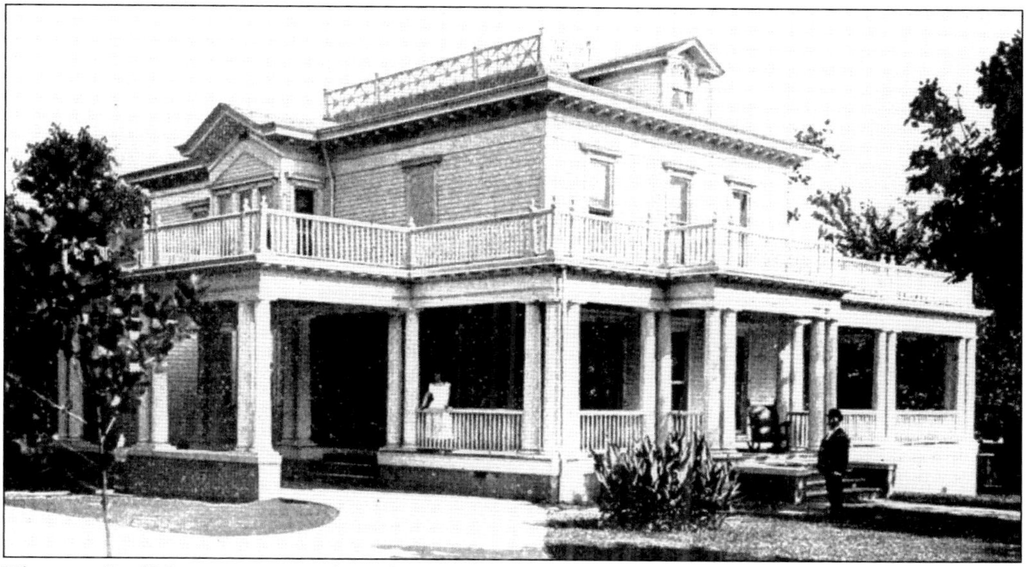

Thomas Griffith was mayor when this was taken in 1901. He is standing in the front by the porch. This is the house on Eighth Street that he swapped for his home on Coolbaugh Street, pictured earlier in the text. That Coolbaugh house is no longer standing, but this structure still stands, almost frozen in time. It remained in the family until about 2003, but no one lived there for any extended time since the 1920s. Gas lamps, the basement laundry rooms, the scullery hand pump, pocket doors, stenciled motifs, and elegant old wallpaper remain much as they have for 100 years.

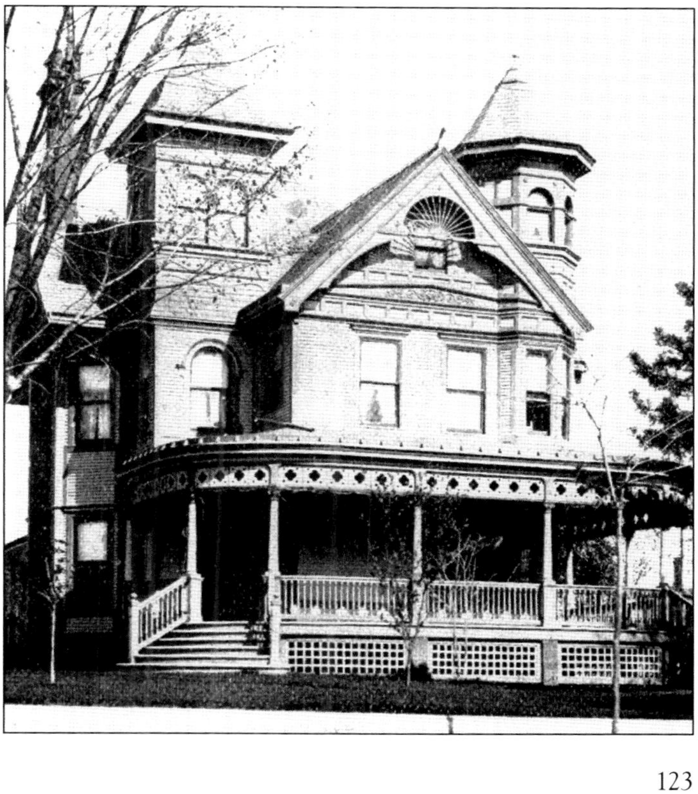

Next door to Mayor Griffith's house on Eighth Street is A. C. Hinchman's home. It was said that this was the house that bootlegging built. Iowa was dry in the 1880s, but if one wanted some whiskey, they could go to Hinchman's drugstore, put $2 down on the counter, and walk out with a bottle. Business must have been pretty brisk. This elegant home has been lovingly restored.

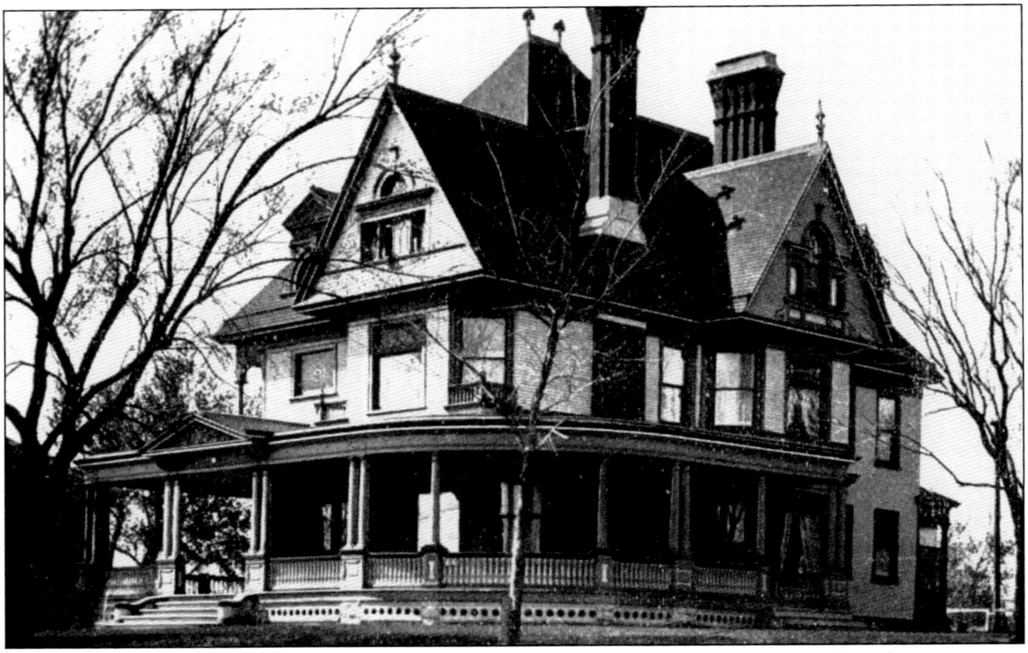

Dan Reifel was a successful clothier who built this beautiful home at 711 Coolbaugh Street. It is another excellent example of the exquisite quality of homes that were being built by successful Red Oak merchants.

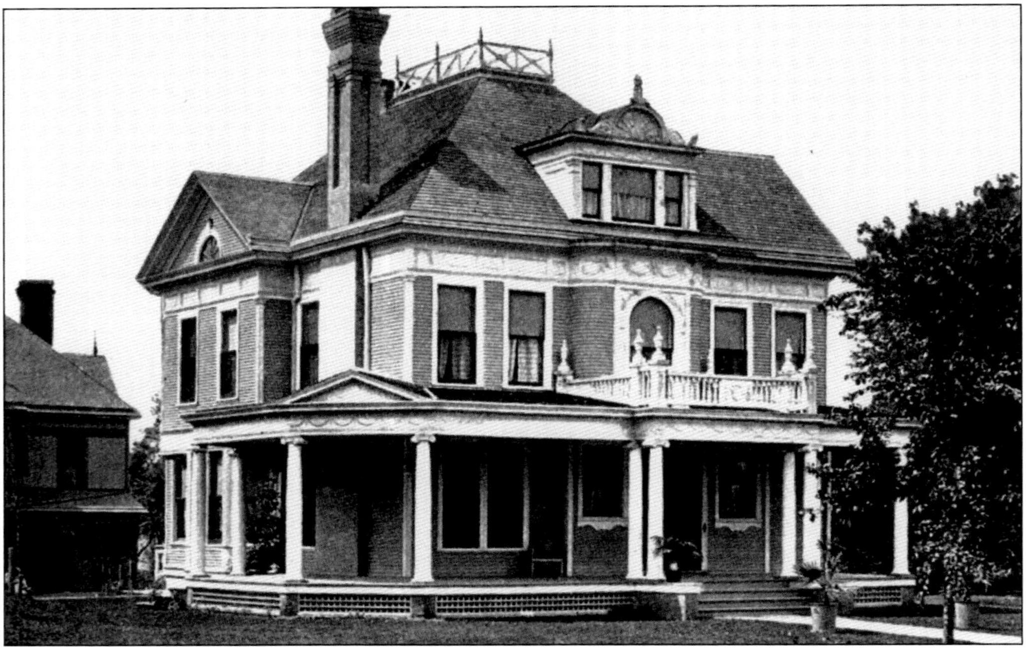

The house that Thomas Dowler Murphy built has been remodeled since this photograph was taken in 1901. The house is in excellent repair, and the family still lives there. Murphy and his partner Edmond Osborne created the art calendar in the late 1800s. The Murphy family has always been supportive of the needs of Red Oak in their many philanthropic gifts through the years.

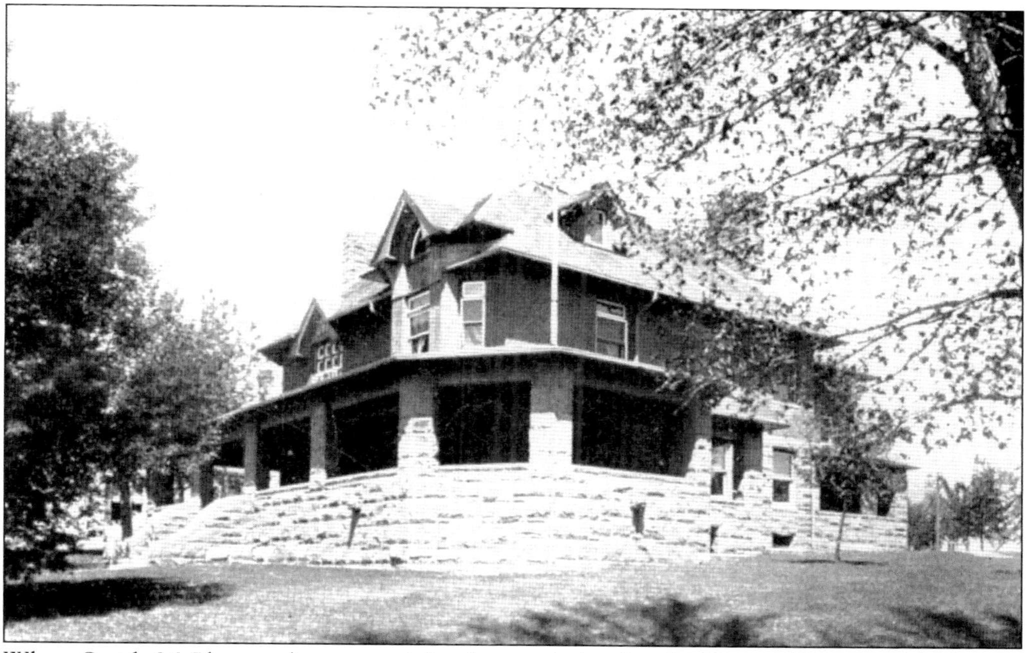

When Smith McPherson became a federal court judge for the State of Iowa he felt that he should have a home that reflected the position he had attained. He had George West design this beautiful home for him at 805 Eighth Street. The home is another example of a well cared for and beautifully restored home that dignifies Red Oak's rich architectural history.

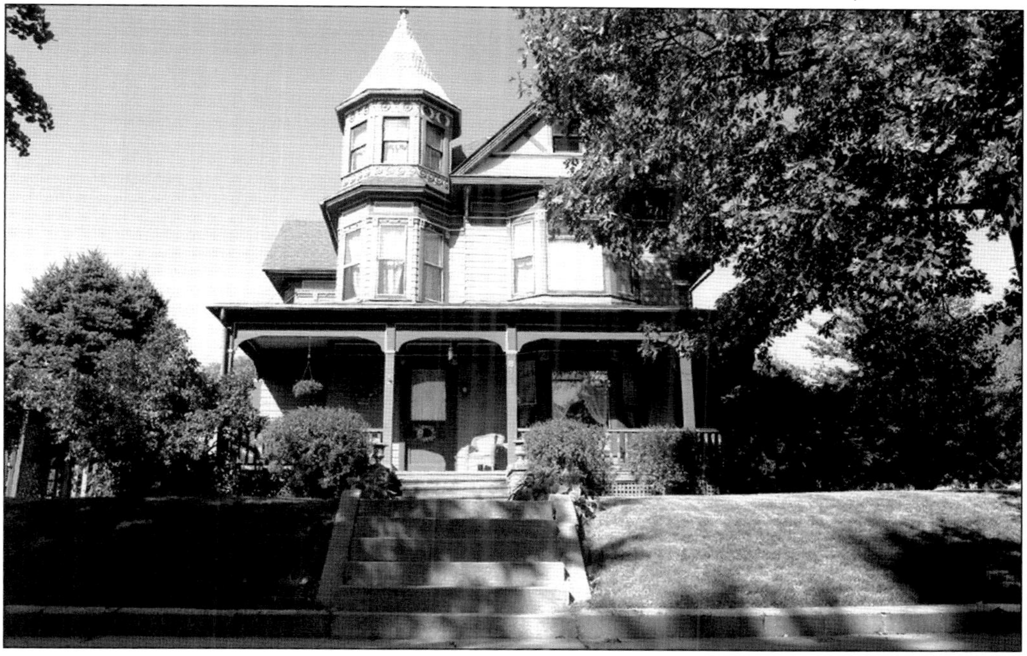

William Maloney was a dentist before turning his attention to the tin trade. He built this house after he retired from dentistry. The details on the turret are unusual in that he used metal instead of wood. This house has been restored with care and attention to detail.

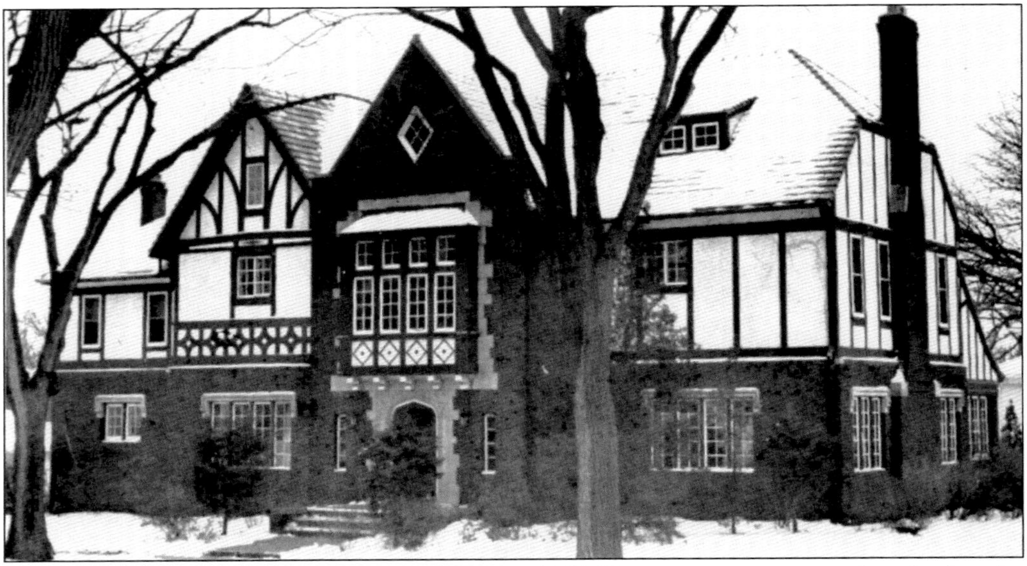

Thomas Jefferson Hysham came to Red Oak in 1874. He was an attorney and studied under Smith McPherson. He was instrumental in raising the money to put a clock in the courthouse tower. In 1895, he founded the Monday Club. His is remembered as the man who defended Rev. Lyn G. J. Kelly, who was charged with committing the Villisca axe murders. He died in 1940, and in 1956, his home was given to the Monday Club. The Hysham House was extensively remodeled from a Victorian structure into a Tudor-style home.

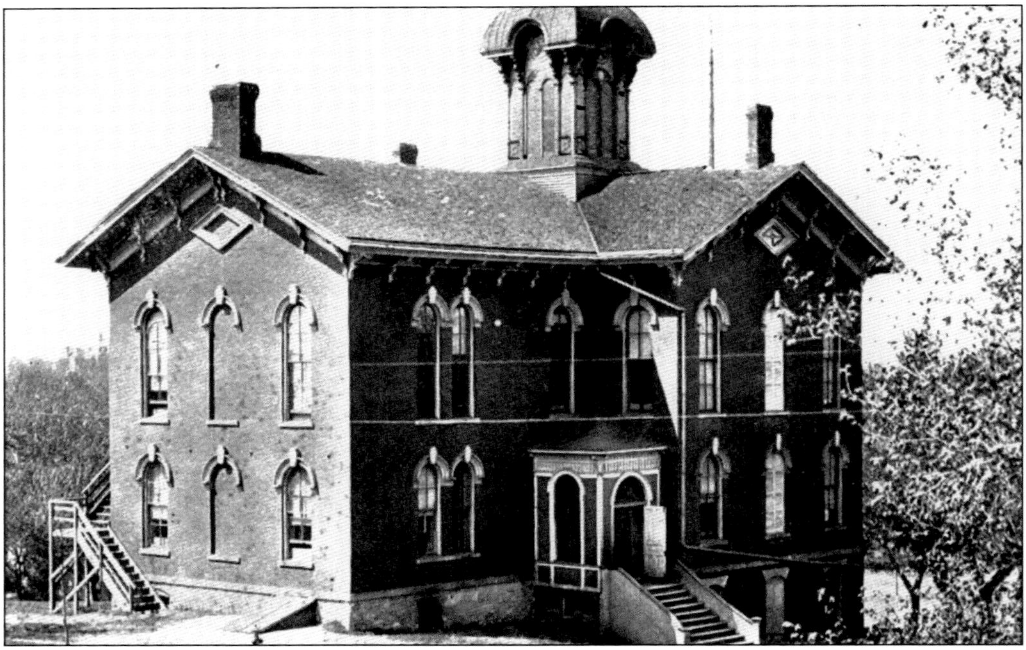

The East Ward, later renamed the Lincoln School, was built in 1870 by George West. Red Oak believed in its future and invested in the lives of the children by providing them with a good education. Sadly all the old schools of this era are gone, replaced by newer more modern centers of education.

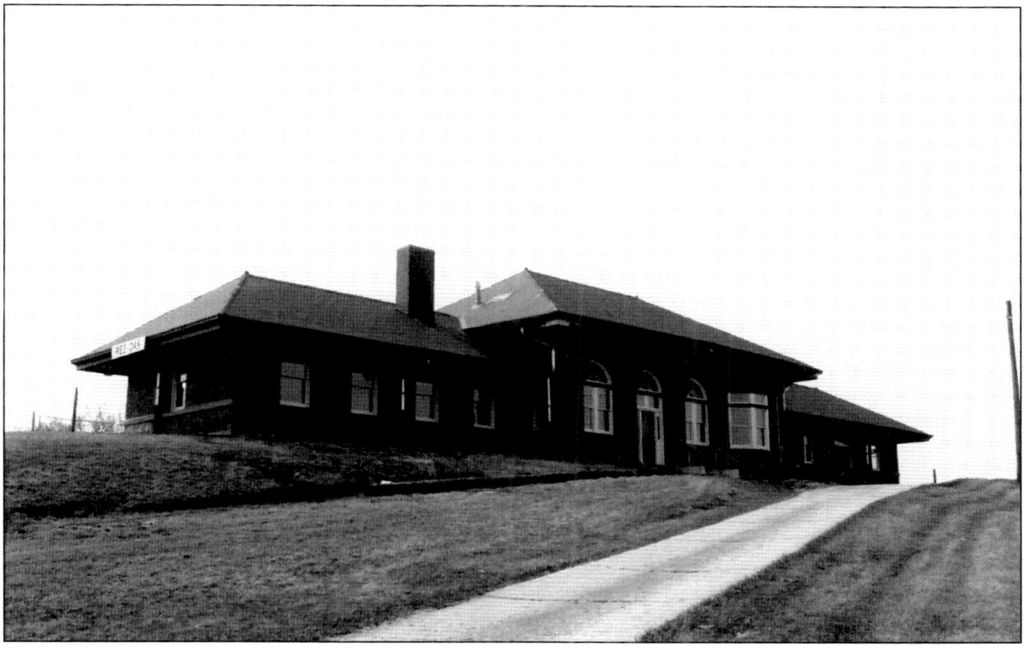

The Burlington Northern Depot and World War II Memorial Museum was restored thanks to Jackie Adams, who had the drive and determination to save the depot and create a museum.

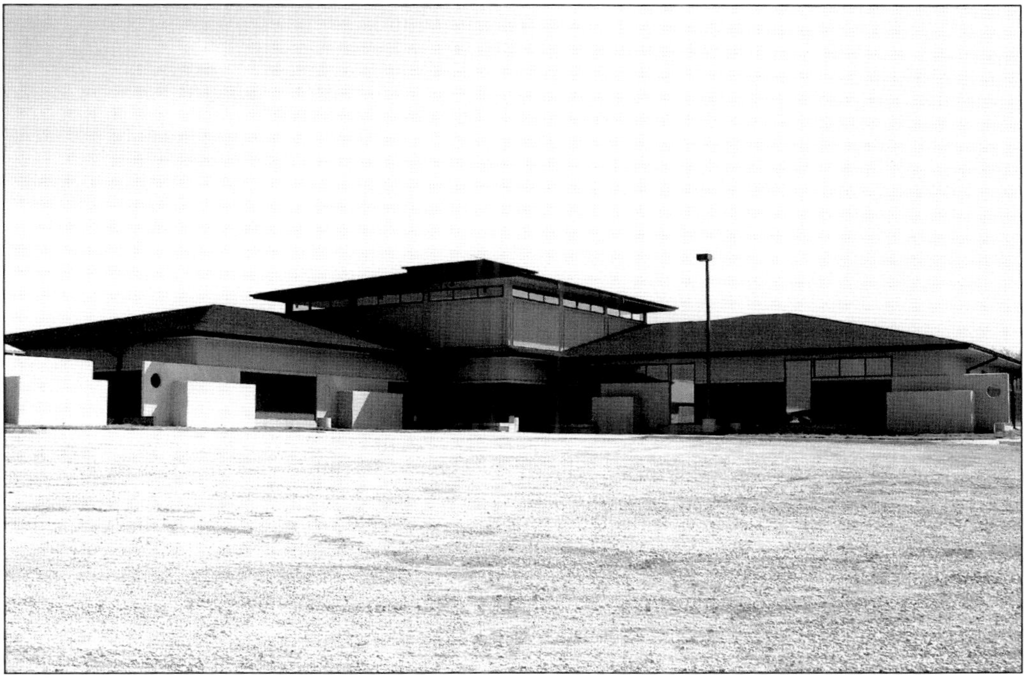

The Montgomery County Historical Society Museum was the dream of Betty McKenzie. Through her drive and determination, she was able to make that dream come true. The new state-of-the-art museum opened in July 2006. Sadly McKenzie died before she could see her dream a reality.